OFF THE RAILS

Chris Hatherly

Chris was born in 1978. When he was fifteen he spent a year in Germany as an exchange student. At eighteen, he rode a bike around Australia in eleven and a half months. He is currently studying psychology at Australian National University and plans further travels with his wife, Natalie. He has also written travel articles for *Australian Geographic*. Chris received the 1997 Australian Geographic Young Adventurer of the Year Award for his around Australia ride. Together with Tim Cope, he also received the 2000 Spirit of Adventure Award for the Siberian recumbent bike journey.

Tim Cope

Tim was born in 1978. At sixteen he travelled to Nepal, and at eighteen was part of a GAP exchange program in England. After a short time studying Arts/Law at the Australian National University, he was accepted on scholarship to participate in the prestigious International Wilderness Guide course in Finland and Russia. At the age of nineteen he qualified as a professional guide – the first Australian to do so. Since the recumbent bike journey, Tim has been part of a world-first expedition rowing the Yenisey River through Siberia to the Arctic Ocean, and been involved in documentary-making for National Geographic and ABC television. He has written travel pieces for newspapers and magazines, and speaks regularly about his travels.

In 2001 he was awarded the Young Australian Adventurer of the Year by the Australian Geographic Society for the Yenisey River journey, and was selected one of the top twenty-five athletes/explorers in the world under the age of twenty-five, by *Outside* magazine in the USA.

CHRIS HATHERLY   TIM COPE

OFF THE RAILS

Moscow to Beijing on recumbent bikes

summersdale

First published by Viking, an imprint of Penguin Books Australia Ltd, in 2003.

1 3 5 7 9 10 8 6 4 2

This edition published in 2004 by Summersdale Publishers Ltd.

Summersdale Publishers Ltd
46 West Street
Chichester
West Sussex
PO19 1RP
UK

www.summersdale.com

Printed and bound in Great Britain.

ISBN 1 84024 398 8

To Mum and Dad,
for your unending love, courage and support, and for letting
me see the world through such a special lens. TC

In loving memory of Jean Brown:
your love made this journey possible. CH

Contents

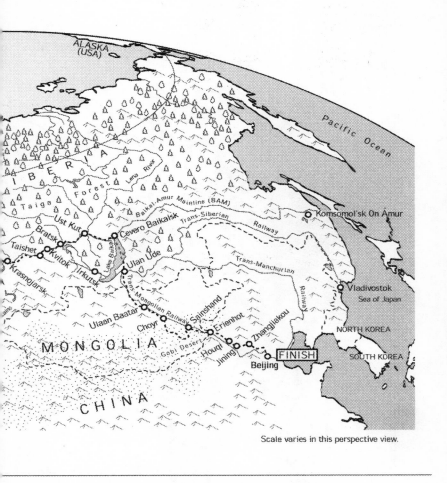

Scale varies in this perspective view.

| Mountains | Rivers | Forests | Deserts |

The recumbent bike

1 24-speed drivetrain
2 Adjustable boom tube
3 Protective PVC chain tubing

4 Thermos
5 Gear lever
6 Handlebars

7 Seat (cover made from trampoline mesh)

8 Backpack (10-20 kg): additional water (5 kg), first-aid kit, toilet paper, stove and fuel, cutlery, plates, cups, cooking pots, folding saw, raincoat/pants, cold-weather clothes, valuables (passport, cash), maps, day pack

9 Sleeping mat
10 Tent

11 Rear panniers (15-30 kg): food, sleeping-bag, clothes, miscellaneous (sewing kits, diary, film and toiletries)

12 Mountain-bike tyre (65 cm)
13 Camera and tripod

17 Spare tyres
18 Road tyre (50 cm)
19 Front suspension
20 Quick release wheel lever (front and rear)

14 Tool kit (10 kg)
15 Water bottles (3 kg)
16 Front panniers (12 kg): food (biscuits, breads, lunches, tinned meat, fresh fruit/vegetables)

Reproduced courtesy of *Australian Geographic*. Illustration by Kevin Stead

Find out what you want, find something you really care about. When you know what you want the rest follows. But don't just drift off into something because it offers security. Security is never worth a damn. We're meant to live and to live means living dangerously, half on the edge of trouble, half on the edge of achievement.

Hammond Innes, *The Strode Venturer*

Foreword

Toward the end of 1999, we began our journey on recumbent bicycles across Russia, Siberia and Mongolia's Gobi Desert, to end in Tiananmen Square, Beijing. We were twenty at the time and spoke minimal Russian. To complicate matters, we knew very little about Russia itself, and almost everyone we spoke to said we were on a suicide mission.

Why did we persevere?

Beyond craving for adventure and wanting to turn a dream into reality, we wanted to prove to ourselves and to others that alternative ways of living exist; that with hard work and perseverance dreams can be made to come true. In the spirit of youth, we believed that the world was brimming with endless possibilities. We didn't want uncertainty to stop us from living our dream.

Writing a book about our experience was something we wanted to do from the beginning. The process would complete the dream, providing the opportunity for us to reflect on our journey and, just as importantly, to share our experiences with others. To do that, we had to write from the heart, honest and truthful.

We approached a few publishers, to no avail. After many frustrating months, out of the blue, came an e-mail from Executive Publisher Julie Watts, at Penguin Books. She'd heard us being interviewed on radio and thought we were 'role-models for young people'. Our chance to run the last leg of the journey had arrived.

Writing the manuscript has proved every bit as difficult and rewarding as cycling across Siberia. To complicate matters, we had agreed to write the manuscript together, alternating chapters throughout the book. After fourteen months of living in the same tent, would our already weathered relationship survive another epic?

In these pages we wish to share the people, landscapes and insights that made the journey special. We also hope that our accomplishments will infect others, so they too may turn half-baked ideas into reality. If two twenty-year-olds can ride 'couches on wheels' halfway across the world, then surely anything is possible.

Tim Cope and Chris Hatherly

Off the Rails

Daring to Dream

Tim

The Finnish border guard looked bewildered.

'Are you crazy? You are sure you want to do this?' He shook his head.

'Yep,' I replied, feigning confidence.

'Well, just be very careful. You know what those Russians are like. Russia is dangerous! Even we Finns don't go to Russia alone, especially for such a long time. But an Australian, by bike?'

With a look of sincere pity he stamped my passport and handed it back. I offered him a nervous smile and strode out of the swish customs building. My Russian chauffeur, Alexsei, was waiting outside.

'C'mon, c'mon, Tim, faster. We are running late!' He nagged in Russian from behind the wheel of his clapped-out old van. As usual he was wearing a worn-out leather jacket and a lopsided baseball cap over his thinning hair.

After several attempts at starting the engine, it spluttered spectacularly into life. I leapt into the front passenger seat and before I had even closed the door, we lurched forward under the rising boom gate.

Then Finland was behind us.

It was only a kilometre or so across no-man's land to Russian customs but it dragged out in a long dreamlike sequence. I held the ill-functioning door shut, and felt my head bobbing up and down with the convulsive rattle of the van. For many months I had been working towards this day but in all that time, I had not clearly thought out the reality of what I had decided to do. My plans were still as vague as they had been from the beginning: I am going to ride a bike with my friend Chris, 10,000 kilometres across Russia, Siberia, Mongolia and China to Beijing.

Between stretched a realm of mythical places, far off wonderlands. I had a vague understanding that between us and the end lay snow, cold weather and even the Gobi Desert in Mongolia. It was a prospect that tempted my imagination and left me feeling frighteningly exposed, naïve and young. The size of the land alone was dumbfounding: Russia and Siberia cover more than twice the mass of Australia. In all that vast landscape, what kind of people would we meet? Would we come through it alive? Was it possible to ride in Siberia? If we did make it, what would I be like at the end? We hadn't looked at any maps beyond the world atlas, didn't know how long it would take, and I had barely been on a bike in the past two years, and then never for great distances.

Ten thousand kilometres? It might as well have been a million. All I knew was that it was a bloody long way. From the outset I had been repressing a fear that maybe I didn't have what it took to endure such a mammoth challenge. I had enough money to live on a budget of US$60 a month – and that was only if the journey took one year. What if it took longer?

My chest grew tight and a tangle of emotion balled up in my throat.

I had been based in Finland for fourteen months. During that time I had grown attached to the country and developed strong friendships. In recent months I had fallen into a comfortable relationship with a Finnish girl. Leaving it behind felt like severing ties with everything that had become a part of myself.

My thoughts were interrupted as the van came to an abrupt halt in front of the Russian border post. I pulled out the little document from my passport and re-read it for the hundredth time: 'Twelve month Russian Visa'.

The fragile bit of paper was the only tangible security I had. I first visited Russia almost a year ago. I had felt an inexplicable connection with the country, as if a part of me had lain dormant and suddenly sprung to life. I had known instantly that Russia was where I wanted to be: to travel, live, explore and experience.

It was also reassuring to think that I was embarking on this journey with a special friend, Chris. I remembered our brief time at university in Canberra, where we had met. In all honesty, I couldn't think of a more ideal partner.

I took a deep breath, clutched the passport and approached the guard on duty. The female guard smiled. Her bright red lipstick contrasted with the drab khaki uniform she wore. 'You are really Australian?' she asked. She made several calls and some officials whisked away my passport for processing.

After some deliberation I was waved through customs. Back in Alexsei's van, I was surprised to find two men squeezed into the front and three giggling women in the back with my gear.

'Let's go, Alexsei. Time to go home!' one of the men roared. He was a little drunk, as were the others. It took me a few moments to realise why Alexsei had been in such a rush: the extra passengers were the border guards who had just finished work.

A shot of vodka was passed over my shoulder, the volume on the crappy stereo went up, and we rumbled into Russia.

It was a short ride to the village of Vyartsila where Alexsei lived. In fact, it was so close that from the village you could just make out a Finnish farmhouse on the far side of the border.

We turned off the main road and immediately slowed to a crawl as the van dipped and swayed through pot-holes. Most pedestrians we passed had their hands out for a lift. Alexsei put his head out the window and yelled, 'Sorry, we are full!'

After dropping off the guards we made a trip to Alexsei's garage, where I helped him load the van with beer and cigarettes. In the morning he planned to drive back across the border with the goods concealed under the seats. His business involved shuttling clients from country to country and selling contraband to buyers in Finland. Everything about his lifestyle contrasted with the ordered and intensely quiet character of Finland.

When the van was packed, we hurried into the village centre under the dim glow of token streetlights.

The moment Alexsei ushered me into his home, I relaxed. His elderly mother was part way through nibbling a dried fish when I entered. She dropped it on the table and rushed to tackle me in a ferocious hug. 'Oh, well done. That's my boy, Tim. Good boy!' she shrieked in my ear.

Alexsei's pregnant wife emerged with her three-year-old son. Soon I was sitting down with a cup of tea and some biscuits, showing my updated photo album. It was my third visit to the family, and it felt as special as the first.

As I sipped the cup of hot sweet tea, I couldn't stop grinning. Everything, from Alexsei's battered van to his improvised career, to the jovial border guards and the family's warmth, indicated flexibility and sense of humour. The thought that I would be immersed in this culture for the next year was nothing less than exciting.

After dinner I strapped my gear onto the roof of the small Lada that would be my taxi to Petrozavodsk, 400 kilometres to the east. There I planned to wait for Chris to phone me with the details of his trip to Moscow. Once the times were confirmed I too would travel to Moscow for our rendezvous.

Before leaving, Alexsei's wife mischievously tucked a bag of hot potato pies into my backpack and I gave her one of the many Australian calendars that I had brought along as gifts.

The Lada is one of the ubiquitous relics of the Soviet car industry. They are like little boxes on wheels with large round headlights, and are often seen conked out on the roadside. I always savoured riding in them, as you can feel every gravel stone and bump. Somehow I preferred that to the dull drone of a modern vehicle in which it is hard to appreciate the speed.

For six hours I sat gripping my seat, keeping the radio at full blast to ensure that both the driver and myself stayed awake. He rocketed along the forest road, treating the unsealed surface like an obstacle course, swerving around mud and football-sized gravel stones, and taking the apex of most corners. Gravel peppered the underside of the car, sending vibrations up through my feet.

At 4 a.m. we slipped out of the forest and the lights of Petrozavodsk came into view. After being checked by road police wielding machine guns, I directed the driver to the suburb of Drevlyanka. At the base of an apartment building, I unfurled my possessions onto the street and watched the Lada putt off into the distance.

'Well, Tim, this is it,' I muttered. Shivering with cold and exhaustion, I climbed the stairs and woke the Kleshenok family. They had invited me to stay before catching the train to Moscow.

The next day I received a phone call from Chris who was in Bucharest. 'Hi, Tim. Can't talk long. I am afraid the visa hasn't arrived in the mail.'

I had mailed his Russian visa two weeks ago and presumed it had arrived. Everything hinged on that bit of paper. If it didn't show up, it would be at least another six weeks before I could get him a new one. Without any control over the situation, all I could do was wait in Petrozavodsk until the visa showed up and Chris could get to Moscow.

On the upside, this would give me a bit more time to rest, reflect on the past and gather my thoughts for the journey ahead.

There was no single moment in which the idea to cycle across Russia began. It was more a blur of emotions and events. Quite simply, a series of chance meetings, special relationships, spontaneous decisions and hard work led me to this point. During my childhood in country Victoria I had spent considerable time in the outdoors: surfing, kayaking, skiing and bushwalking with my father. Even so, I could never have predicted winding up on this journey.

If I had to pick a starting point, it was probably when I was fifteen. While playing basketball at school, my left femur snapped clean in half in a freak accident. I can still vividly recall the resounding crack and the world spinning in a kaleidoscope of pain. To correct the break a steel rod was inserted down the femur from my hip to my knee; and despite a successful operation the leg has been a little shorter ever since.

The following year, after some intense rehabilitation and training, I trekked in Nepal with a group of students and my English teacher, Rob Devling. It was my first time overseas and I returned home with a broadened view of the world. Up until then I had naïvely presumed that the majority of people in the world lived like us in Australia.

A pivotal friend who influenced my direction was Bruce Cooper. I met the tall, athletic ginger-haired Scotsman while working at a children's adventure camp in England. I was eighteen years old at the time and had deferred my Arts/Law degree for a year to travel and work in Europe. One afternoon he introduced me to the mountains of Wales, the first of many trips. I recalled the blue sky and the way the peaks cut a jagged horizon. There was the crisp air, the pain in my legs and our high-spirited discussion of dreams and hopes. The sweeping space and heart-in-the-mouth views gave me a great sense of purpose.

I met Chris Hatherly the following year at Australian National University. He was studying an Arts/Science degree and, like me, had deferred for a year. In his year off he had travelled 20,000 kilometres by bicycle around Australia. We struck up a friendship on the spot. As neither of us was comfortable with the prospect of four or five years of studying, we spent much of our time musing over a world map. We believed that dreams could become reality, and that there could be nothing harder than working nine-to-five in an office.

Then, just three months into the first semester, an opportunity arose out of the blue. Chris's father brought home an advertisement for an International Wilderness Guide Course. It was a year long course based in Finland, including study placements in Russia and England. There were sixteen places offered worldwide with a scholarship.

We both applied and made it through to the final phone interview. As luck would have it, I was accepted but Chris was not. A couple of months later, I deferred my course yet again and was on a plane to Helsinki.

My interest in Russia and the north was fuelled during the wilderness course. The first of a series of training journeys was a three-week hiking expedition in a remote part of north-west Russia. The old-growth forest that spread out like a sea to every horizon was a sight I could never forget. The only signs of civilization were several abandoned villages. It struck me that in Russia lay a chance to live out childhood fantasies of exploration. I had always dreamed about going back in time to experience the virgin landscape of Australia and its Indigenous peoples. I desperately wanted to know how it felt without the presence of white settlers. Maybe in Russia I would experience genuine wilderness and the authentic culture that I craved.

On return to Finland I began to study the Russian language. Later that year, on my twentieth birthday, I found myself embarking on one of three expeditions to Arctic Lapland. Everything I saw and experienced in the following two weeks, from reindeer running stiff legged across the snow, to the northern lights, felt as vivid and biting as the cold. It left me overwhelmed and intoxicated in a pure, magical way.

I had expected to tire of the north once the novelty wore off. As my year in Finland progressed though, the exact opposite happened.

With each visit into the forest, I became aware of yet another level of subtlety. Sometimes it could be just a bird, the way sunlight slanted through the canopy, the feeling of brushing by the pine bark, or even just a slightly different aroma. It intrigued me that the forest the Russians called the taiga stretched almost unbroken from Scandinavia to the Pacific. When considered as one large tract of forest, it is the largest in the world, constituting 22 per cent of the world's forests and covering an aggregate area the size of Australia; it contains some of the greatest tracts of wilderness left on earth today.

Upon returning to civilization, I reflected with disappointment that I had only just begun to tune into the forest environment. I always felt like the chance to deepen the experience was being cut short and craved a longer, drawn-out journey.

Throughout this time Chris and I kept in contact by e-mail. In January of 1999, his idea of taking horses from London to Beijing evolved to riding recumbent bicycles instead. He planned to start from London in May and cycle through Europe over the summer. After completing my course in September, I planned to meet him in Russia. From then on we envisaged cycling together across Russia and Mongolia to Beijing.

Early on, even before we had settled on the idea, I knew what kind of experience I wanted. I had learnt that it wasn't the spectacular moments that made journeys special for me – they were always transient and rare. It was finding enjoyment and a deep satisfaction from the ordinary and routine that was most important. And the only way to do that, I thought, was to get to know a place deeply. To do that would take time and patience. I wanted to make the taiga forest, Russia and its people my focus.

Essentially, I wanted to experience Russia and not just see it.

The last two months of the course were highly intensive with exams and tests, and I felt guilty about not being able to help Chris with the sponsorship drive. His e-mails were nothing short of inspiring. Sometimes he would write about an incredible number of businesses that he had faxed, and say that there was an inkling of interest. At other times he sounded dejected and downright convinced that he was not getting anywhere.

The day before he flew out of Sydney, he surprised me with some news – his girlfriend Natalie Chan would join him from London to Romania. Interestingly, Nat also studied in Canberra and had lived a few doors from me and Chris. It seemed that things were working out in a serendipitous way.

At the end of the wilderness guide course, I moved into a canvas A-frame 'trapper's tent' in the nearby forest. The frame was made of branches cut from the forest. I had twenty-five dollars left and my return ticket to Australia had been forfeited. Using the tent as my base, I worked eight-hour days for the forestry college, repairing outdoor equipment. In my spare time, I went about finding sponsors, organising our twelve-month Russian visas, and trying to nut out a basic plan for our journey. Integral to our adventure was my desire to inspire young people. To this end I e-mailed about 2,000 schools in Russia, hoping to visit some along the way. We planned to use our website to post stories for students in Australia, Russia and Finland so that they could keep up with our progress.

With a month to go before departure, my e-mails and letters to sponsors, the media and schools proliferated. Every time I received an update call from Chris, it was a reminder that time was running out.

One morning a big package from Australia arrived via courier. Attached to it was a note from Chris: 'What do you reckon, mate? A pretty good Christmas present from sponsors!' I tore it open to find 100 rolls of Kodak slide film, Gore-Tex clothing from Mountain Designs, bundles of thermals from Everwarm and a whole host of other goodies. For the first time the journey began to feel real. My bike, however, was yet to arrive. It was still being custom made in Canberra by Wayne Kotzur. My share of the sponsor funds from *Australian Geographic* was going to be just enough to pay for the bike and its shipment to Finland. In the end Wayne waived the courier fee in a gesture of support.

My finances were still looking scarce, even with the money that I was saving from work. I had discovered that while it wasn't too difficult to convince companies to sponsor us with products, procuring cash was almost impossible.

I decided to call John and Alison Kearney, distant relatives who lived on the Gold Coast in Queensland. They had been following my progress since the course in Finland and had already backed me with generous support. I was bowled over when they agreed to support me with some much-needed funds.

One week before I was due to leave Finland, I finally received our Russian twelve-month visas. It had been a long process that included, among other things, getting HIV tests.

The evening after receiving the visas, I was sifting through my things when I came across a letter from Australian National University in Canberra. It read: 'If you have not re-enrolled or applied for further deferral by 1 June then it is assumed that you have abandoned the course.'

Although I had not intended to return to study Law immediately, the security had suddenly vanished. Officially, for the first time, I was technically not 'in-between' anything. A rush of emotion flushed my system. It felt so reassuring that I had now irretrievably committed to my dreams.

The last few days were a whirlwind of tying up loose ends. With first aid in mind, I visited the local doctor who was more than happy to give me free advice, a bundle of bandages and sterile syringes, tubes and even stitching needles. One of my fears was running into health problems or sustaining an injury in the middle of Russia. Fortunately, my parents funded my basic travel insurance for twelve months.

On 6 September, three days before I departed Finland, the bike finally arrived. All that was left to do was pack up and leave. On 8 September, I loaded up my gear into a friend's hatchback and drove to the train station. From there I headed towards the border.

The phone rang and I raced to pick up the handset. I had been in Petrozavodsk for a week, waiting for the visa to turn up in Bucharest.

'Tim, did you get my e-mail?' Chris shouted down the line.

'No.'

'I got the visa! I've been looking in the wrong post office all along!'

The next night I found myself on a rickety overnight train service to Moscow. As the train hurtled into the night, it felt as if a chapter in my life was ending and a new one dawning.

I had barely spoken to an Australian face-to-face for fourteen months. What will Chris look like? How will he have changed? I really couldn't even begin to fathom the journey ahead.

Before drifting off to sleep a new thought came to me.

Chris and I had been following such different paths over the past year or so; we were both fiercely independent. What if he had different reasons for doing this journey than I did? Would we get along, or would this be the beginning of a long, drawn-out conflict?

It left me feeling a little sick in the pit of my stomach.

Sad Beginnings

Bucharest – Moscow – Elbrus

Early Autumn 1999

Chris

For me, the expedition began with a piercing train whistle, a broken heart and a flood of tears. It was 23 September and the train was lurching slowly out of Bucharest. Outside, standing on the platform, was my girlfriend Natalie – looking beautiful, terribly out of reach and desperately close to tears.

After nearly five uninterrupted months of cycling across Europe together, the day had finally come for us to part.

Nat walked along the platform, hurrying to keep pace with the carriage. The gap between us was too great to reach across, but we tried anyway. We blew kisses, vowed our love and struggled to smile into each other's hearts. Then the platform ended and the train picked up speed. It whistled, rounded a bend and, two seconds later, Nat disappeared.

That was the point when my heart broke. I slumped back into my seat and my head sunk into my hands.

We'd known each other for only two years and been in love for less than half of that time, but the months together had been so close to perfect that already it felt as though our relationship was ready to move on. I wanted to spend the rest of my life with Nat, and yet here I was, allowing circumstances to wrench us apart. If all went according to plan – the horrible plan, I thought for a moment – we wouldn't see each other for over a year. I'd committed to this expedition before our relationship had started and all along I'd believed that it was the right thing to do. What would be the cost? If we could both survive the next months and still be in love at the end, then we would each have grown. But if not?

I broke down, succumbing to desolation and a flood of tears. I wished with all my heart that the whole thing wasn't happening.

And that, for me, is how the expedition began.

It wasn't the beginning of the journey, of course. I was an Australian taking a train from Romania to Moscow, and I'd obviously done a bit of travelling to get there. But in the two years between the decision and the destination, that moment when I lost sight of Nat was the moment in which the fun and excitement of the holiday ended and the challenge of the adventure began. I was leaving Nat and the comforts of Europe behind and heading out into a vast unknown. There, I was to meet Tim, a friend I hadn't seen in sixteen months, and together we were hoping to cycle to Beijing. It was going to be a hell of a challenge, not only for Nat and I, but for Tim and I.

The train rumbled on and the days and nights merged. I paid little attention to anything – even the need to eat. I remember once looking up from a patch of torn fabric on the seat opposite and realising that I'd been staring at it for hours. I lifted my gaze to the window and noticed the gold-plated, mushroom-shaped cupolas of a dazzling cathedral sliding by majestically. I returned my indifferent gaze to the torn seat, and it wasn't till an hour later that my stirring consciousness registered that I'd just seen the grand cathedral of Kiev. I thought about it for a moment, then returned to the cold comfort of my gloom. I just didn't care.

Occasionally, my depression lifted and I was able to reflect on what the beginning of such an adventure might mean. My thoughts drifted backwards over all the events that had brought me here, and forwards to the vast uncertainty that lay ahead. Backwards was safe: there was no unknown and nobody in my past had ever tried to kill me. But forwards was something else again. For months, people had warned me against going to Russia. 'It's a country of desperate poverty,' they said and predicted that I – a rich foreigner – would be mugged, robbed and killed as soon as I crossed the border. Previous experience had taught me to ignore such warnings. The people who made them generally had no first-hand experience of what they were talking about, and often they were simply voicing the sorts of fears that would always stop them reaching out to achieve their own dreams. On the other hand, I had only a very basic knowledge of the Russian language, knew almost nothing about the country or culture, and I was about to be dumped out into the mega-metropolis of Moscow on my own. I was, to say the least, a little scared.

I remembered the day the first seed of the trip had been sown. It was two years ago – I was eighteen at the time – and halfway through my first big adventure: a year-long cycling trip around Australia. I'd met an American man in a pub in Darwin. His name was Tom Stone, a retired US soldier. He'd been on the road for the past seven years, walking most of the way around the world! His stories of Russia captured me in particular.

'It's a beautiful country, Chris, totally wild and free. The people are so down-to-earth and friendly. I spent over two years walking there and I stayed both winters with locals in these tiny Siberian villages. If you ever go, think of me, and always remember the bum!'

I thought that he'd been describing himself as a 'bum', but later I realised that I'd simply misheard his strong American accent. He'd actually been telling me to remember the highlight of his journey: the BAM railway through Northern Siberia, one of the longest and most remote working railway lines in the world.

I remembered the university in Canberra where I'd first met Tim. We'd spent a crazy few months poring over maps and dreaming of adventures, until he won the scholarship to train as a wilderness guide in Finland. I spent the rest of the year seriously doubting my reasons for studying until, finally, goaded into action by Tim's e-mails from the Arctic, I dropped out of my course and set about organising an adventure of my own. After a few half-baked ideas, several themes finally merged and I set my mind on Russia. I let Tim in on the idea and it turned out that he was keen on coming too! And so the adventure was born.

We had very little information and no real idea what would be in store for us. But then, we were teenagers and we just knew that we could do anything. What we lacked in knowledge and experience we could always make up with enthusiasm. All that remained was to organise the details and the logistics and the not-so-straightforward matter of finding AU$30,000 in sponsorship to cover equipment and other expenses. In the last months of 1998 I set to work and quickly realised that most companies were reluctant to hand out cash. I made little progress and procrastinated heavily. And then Nat came along.

Nat decided to defer her studies in psychology for a year and come travelling too. She worked in Sydney as a taxi telephonist while I worked the evening shift at a frozen foods factory in Bathurst, packing icy-cold fish-fingers and counting down the hours till knock-off time in dollars and cents. I spent my days on the phone, calling hundreds of media outlets and thousands of potential sponsors, and trying to crack the vicious circle of needing publicity to attract sponsors while needing the credibility of sponsors to interest the media.

On the weekends, Nat and I would meet at Katoomba – halfway between our homes – and explore the deep river gorges and the soaring, wild ridges of the beautiful southern Blue Mountains.

In mid-April of 1999, after months of minimal success, everything finally started to come together. As the list of sponsors began to grow, others were encouraged to join the show. The wagon started to roll and in the weeks before I flew out to London, couriers were arriving at the door every day, carting a range of boxes with all the different bits and pieces of gear that Tim and I would need. Together we were given over AU\$20,000 worth of equipment from forty different sponsors. It felt like a monumental achievement, but I still didn't have enough cash for an aeroplane ticket. I spent a few days in uncertainty, until my beloved grandmother stepped in with a loan.

I flew out of Sydney on 14 May 1999. The final week of last-minute preparations had been so exhausting that I slept for twenty hours straight. I arrived in London to meet Nat; she had taken a different flight. Together, we sat at a bus shelter outside Heathrow airport, rebuilding our bikes and packing our gear under a sky of heavy grey clouds.

And then we were off. The first pedals of an incredible journey. All the stress and the months of worry fell away and we lost ourselves in the beginnings of a beautiful lifestyle of gentle, easy cycling.

We spent the next four months cycling east through the countries of central, southern and eastern Europe. We stuck to back roads, camped in secluded forests and generally planned our route day by day. We had many rewarding encounters with locals and occasionally we'd leave our bikes to canoe down a river or go walking in the mountains. At other times, when the roads took us through cities, we'd stop off at an Internet café to contact friends and family.

Throughout, I stayed in regular contact with Tim. He'd solved our biggest problem and found a way to get year-long Russian visas! The embassy in Canberra had refused point-blank, saying that it was impossible; people from the various Russia-focused Internet newsgroups I'd checked out agreed. Tim had come through though, and now he was well on track for our meeting in mid-September.

Nat and I were less successful when it came to organising visas for the Ukraine. First, the officials said 'no'. Then, 'Yes, but it will cost you.' They were sticking to the old Russian system of communist tourism, which stipulated that we needed to have pre-booked accommodation for every night of our stay. Furthermore, the only official travel agent authorised to make such bookings gave us starting prices in the thousands. In the end we gave up and set our sights on Romania instead. There, I would collect my Russian visa and take a train to meet Tim in Moscow, while Nat took a bus to Istanbul and continued cycling in Turkey.

We reached Bucharest a month later only to find that the Russian visa had not arrived. For Nat and I, this came as an executioner's stay. We spent the week before the visa was finally tracked down wandering around the city, hand in hand. After this extra time, in a strange way, we felt more prepared for the separation than we would have otherwise been.

Two days later, I was standing on a station platform and shivering with my hands under my armpits and my chin tucked well into the zipped-up collar of my polar fleece. The roiling grey sky had descended during the trip from warm, sunny Romania and was now skimming the tops of the featureless, eleven-storey concrete towers that served as homes for Moscow's millions. A piercing cold wind was howling through the station, bringing with it an angling, icy sleet that defeated the design of the broad roof stretched over the platform leaving me with nowhere dry to stand. Milling around was a bustling crowd dressed in bleak colours that matched the weather. Above each platform were signs giving meaningful information to everyone but me. Beside the few inconsequential words that I remembered from my brief study of Russian at university, the only thing I could understand was the big clock mounted high above the entrance to the station. It was 11.30 a.m.

I'd been in Moscow for three hours and spent most of that time confused, cold and just a little terrified. I managed to change some money at a rate that I was sure had suckered me right in. I couldn't understand what the man was saying – I'd simply handed over my American dollars and hoped for some change. Finally, I managed to cross town on the underground system and get to the station where I was supposed to meet Tim. His train was late. Unable to ask what was happening, I could only stand and wait, feeling very much alone.

Finally, at midday, a shrieking train ground to a shuddering halt at platform five. I hurried along, eyeing the doors to each of the carriages until I reached the very end. There, standing behind a huge pile of boxes and bags, was a figure I recognised in an instant. Tim!

Eight hours later, we were on a rattling train that was hauling us south through the night, towards the Caucusus Mountains. Tim was describing our destination: Mount Elbrus, at over five and a half thousand metres, is the highest peak in Europe. We had been planning to climb it as a way of kicking off the journey. Next to Tim sat Stas, an expert mountaineer from Petrozavodsk. He had agreed to be our guide on the mountain, yet he spoke no English. I turned back to Tim, who was still gushing with an unbroken stream of enthusiasm. We had barely spoken since Tim had left for Finland, yet here he was in front of me, bigger than I remembered, and hairier too!

We chatted into the evening and I soon realised that we had both changed a lot. I had no doubt that we would have an amazing time together, and that we'd both meet the challenges of the year head on. But would we still share the same spark and the same values that we had over a year ago? Somewhere, in the back of my mind, the first seeds of doubt were beginning to grow.

We got ready for bed. Tim had a top bunk sleeper and I watched as he climbed up to make his bed by stepping on the lower occupant's pillow. I cringed as the owner of the bed glared furiously at Tim. This was an aspect of his personality that I'd forgotten. How to describe it? An ability to concentrate on one thing at the exclusion of all else.

I remembered back to the first day I'd met him – the second person I'd gotten to know at university, just after meeting Nat. We'd sat down to eat sandwiches at a barbecue before becoming engrossed in each other's stories of adventure. Two hours later, Tim's conversation faltered as, all of a sudden, he almost fainted with hunger. He'd been clutching a sandwich for two hours without taking a single bite.

I settled down in my bunk and tried to take in the day. It was only two days since I'd left Nat and although the pain of parting was still very clear, recent events had forced me out of my reverie. Tim was a fantastic guy and a great friend, but he was certainly not Nat, and I would have to try hard not to let the pain of separation affect our friendship. We had both changed, moving on and developing in ways that were yet to become clear. Adjusting to the changes would probably be a lot of work for both of us.

Not for the first time, I wondered if what I was doing – this year of adventure in Russia and Siberia – was *really* what I wanted to do.

Ten days later, dishevelled, sunburnt and dehydrated, I limped down to the bus stop on a badly sprained ankle to wait for a lift back to the train line. In the past week, I'd climbed a gigantic mountain – twice – and started getting to know Tim again. Elbrus had taken its toll. Tim had come within an ace of the summit before having to turn back with severe altitude sickness. On the way down from a second attempt, I'd fallen on a steep slope and been lucky not to break my leg. The scenery had been stunning, but we'd spent more time acclimatising than actually climbing. This meant long hours sitting around in the scorching sun. We'd talked a lot about our plans. Tim had never really travelled by bicycle before and I wasn't sure if he understood what the lifestyle would involve. A lot of riding basically. I could only hope that the day in, day out cycling routine that I loved would suit him as well as it suited me.

Tim was probably thinking similar thoughts about me. He had talked for hours about his love of the northern forests and the Arctic, but never having experienced them myself, I couldn't yet share his enthusiasm.

For me, there was a big question mark hanging over the expedition. I felt that it was still too soon to know how Nat and I would handle a year apart. As big as my commitment to Tim, to the journey and to our sponsors was, Nat would always come first. If the time and the distance began to seriously threaten our relationship, I would be back home on the next plane. I'd admitted as much to Tim – shocking him, I think, and adding yet another layer of uncertainty to the journey.

If nothing else, we had a starting point. We'd decided to begin our bicycle travels in Petrozavodsk rather than Moscow, as this would give us a little while to build up the bikes and get organised among friends. This route would also be a more scenic and isolated way through the north, instead of the dense belt of population surrounding Moscow.

We'd been together for nearly two weeks, but the adventure had just begun.

Breaking the Ice
Petrozavodsk – Babushkina
Autumn 1999

Tim

I rolled my shoulder and watched the last heavy bag hit the tarmac with a satisfying thwack. Our combined gear of backpacks and boxes now stretched along the edge of the platform. We had just arrived in Petrozavodsk on the overnight train from Moscow. Sleet was falling from a leaden sky.

The past few days had been plagued with disappointment about failing to reach the summit of Elbrus. It had left me feeling subdued and pining for the familiar northern forests of Russia and Finland. More worrying was Chris's sadness about leaving Nat. He seemed to be wrapped up in his own notion of how the journey would turn out, his moods distant and hard to gauge.

'Well, Tim, it's time,' Chris proclaimed. He looked surprisingly refreshed and excited.

'Time for what?' I asked.

'To build the bikes, of course.'

'You what? Here?'

He was already ripping open the box that contained the bicycle parts.

I had never seen a recumbent bicycle before and certainly never ridden one. It worried me too, that my brief cycling experience amounted to no more than learning how to patch up tubes and adjusting a seat.

'Tim, can you get me a bolt?' Chris asked, as he worked away at a dizzying pace.

I peered into a bag packed with an array of shiny metal things.

'Chris, mate, is this long bit or the round screwy bit the bolt?' I enquired, as he paused in astonishment.

'The long thingy.'

Eventually, the boxes were discarded and I looked at the transformation. To me, with its shiny new parts and blinding white seat, the recumbent looked like a raised deck chair on wheels. The pedals stuck out over the top of the front wheel, which was smaller than the back wheel. Its steering system consisted of joystick-like handles that stuck up on either side of the seat. It was hardly the kind of bike that I had envisaged. However, seeing it for the first time rekindled a sense of excitement.

A little gingerly, I clambered onto the contraption and lay back, semi-horizontal. The seat was made from a taut mesh similar to that used on trampolines, and extended high enough to support my lower neck. It was surprisingly comfortable, not unlike sitting on a couch.

Passengers dressed in fur from head to toe stopped and stared down at us. I was acutely aware of how low to the ground I was sitting. My eyes were at hip-level with the onlookers.

Chris held the bike while I rested my feet on the pedals and waited for a push. I clasped the steering and with a jerky swivel faced headlong down the narrow platform.

Then I was off.

Being so low to the ground, it felt like I was riding through the land of giants. Then, suddenly, I began to tilt to one side. Attempting to avoid a fall, I turned the wheel, only to cut a path straight for the crowd. A plump woman yelped as she dived out of the way. The edge of the platform reared and the long drop to the tracks below came into view. Unable to find the brakes, I slammed my feet down, narrowly missing the fall.

By the time sixty kilograms of gear was loaded onto the bike, I was struggling to keep it upright. Then, with a lot of patience and coaching from Chris, I covered the first two kilometres in two hours. After the umpteenth crash I lay dejected beneath the tangle of bike and bags. My clothes were wet from numerous falls. Chris closed in with precision, gently clasping his brakes.

'Well, only ten thousand kilometres to go!'

We spent the next week in Petrozavodsk making final preparations. Petrozavodsk is a small city situated on the shores of Lake Onega, part way along the train line from St Petersburg to Murmansk. It is the capital of the small republic of Karelia, one of many republics that make up a large part of the Russian Federation.

From Petrozavodsk we planned a route east through the forest towards Vologda. By nature it was a northerly, isolated route that posed some uncertainties. We were well into autumn and there was a thin line between it and fast-approaching winter. Would the roads be in good enough condition to ride on? What would happen to the bikes in extreme cold?

Having studied a road atlas, we had a vague idea of our route for the first 100 kilometres east of Petrozavodsk. The atlas had a scale of 1:1,500,000. On this scale 100 kilometres amounted to about 6.5 centimetres. Beyond that lay about 10,000 kilometres of the unknown.

On a day when the first snow clouds of the season shrouded the city, we put foot to pedal and turned our backs on the grey apartment blocks of Petrozavodsk. I wavered all over the road in an attempt to miss frozen puddles and dodge cars and buses. Beyond the edge of town traffic petered out and we passed into the forest. With the city behind us, I became aware of the whir of the pedals and the icy wind that brought with it scattered flakes of snow. My lungs filled with icy air. It was below zero. The wind left my cheeks parched red and my fingers stung even as a sweat built up beneath my beanie. It occurred to me that from behind Chris looked like a little hunchback ambling along the road. The recumbent, leaden with equipment, looked nothing like a bike. I could understand why from a distance people had mistaken Chris for an invalid in a wheelchair.

At lunch we huddled, shrinking into our Gore-Tex jackets, on the shores of Lake Onega. Onega is the third-largest lake in Russia. It is connected to the Ladoga lake system which, in turn, flows into the Baltic Sea. Swells crashed onto the rocky beach and a light veil of snow on the horizon made it appear like the sea. Every sensation was vivid and striking. Life in the city had been like sleepwalking, by comparison.

I wondered how long it would take before the weather closed in altogether. Once it became too cold we planned to abandon the bikes and return to them nearer to spring. We guessed that there would be at least three months when cycling would be out of the question.

As the light faded, we pulled off the road and came to a halt 100 metres into the forest. Reaching above the tree line the crowns of ancient pines were catching the golden glow of the sinking sun.

It was time to introduce Chris to the taiga. Taiga is the Russian word for the boreal forest that stretches from Finland right across Siberia to the northern Pacific. To the north it reaches as high as the Arctic and sub-Arctic and peters out at its southern-most extreme on the steppes. The primary tree varieties that constitute the taiga are pine, spruce, birch and larch.

Our camping equipment included an axe, a couple of billies, and a Finnish-made shelter called a *loue*. Chris also carried a tent. The *loue* is like a light-weight tarp that when set up forms an open semi-circle. It requires the use of three poles – usually tree branches – and resembles half a tee-pee. The fabric inside of the *loue* is a silver reflective material so that when a fire is lit on the open side, the heat radiates with remarkable constancy. Contrary to its appearance, it is very warm.

'But what if it rains?' Chris asked, dubiously.

'Well, before we set it up you just have to check the direction of the wind,' I replied.

'But what if the wind changes direction? I'm stuffed if I'm going to trust this thing!' he said.

Biting my lip, I took the axe and made into the dense stand of pines and spruce. In the still of dusk, I chopped at logs for firewood until my eyes lost focus out of sheer hunger. Before returning to camp, I let my breath slow until I could just hear the odd creak of a tree branch. 'Finally, finally I am here ...'

After the meal, we retreated to write our diaries. Light danced on my diary pages as I wrote. The embers eventually faded, glowing orange with every random breath of wind. I lay on my back, peering past the silhouettes of pine and spruce fronds to where stars glittered. Tucked into my warm sleeping bag, only my face felt the crisp frost that was falling like a blanket.

Our route for the first few days followed the shore of Lake Onega, before turning east. The road deteriorated into a muddy dirt track with fist-sized gravel stones and ridges of bulldozed dirt. This was marked as 'covered' rather than 'sealed' on our cheap Belarussian-made road atlas. For most of the time Chris rode far ahead of me.

Meanwhile I struggled to stay upright, let alone cover distance. It would be two weeks before my first crash-free day.

The weather greyed further and the daylight hours shortened. Even at noon the forest cast a foreboding shadow across the road. The icy wind cleaned away the last brittle leaves of autumn, leaving the stark skeletons of birch and aspen trees. Days seemed to merge into each other as we passed through forest broken only by villages.

Our approach to the villages usually went unnoticed – until, that is, the first dog started howling. Within seconds other dogs would join the chorus and a cacophony of barks and growls would be echoing through the damp air. For every dog that ran to the end of its chain and retreated with a choking yelp, there was another that ran free. Sometimes we had as many as ten dogs in hot pursuit as we made a dash for safety. Being low to the ground made the experience particularly harrowing; our eyes were at the same level as the dogs'. Being face to face with salivating, teeth-baring, wolf-like mutts was the most dangerous aspect of our daily routine, closely followed by the petrol tankers that roared along the forest roads.

Time on the bike quickly became characterised by bouts of hunger that often coincided with crashes. Half an hour after a good serve of porridge, I would feel my stomach begin to cave in until it felt like the wall linings were resting on one another. In this state my reactions became slow and my dilated eyes began to lose focus. To counter this, I introduced Chris to *pryaniki* biscuits. These thick sweet delights quickly became an important part of our diet; with a bag stuffed under our seats we were able to eat on the move.

As the days passed, I was getting to know Chris a lot better.

One night I lay in my sleeping bag, feeling my legs and back relax for the first time all day. Chris lay at the other end of the shelter in his sleeping bag so that our feet met in the centre. The fire lit up a crescent-shaped amphitheatre of thick moss and a few scraggy blueberry bushes. Now and then sparks rose like fireflies into the night before blinking out in the darkness.

I found it ironic that in this calming hush I was being driven mad by noise. Chris was finishing his dinner and each spoonful sounded like the rasp of sandpaper. Ever since I can remember I have been irritated by the noise of people eating and breathing heavily; it's some kind of hypersensitivity, I guess.

Eventually, he finished eating and tossed the pot clear of the shelter.

'Well, mate, made a nice smoke catcher tonight, didn't you?' he said, with a cheeky smile.

The smoke from the fire I had made was pouring straight into the tent.

'I swear the damn wind has changed direction,' I replied.

Feeling too tired to study Russian, I put the dictionary away and lay back. Now there really was just the crackle of the fire and a subtle flaring every time an unburned twig caught alight.

Chris broke the silence. 'You know, Nat and I talked about getting engaged.'

I let the crackle take over for a few moments. Then I sat up, coughing and spluttering in the smoke. 'Chris, mate ... did you really ... you really discussed getting engaged?'

'Yep, sure did,' he replied. As the fire painted his cheeks and broad jaw in a golden orange, the vague hint of a smile crept over his face.

'Jeez, that sounds bloody serious!' I said, laughing. 'But how do you know to make such a big decision?'

'Trust me, Tim, you just know. When I was waiting in Bucharest with Nat, I just knew. There are probably a handful of people in the world that I could build a fantastic life with and she is one of them.'

He went on to describe the life that he and Nat would have together in Australia. She would continue to study while Chris found a way to earn money to travel. Later on they would start a family. He even had an idea of the kind of place they would settle down in!

It struck me that I didn't have a clue about my future. Beyond this journey was just a big unknown blank. I did not have the slightest idea what I would do when I returned to Australia. I wasn't going to study and I would probably have a big debt. What did Australia mean? Surely I would feel like a fish out of water back there. It was here in the northern forest that I felt most alive.

That Chris and I were embarking on the journey with a similar mindset had always been reassuring. We had abandoned our university degrees to pursue a common goal. In doing so, we cast our futures into uncertainty. Even if the trip ended in disaster, at least we were in it together, and could find comfort in knowing we shared the same fears, trials and tribulations. Now it was clear that we were living two very different realities. And, although we were on this journey together, it was going to be a solitary challenge, like living parallel lives.

I was sure of only one thing: this trip was what I wanted to do.

The next morning I awoke to the patter of rain on my face. I forced open my eyes to see the dark skeletal trees spiralling out of sight into a heavy mist. I had rolled clear of the shelter during the night. Rather than lie awake, I decided to get up and prepare the fire. In any case, I was on breakfast duty.

After porridge, I carried the dirty dishes to the frozen puddles by the roadside ditch. There I broke the ice and with numb fingers scraped at the burnt porridge on the bottom of the pot. Afterwards, I packed slowly and stretched before putting feet to pedals.

At the first turn of the crank a hot rush of pain shot through my right knee. I rode for five metres before the wheels slipped and I was sent skidding on my backside; the muddy surface of the road was covered in ice.

As the day progressed, the pain in my knee, which had begun as a niggling problem a day earlier, continued to worsen. With every turn of the crank, it felt like a nail was being hammered into the side of my kneecap. By afternoon I was using only my left leg to pedal. Chris, although concerned, seemed agitated by the slow pace. The low clouds continued to precipitate a cold rain, adding to our woes. Snow or sleet would have been more pleasant.

Upon arrival in the village of Skokovo, we decided to call it a day. I hoped that a Russian *banya* might treat my knee. It would also be a chance to wash for the first time since leaving Petrozavodsk.

A couple of derelict wooden houses came into sight. The lifeless grey structures leaned into the long wet grass, the front doors hidden from view. Even though it was cold, no smoke appeared from the chimneys. It reminded me of a peasant village out of an old film that I had seen about the Black Death in Europe. I expected to see a half-naked, bearded group of God-fearing men walk over the rise, whipping themselves on the back to free their lives from sin and avoid the plague.

One hundred metres on, we passed out of the village. We doubled back and I approached one of the log houses. It stood in a muddy yard and had but two unbroken windows. Half the logs were rotten, the ends frayed into splintered pieces. Through a window I eyed some movement. 'Excuse me!' I cried.

A balding old man with a bushy beard appeared at the door. He looked bemused, but not unfriendly.

'I was just wondering if we could have a *banya* at your place. We have been riding for days and I've hurt my knee,' I fumbled in Russian.

He scratched at his thinning hair, revealing more bare scalp. 'Sure,' he said.

We followed him into the house and sat down for a cup of tea. The table was smeared with brown muck that was obviously the leftovers from years of tea-drinking and greasy food. In the light that drifted through a window I caught glimpses of the man's clothing, which consisted of layer upon layer of jackets and jumpers without elbows, and broken zips that had been replaced with safety pins and make-do buttons.

As we drank our tea, I noticed that whenever we weren't looking at him his eyes darted up and down, studying us.

Eventually the *banya* was ready. *Banya* is a concept very similar to a sauna. Stones are heated over a wood stove in a small room. Hot water is then thrown onto the stones to create a steam bath. The temperature can rise to around 120 degrees Celsius but usually hovers at about seventy. By beating the skin with birch branches, and leaving and entering the *banya* several times, circulation is stimulated, skin pores are cleansed and blood pressure drops. For this reason *banya* is used as a form of relaxation. However, the primary purpose is for washing. In most Russian villages there is no running water so *banya* is the logical place to wash, especially in winter when the temperature can drop well below minus thirty.

This *banya* was probably the most rundown I had ever seen. The overcast sky was visible through gaps in the roof and walls, providing the only form of light. Steam rose with a hiss and beads of hot water began to form over my body. I felt around in the dark until I found a rusty steel tub of warm water and used it to douse my skin.

Then, while Chris washed, I stood naked in the yard, steam pouring from my body. My moment of reflection was broken by a petrol tanker that came to a screeching halt in front of the house. The driver's face appeared at the window. 'Hey mate, have you got a lighter or matches?' he cried, cigarette dangling from his mouth.

'Um, no ... sorry,' I replied.

As he drove off, I scampered back into the warmth. My knee had begun to throb again.

By the time we rolled out, it was dark and raining again. We waved goodbye to the man whose name we never learned. With wet hair cooling, we pulled into camp 200 metres from the village and struggled to get a fire going.

I rushed to write in my diary as if it was the only security left in the world. Chris lay sullen in his sleeping bag. The lack of distance covered had evidently left him frustrated. His eyes, as they so often did, peered into the night straight past me. I began to feel that his indifference masked anger, which left me feeling guilty. More than anything, he was probably thinking of Nat.

As the fire fizzled out in the rain, so too did our morale.

I managed to cover three kilometres the next day, with a clumsily wrapped bandage on my knee. Then I came to a halt. Chris screwed up his face. I had the feeling that he suspected a conspiracy or hoax. We were not achieving the daily average, but there was no choice. We had to stop at the next village.

At first sight, the village of Novi Vashki didn't appear any better than Skokovo. I was pleasantly surprised, however, to find a shop among the three or four wooden homes.

We sat out the back of the shop on a slab of concrete eating lunch. The temperature had risen slightly and the puddles and frozen dirt had turned to sticky mud. Dollops of cow dung were flying periodically out the window of a nearby house.

While I cut the loaf of bread, Chris wandered off to find water.

'Jeez, we can't drink that!' I shrieked. He was dipping the billy into a muddy puddle.

'It's all right. During my bicycle journey around Australia, it was just a matter of choosing the puddle with the least cow shit ... Oh that looks like some nice ones over there,' he said, his eyes lighting up.

It was obvious that we could not continue with my injured knee. Over jam sandwiches we decided that we would hitchhike to the small city of Vologda, 200 kilometres to the south-east. There I would find a hospital and get some advice. But first we needed to solve the problem of where to leave the bikes. Within seconds of entering the shop we were surrounded by three or four babushkas, all vying for the honour of being our hosts.

'Oh, good boys, good on you, well done!' they uttered, shaking their heads and tut-tutting. I looked down to see faces squeezed into neatly tied scarves.

'I'll cook you pancakes!'

'I'll make you fish pies!'

'Do you like cottage cheese?'

Finally, we chose a woman who muscled her way to the front midway into the scuffle. The others winked in approval. She had been the woman shovelling the cow dung out the window, and she wasted no time in ushering us back home. Under orders we hauled the bikes through the front door and plonked them in her tiny kitchen. The table had to be removed so that they would fit.

'Are you sure about this?' I asked, uncertainly.

She wielded a fist as her face screwed up like an old walnut. 'Don't worry about it! They are staying here!' she thundered, breaking into a cackle. She didn't tell us her name, suggesting that we should address her as Babushka or Baba, the Russian term for an elderly woman or grandmother.

We said goodbye and wandered back to the main road to begin the trek to Vologda. In vain we plodded on with our thumbs out, hoping to encourage some traffic to appear. Every half hour or so the faint whine of a vehicle could be heard in the distance. Eventually a car appeared, rising and dipping in the potholes, only to whoosh past and shrink into the horizon.

By the time the mist began to fall we sat dejectedly by the roadside. Chris inspected an abandoned shack nearby and proclaimed that if we broke through the window we could sleep on the wooden floor. Several hours later we had given up all hope when a bus came to a halt and the driver ushered us inside.

For the next three hours we held onto the seats as the bus hurtled through the darkness, swerving around unseen potholes and hitting bumps with frightening abruptness. Meanwhile, our fellow passengers nursed bottles of vodka. We were eventually dropped off in the centre of the city and found our way to an impoverished dorm beneath an Orthodox church. After haggling with the manager, she agreed to let us stay for two dollars.

In the morning I awoke to the daunting task of finding a doctor. It was a shock to be back in civilization. Grand, onion-shaped domes rose in a sparkle of gold above the inner city paved with cobblestones. Rows of small box-shaped kiosks lined the streets and babushkas sat on every corner selling sunflower seeds out of glass jars. At first light, Chris had gone off to find access to the Internet.

I boarded a bus that took me into suburbs of faceless apartment blocks and stumbled into what I hoped was the hospital. After failing to understand a single word spoken by the receptionist, I was dragged before a glaring nurse. As I told my story, she softened and her pursed lips broke into a smile of pity.

After a series of phone calls, I was led upstairs to a waiting area where a long queue of angry-looking patients stood outside a door. It was the X-ray room. The door opened and a short, plump woman poked her head out. 'Come here now!'

she waved. The queue turned with a collective groan. Some began to shout but the nurse was adamant. 'He is a special boy from Australia and needs attention for his knee. He is on a cycling expedition!'

Several hours later, after a confusing X-ray process and a visit to a specialist, I was given a tube of cream and advised to apply it three times a day.

We left Vologda feeling positive. Chris had received some e-mails from Natalie, which seemed to release some of his tension. I only hoped that the cream would work on my knee.

At eleven that evening we found ourselves outside Babushka's house in Novi Vashki.

'What do you reckon, should we knock?' Chris said over the thud of a million raindrops.

'Yeah, I guess so.'

After knocking failed to rouse Babushka, we lobbed a few rocks onto the roof. Soon we were greeted with a toothless smile and an enormous platter of pancakes, potatoes and cottage cheese.

At six the next morning, I woke up as Babushka screamed obscenities at her cow. It lived in a room attached to the house, and from my bed I could just see it being wrestled for the morning's milk. Babushka laughed as she kicked the cow in the behind. 'Good girl, good girl,' she said, in a caressing voice. Then, suddenly, the animal flinched and the bucket tipped over. 'Stop it! Be still you brat! Just wait, I will get you for this!'

My knee was the next task of the day. After flicking through a couple of thick herbal-remedy books, she took Chris out into the front yard where they dug some mud and clay. Soon I was presented with a plate of steaming mud-pie. Babushka swung a nut on a string over the mud, watching it with a keen eye. She called it a *gaika*. If the nut swung towards me, it meant that the clay held positive healing powers. If it swung in the other direction, it meant that it was bad.

In her shaky grasp, the nut began to swing towards me.

'See, you see, this clay is for you!' she cried.

She lowered the plate to my knee. As she prepared to mould the mud onto my leg, I noticed something strange: the clay appeared to be moving.

'Chris, this stuff is full of ants!' I shouted.

Babushka looked closer and quickly reversed the swing of the *gaika*. There were no excuses next time round, however, as a lump of clay was padded to my knee and wrapped in tea towels.

Breakfast put a halt to further activity for the day. Three enormous bowls of porridge with four jugs of fresh milk were followed by copious amounts of pancakes, tea, bread and potatoes. As the patient, my role was to lie still and cope with a bloated belly. Meanwhile, Chris helped chop the wood and drag extra water from the well. The yard was a ghastly sight. The temperature had risen above freezing and turned everything into deep sticky mud. A few narrow planks laid down on blocks of wood formed a raised path above the slush.

Around midday a middle-aged man with a ruddy complexion came, pleading for a bottle of vodka. 'I need a bottle ... please, just one!' he begged.

'Oh, goodness me, you should be out cutting your wood and working your potatoes! Go home and do something!' Babushka replied, refusing to be persuaded.

In the evening another man and his wife came to visit. The man was tall and gaunt. Soon after arriving, he began asking for vodka, and after some argument Babushka handed over two bottles. Within an hour sweat was dripping from his brow and two empty bottles sat by his feet. His wife explained that their family earnings totalled AU$17 a month. They had two young boys of ten and twelve years of age. When it was time for them to leave, he collapsed in the arms of his wife.

Night came and after another enormous meal, Babushka struggled up the ladder to rest with a sigh of relief on top of the brick furnace where she slept each night. I was woken hours later by a constant knocking at the front door. Babushka eventually stormed out, swearing at yet another man begging for alcohol.

Unfortunately, being awake made me acutely aware of a terrible rumbling in my bowels. It felt like any sudden movement would bring the contents gushing out. Earlier in the day, Chris and I thought it peculiar that Babushka had stated quite clearly that there was no toilet; we were instructed to find a place in the front yard. Taking my jacket I tiptoed through the kitchen, fumbling for the door handle in the dark. Eventually, I made it outside, leaving the door ajar to make things easier for my return.

I poked my toes into my shoes and shuffled out along a plank. It was raining and the muddy slush in the backyard was as black as the sky. Unfortunately, I hadn't been able to find any toilet paper, but that was the least of my problems. As I stepped off the plank and shuffled on, one of my shoes remained stuck in the mud. It didn't matter anymore. Resting against a heap of firewood, I squatted ... and slipped.

I managed to steady my footing but it was too late. A pungent smell wafted from below. Some quick thinking was called for. I had to get out of my pants and get rid of my underwear – carefully. All was going smoothly until I hit my right knee. The huge clump of clay made it almost impossible to roll down my pants. Desperately, I fiddled with the knot in the tea towels.

Finally, I removed the tea towel and my pants, and found myself with the soiled culprit in my hand. Then came movement from inside the house.

Frantic, I lifted a few logs and stuffed the underwear into the mud. With quivering hands, I wrapped the clay back onto my leg and pulled on the trousers. Just as I found the lost shoe, the door opened and I was blinded by the light of Babushka's torch.

'Oh, Tim, it's only you. What are you doing?' she asked.

'I was just going to the toilet,' I replied.

I never told Chris about the experience, and never let on that what I'd left in the woodpile was my last pair of underwear.

The following day it was time to test my knee. Out on the muddy street, it was clear that neither the clay nor the cream had helped. The same nagging pain flared, making a 300 metre ride an excruciatingly long distance. It was bitterly frustrating and disappointing that such a small injury could cause such havoc. If it were major, at least I would have known with certainty that I couldn't go on! We had ridden just 400 kilometres in a 10,000 kilometre journey.

As a last resort we walked to the nearby town of Lippin Bor to look for another doctor, to no avail.

By the time we stumbled back to Novi Vashki another huge meal was waiting for us, and Babushka wasn't taking no for an answer. After squeezing in half a dozen eggs, piles of drop scones and cottage cheese we lay on the couch.

'Christ, at this rate we won't be able to ride by the time we get out of here!' I said, with a groan.

'I know,' Chris replied, with a giggle.

Moments later, Babushka wandered in to inspect my knee. 'So, how is it feeling?' she asked.

'Um, well, it's not any better,' I said, in a near whisper.

'Well then, you know what we have to do? If the clay hasn't helped, then you will have to urinate on your knee!' She said it with all the seriousness and iron-fisted determination that she brought to all her tasks. I had to do some fast talking.

After convincing her that the clay had worked a treat, we wheeled the bikes out onto the street. We hugged and thanked her profusely. I promised myself that I would never forget her zest for life and the way she battled her cow with such humour.

Back on the road there was a sudden rush of tension. Chris's legs moved faster and faster as if he were in a race. Several kilometres down the road I decided to re-apply the cream. No sooner had I done so than the pain went – it literally vanished.

'Chris, mate, I don't want to jump the gun, but I think that cream works!'

'What, really?'

'Yeah, I think I have just been going about it the wrong way. This must be some kind of anti-inflammatory.'

Two days later we made camp on the sandy foreshore of a lake. For the first time we used the tent, and in the morning I awoke with the ugly task of preparing breakfast. As I rose my shoulder brushed against the tent wall, setting off a shower of ice particles. The rush of cold was instantaneous, as the warmth was wrenched from my thermal underwear.

At first I tried to get the stove going with bare hands, but my fingers quickly numbed and became stiff as wood. After putting on gloves, it was a relief to see the petrol stove burst into life. The only problem was that our water bottles were frozen solid.

Taking the axe and a shopping bag, I made for the edge of the lake. A golden pin-strip on the far side forewarned of the approach of the sun. It would be a slow process, though, and wouldn't come into view until after 9.30 a.m. Even so, the glow was just enough to give a gleam to the polished veneer of ice. After a flurry of chopping, I made my way back to the tent with the bag full of jagged ice shards.

By the time we were getting stuck into the porridge, the sun was just nudging over the horizon into a clear sky. The foreshore looked like a desert plain, dotted with tufts of long spinifex grass. Sand dunes encrusted with sparkling ice crystals rose along the shore. In his puffy down jacket Chris looked set for the North Pole.

In the excitement, I took out the digital video camera Chris had picked up in Sydney before flying to London. We had a whimsical idea that if we filmed enough footage we might be able to make a documentary about the journey.

'C'mon, Tim, we haven't got time!' Chris snapped.

'Why? This is probably the most stunning morning we've had. It will only take five minutes!' I replied, opening the lens cap.

I filmed Chris riding along the frozen sand, his tyres leaving not the slightest trace. After reclaiming the camera, he pushed off towards the road.

After the first few turns of the crank the cold penetrated to the bone. The razor-sharp air cut through the gloves until my fingers were numb. I dreaded the re-warming routine that made my hands feel like they had been hit with a hammer over a red-hot anvil.

Although the sky was cloudless, particles of ice floated down like tiny pieces of shredded cellophane. Now and then a truck whooshed by, sending a plume of white that collected in my mouth and eyes, forcing me to blink continuously.

Chris was a speck in the distance, no doubt pedalling at full speed to get to the Internet in Vologda. In an effort to catch up, I pushed my legs as hard as I could.

It was after Chris cycled straight through the first village that I began to worry. I was hungry and we were out of biscuits. By the time I caught up, I was in a state of hypoglycemia, near collapse.

'Chris, I really need to get some biscuits,' I said, eyeing a village 200 metres further on.

'No way, mate, we've got to get to Vologda. I am not stopping before lunch,' he said.

I looked at him, trying to hold in my frustration.

'Well,' he said, looking at the map, 'what about this village here? It's only another six kilometres.'

'All right, fair enough,' I said, satisfied that we had reached a compromise. We pressed on.

I was riding alongside Chris as we approached the turn-off for the village. I veered towards the houses, but Chris didn't budge. I stopped on the far side of the road. 'Chris! What are you doing? We agreed to stop for biscuits!' I yelled.

'Yeah, well I'm not stopping. I'm going to Vologda and I don't even want *pryaniki*!'

Didn't he realise how hungry I was? Or maybe he didn't care.

'Well, give me the group wallet and I will buy the *pryaniki*!' I yelled. Chris did a semi-circle, lobbed me the wallet and rode off.

There was no time to waste so I released the brakes and rolled into the village. My eyes darted in search of a shop. 'Where can I buy biscuits? Where can I buy biscuits?' I yelled at pedestrians, until a frightened looking woman pointed me in the right direction. To my horror there was a queue outside the kiosk window. Five minutes later I stood drooling over the *pryaniki* display.

I purchased a bag, stumbled two metres onto the curb and devoured half a kilogram. Only then did my heartbeat slow and the world come into focus.

With renewed energy, I returned to cycling. My anger and frustration balled up in my chest. I wanted to tell Chris exactly what I thought of his behaviour. As I became lost in my thoughts, I heard a familiar voice.

'Tim, hey, Tim!' Chris was sitting in a bus shelter. My fury faded as I was greeted by the warm soup he had prepared. As I slurped it down, I noticed that he was even more pissed off than me. 'You know I've had to wait for half an hour. My toes are getting cold,' he said, finally.

'If you had come to the village that wouldn't have happened,' I replied.

'Tim, it's pretty obvious that you are eating more *pryaniki* than me. I think it's time that you bought your own.' He was referring to the fact that we were buying all food with our pooled funds.

'Okay, fair enough. But do you understand how bloody hungry I was back there? I was desperate.'

'Yeah, well, at this rate we are never going to get to Vologda, let alone China.'

'Chris, mate, I am cycling as hard as I can. If we don't make it, we don't make it. But I am trying.'

'I don't know about you, but I'm going to get to Kirov before we stop for winter. We just have to!'

'But Kirov is another nine hundred kilometres or so! What about the cold? And what if something happens? We've got to expect the unexpected.'

'Yeah, but the unexpected almost never happens! If we set our goal at that, then that is what we will achieve.'

'Sure, mate. All I'm saying is that we do what we can without bloody killing ourselves.'

Later that evening we arrived at Vologda just after sunset. People were rushing about in their winter furs, treading carefully on the ice-encrusted streets. I hoped that a night in the warmth would do us the world of good.

Upon arrival, I stepped off the bike and stumbled about unsteadily. My feet had frozen up to the ankles and felt like iceblocks hanging off the end of my shins. The pain was excruciating as I stamped life back into them. Eventually, we made our way back to the dorm in the basement of the old Orthodox church.

At first light Chris was gone like a rocket. I knew I would find him at the telegraph station, on the Internet. We spent the afternoon doing the food shopping for another two weeks of riding. The markets were cluttered with an influx of new fur hats and coats for winter. As we wandered along the boot aisle, I eyed a pair of *valenkee.*

Valenkee are knee-length boots made from felt. They are traditional and still used all over Russia in winter. I thought, fleetingly, about buying a pair but decided not to when Chris objected to the idea.

By the time we reached the outskirts of the city the following morning my toes were already numb. The ditches were no longer covered in a thin layer of ice, but were solid to the bottom. Even at midday the sun failed to rise above the tree line and lift the shadows. There were only five hours of daylight and we 'had' to keep up an average of seventy kilometres a day.

It wasn't long before we invented the 'cold feet dance'. This involved getting off the bike at regular intervals and jogging on the spot until life and warmth flowed back down into our feet. The road cut straight into the forest; we were back to passing tiny wooden villages.

In the evening we pulled into camp only to discover that the tent pegs couldn't be hammered into the frozen earth; a few ended up bent at right-angles. At dinner we raced to finish our stodgy macaroni and sardines before the bottom layer froze to the base of the pot. It took hours for my toes to warm up in the sleeping bag and I felt as if I wore slippers of cold around my feet. At minus 20 degrees Celsius it was by far the coldest night of the journey.

The following morning, riding became almost unbearable after the first two minutes. I wanted to cry from the pain as my feet froze and frost collected on my eyelashes. Eventually the lashes fused together and I struggled to pry them apart. My nose wasn't coping much better. With every breath the nostril hairs turned stiff with ice. Before too long there were mini icicles growing around my mouth and under my nose. I wore full Gore-Tex gloves, a balaclava and a down jacket. My footwear, however, was just a standard pair of leather hiking boots. Amazingly, Chris wore a cheap pair of Romanian-made runners and seemed to hardly feel the cold.

For several days we powered on in freezing conditions. We started the day in darkness and ended similarly. Chris rode ahead for most of the time, increasingly dissatisfied with the distance we were covering, which amounted to between fifty and sixty kilometres a day. I felt miserable and exhausted, unable to really connect with the land or with Chris.

At about three o'clock in the afternoon of our fifth day out of Vologda, I caught up with Chris and stopped for another dance on frozen toes. A dark wall of clouds was marching in from the east. The sunlight was fading quickly as Chris mounted his bike and rode out of sight. I too climbed back onto the bike, taking solace in the fact that it had been the last dance for the day.

When I looked at the sky, the clouds had already hit and a white curtain was sweeping over the forest. Soon I found myself beneath snowflakes that fell as large as butterflies. In minutes the road was layered in a murky white, the forest barely distinguishable from the sky.

I cycled on for what seemed an eternity, looking for signs of Chris's camp or tyre tracks. The light disintegrated into a dark blurry grey, making it difficult to stay on the road. Beyond a five-metre radius there was just a sea of white. Had Chris gone further on?

I cycled until even the grey faded and I knew it was well beyond sunset. 'Chris, where the hell are you?'

Finally, I gave up and rolled the bike off the road to set up the shelter.

We had not anticipated splitting up; and as I went through my bags I grinned. I had all the cookable food, but Chris had the pots. I had a torch but he had the batteries. It was pure luck that I had an unopened bag of *pryaniki*.

Comfortably, I wriggled into bed with the sweet taste in my mouth. When I stopped eating or moving, there was just the sound of snow peppering the shelter. No munching, brushing and breathing. And yet there was no one to talk to, either.

Next morning, I was on the roadside at first light. The snow had transformed the landscape. Gone was the mud, the stark skeletons of trees and the mushy greys. Everything shone a glaring white. The trees looked as if they were in full bloom with puffy white flowers. The road looked like a frozen river winding through the trees.

For three hours I waved down traffic. 'Have you seen a foreigner on a strange bicycle like this?' I asked, only to be met with negatives.

Eventually, a black speck appeared in the distance. At first I grimaced, but as Chris came closer, I couldn't help smiling. 'Good morning mate!'

'Morning,' Chris replied. 'I guess you'll be wanting breakfast then! I don't suppose there are many *pryaniki* left?' He wiped the snow from his brow and giggled.

'So what happened?'

'Well, I went to make camp and left the flag out on the roadside. I thought it strange that you didn't arrive and when I went back to check, the flag was covered by snow. Sorry, I slept in a bit this morning.'

We told our stories over a double serving of glorious porridge and even did some re-enactments for the video camera. Something about the break had cleared the air. What's more, my toes were feeling better and the novelty of riding in the snow beckoned us back to the road.

Less than three kilometres further on the forest widened and we entered the large village of Babushkina. I chuckled at the name – it was so similar to babushka. Was it a village of bubbly, rotund old women?

The greying homes didn't look quite so drab in the snow. Smoke puffed away in every chimney and vanished into the clear air above. A lack of *pryaniki* and fresh bread was a good enough excuse for stopping.

While Chris wandered into the shop, I minded the bikes. A trickle of pedestrians shuffled through the snow in long fur coats. Two women took a long sideward glance before moving on. I watched curiously as they went ten metres and doubled back. Again they passed me without saying a word. By the time Chris came back they had walked by three or four times. As I bit into a fresh *pryaniki* they plucked up enough courage to approach.

'Excuse me, boys, do you mind if I ask where you are from?' the older of the two asked, nervously.

'Of course we don't mind! We're from Australia and we're going to China,' I replied.

'Oh, you poor boys, aren't you cold? How about some hot mushroom soup, how does that sound?' she enquired.

I looked at Chris, whose eyes suddenly lit up. A smile cut across his red chaffed skin.

We followed our hosts into a sleepy little cottage. The warm air hit me like a wall making my face and eyes tingle. We were ushered to a table and, for the first time in a week, I removed my beanie and tried to bring some dexterity to my fingers. I felt like a lump of butter melting in the sun.

It made me realise that for what seemed like an eternity, the cold had dominated our lives. There wasn't a moment when it hadn't been a source of anxiety or pain. The only time we had been warm was in the sleeping bags at night.

The older woman introduced herself as Tatyana. 'Here you are boys, eat up!' she demanded, placing a bowl of mushroom soup before me.

Without hesitation, I plunged in my spoon. The hot liquid ran down my throat to fill my stomach as if it were an internal hot-water bottle. As the heat radiated and thawed me, the feeling was nothing short of divine. But this rare opportunity to relax didn't last long.

Almost immediately, my toes began to throb and sting with the rush of blood pumping through my limbs. I stopped short of finishing the soup and ever so subtly slid my socks off under the table.

A large purple blister, the size of a big bulbous marble, was hanging off the end of the big toe on my left foot. There was a similar blister on my right foot, only pale white in colour. They looked lifeless and artificial, like light bulbs screwed onto my feet; I could only feel my big toes from the first joint. Somehow, it didn't register that they were part of me. Then I wanted to throw up.

The world came zooming into focus with a dizzying punch. I tried to process the situation but my brain just seemed to short-circuit. For a while I stared into the swirls of chopped mushroom and drips of oil in the soup.

Eventually, I nudged Chris and gestured towards my toes. 'Chris, mate, I don't know what to do. I think I might have ...' I whispered, too scared to say the word.

He looked down, a little puzzled. There was a sense of blankness about him, like he had no way of grasping the gravity of the situation. Suddenly, I felt disconnected from him – I had frostbite and he didn't. I was cut off in a world of trauma that he couldn't possibly understand or do anything about. Would he ride on without me?

Then my feelings turned to anger. How stupid and weak had I been? I had been blindly riding while my toes froze. I had trained in these conditions for a year and knew the risks involved. But, I had felt guilty for having cold feet and for complaining.

Long after this incident had passed, Chris and I discovered that there was one reason for the frostbite that neither of us had foreseen. The laid-back position of riding a recumbent bike meant that gravity didn't aid the process of blood circulation to the feet. Furthermore, the pressure of our feet on the pedals squeezed the blood out of the toes. This meant that our toes were much more susceptible to frostbite than if we had been walking in the same conditions. In my opinion, I still had the ability to judge how cold my feet were; my error was inexcusable.

Tatyana eventually caught onto what was going on and lifted the tablecloth for a look. Her scream confirmed my worst fears. 'Frostbite!'

Within seconds Chris and I were bundled up in two heavy winter coats. Tatyana took one look at my hiking boots and tossed them aside contemptuously.

'Well, of course you've got frostbite! These are terrible-quality shoes, not made for the cold! I take pity on you. Here, take these *valenkee*.'

I slipped my feet into a pair of the knee-high felt boots, completely defenceless against her finger-pointing.

She grabbed me by the arm and marched down the street with Chris in tow. It was snowing heavily. Through clouded vision I caught glimpses of wooden homes draped in snow, that gradually crept over the roof edges, obscuring all but the walls. It looked like the closing eyelids of a creature going into hibernation.

Tatyana had given Chris a woman's coat decorated with colourful floral embroidery. With large snow flakes catching in his eyelashes he looked like a Russian drag queen. Somehow it fitted into a world that was fast becoming surreal.

Just before we stormed into a derelict looking building – the medical clinic – I turned to Chris.

'Mate, no matter what happens, if I have to be operated on, I want it to happen in Finland – just not here.'

Inside, Tatyana dragged us past a rather subdued queue, wielding me as if I was a formidable weapon. 'Australians! I have an Australian! I am coming through! Make way!' she screeched. We stumbled into an office to be met by an astonished doctor and patient. The uncomfortable silence was shortlived. Tatyana bleated out the gory details. 'This young man is from Australia and he is riding to China, but he has frostbite! I had to bring him here!'

The doctor, who was middle-aged and of Dagestani descent, looked contemplatively at me. I took note of his olive skin and deep-set eyes that were fringed by dark bushy eyebrows. 'Just take your socks off. Just take them off and show me!' he said.

Pinching the end of the first sock, I pulled it off slowly and then removed the other one, oblivious to the fact that I had daintily dropped them onto the doctor's telephone. After two weeks' wear, the smell was overpowering.

After screwing up his nose in distaste, the doctor seemed to collect himself and focused on my toes. 'Well, Tim, what are your plans? Because I am going to have to operate immediately, and you will have to stay here for ten days. You could get gangrene if you leave it much longer.'

Next, I was pushed through another door and onto a cracking vinyl bench. A nurse washed my toes with disinfectant, and from the corner of my eye I noticed a glint of metal – the doctor was sharpening a pair of deadly looking scissors.

'What are you doing? What are you doing?' I asked.

'Oh, nothing, nothing,' the doctor replied, chuckling. Frantic, I pulled out my pocket dictionary and began looking for words like 'painkillers', 'antibiotics', and 'numb'.

'What, are you going to read while I do this operation?' the doctor asked, with another chuckle.

Finally, I found the word for numb. But even as I said it, it was too late. With a snip two pieces of flesh were carved away, wrapped up in tissue paper and thrown into the bin. There was no pain.

'Look, look!' said the doctor, with a grin.

I peered at what I thought were the bloody stumps of my toes. 'Bloody hell, this crazy bastard has just cut my toes off!'

To add to the confusion, he told me he didn't expect payment, but asked if I could bring a baby kangaroo as a gift next time I visit Russia!

Chris was next in line, but fortunately he wasn't diagnosed with frostbite. A couple of days later, however, late symptoms of frostbite emerged and he too had some flesh removed.

Back at Tatyana's, I was put to bed and flattened with heavy blankets. Then she put on an old LP record. The tunes were slightly warped and crackly, but it didn't stop her from swinging a bemused Chris around the room in a dance.

All I could do was take pain-killers and wonder whether it was all a bizarre dream. Unbeknown to me, Tatyana and her daughter Lena had agreed to accommodate us for the ten days. And so our residence in Babushkina began.

Despite the distressing events of the day I was feeling grateful, and at ease by evening. As it turned out, the house didn't belong to Tatyana, but a seventy-five-year old babushka named Galya. Tatyana and Lena were visiting from their home in far-north Russia.

When Galya walked in the front door, she looked like a big round bundle of fur. I had expected a look of confusion when she saw a stranger in her bed, but nothing could be further from the truth. There was no hesitation, or even a look of suspicion; her entire being positively oozed with kindness.

It was made clear to us that we had been embraced with the care and support of a family. For the time being, Tatyana would be our mother, Baba Galya our grandma, and Lena our sister.

Tatyana was already busy organising our schedule for the next two days, ringing up countless friends and booking dinners and lunches. She was a short plump middle-aged woman with perky cheeks, wide eyes and a ∪ shaped smile. Her voice was rough and raspy and always on the verge of laughter. In no time at all we had gone from being independent boys on bikes to having our lives run for us.

Our first Baba Galya meal was a sign of things to come. The table was piled high with pancakes, fish pies, fried potato and preserved cucumber. This was followed by cottage cheese mixed with homemade blueberry jam. Almost everything was drowned in oil or salt, or both.

'Eat, eat, boys! You are eating terribly, you have to eat!' she shrieked, giggling contagiously. Her large fleshy face was framed by a red scarf, and her mouth was unusually small, like a card slot. Her forearms, in line with the rest of her body, were like large sticks of salami, not tapering from elbow to wrist. Her fingers were small and babyish, but obviously quite strong. Like Tatyana she was a little bit cheeky.

Along with dinner came the compulsory shot of vodka, which was produced with a wry smile from under the table. 'Now, Tim, a little bit of vodka is good to whet the appetite and wash the food down! But only a little. Baba Galya is a good girl, she only drinks *chuut-chuut* – a little,' said Baba Galya, with a smile.

'Yes, but I know what a Russian "little" means!' I replied, indicating a full glass. Everyone roared with laughter.

Baba Galya shot back a glass of vodka and turned to me. 'So, Tim, was that *chuut-chuut*? Would we be guilty if we drank some more?'

'Maybe, maybe not,' I replied.

'Oh you, Tim! Then "maybe" it is not naughty and we will have some more!'

At some point in the conversation, Chris and I decided that Baba Galya was the equivalent of a local queen. We began to call her Queen Galya, which brought about more boisterous laughter. Later on, to add to the nonsense, Tatyana told us of her plans to marry Gorbachev and to visit Australia with him.

Lena was twenty-eight years old, and a unique person in a tragic situation. She was tall and slim with long blonde hair and striking features. Two years earlier she had lost her voice and never regained it. Since then she had lost her job, her health and her boyfriend; and in her own raspy words become 'wooden' because people treated her like she was devoid of intelligence. When she attempted to speak, it was in a whisper that was obviously painful. This didn't stop her laughing though. In fact, happy tears came to her eyes and rolled down her cheeks several times over dinner.

When Chris and I eventually stumbled to bed we were holding our full bellies. Baba Galya and Tatyana did the rounds, tucking us in, turning off the light and saying goodnight.

I was woken in the predawn gloom by Baba Galya. She was carrying a bundle of firewood from outside. It must have been freezing. Soon I could hear the crackling of firewood and the sizzle of fresh pancakes. I went to sleep again, and was woken by the sweet smell of hot food. The sun was up and Tatyana was babbling away energetically. After checking my temperature, I hobbled to the table. 'My temperature is still fine. So far so good,' I said, to the relief of everyone.

Breakfast was no less extravagant than dinner, with delicious pancakes, cottage cheese and soup. It came with a healthy serving of Baba Galya's favourite food, *sala*, which is salted, often smoked, pig fat. It is eaten in great quantities during the winter in Russia and the Ukraine.

'Baba Galya loves *sala*!' she said, while nibbling on the white pieces of fat. I had also grown to love it and devoured countless slices along with bread and whole cloves of garlic. Chris, on the other hand, had reservations about eating pure chunks of fat.

Once again we ate to bursting point and were left feeling like immovable blobs. We had only stopped riding for a day, but if this kept up for ten days we would most certainly be overweight by the time we departed.

As we began to pack up the breakfast mess, I heard Tatyana use a word that was unfamiliar to me. 'Tatyana, what does *szhopa* mean?' I asked.

She laughed and so did Galya. 'Hey Baba Galya, show Tim what a *szhopa* is!' Tatyana demanded. With a cackle Galya turned around and slapped her bum. Arse, it meant arse!

Our day was mapped out by Tatyana. After breakfast Chris helped cart water from the well. The water had frozen overnight and they had to break the ice with a long pole before lowering the bucket.

Then there was the firewood collecting, and gathering of potatoes in the cellar. It struck me that Galya was one of the most energetic and lively seventy-five-year-olds that I had ever known. Just the mere fact that she had to keep the fire going at all times would have been hard enough.

At lunch we had guests from across the street. Baba Sveta, as we came to know her, had the same humour and zest for life as Galya. Together they were unstoppable. Baba Sveta, her daughter, and her grandaughter were all keen to see my photo album from Australia and talk about the adventure. I was glad that 'frozen toes' wasn't the main subject.

In the afternoon I had my first appointment with the doctor. He removed the bloodied bandages to inspect for any signs of infection, and I was relieved that only a small amount of flesh from the end of my toes had been removed. It would probably grow back without scarring. Whether the nerves would return or not was another question. One thing I knew very well about frostbite was that even after a mild dose, the affected part of the body would be permanently susceptible to cold. In any case, it was encouraging to face up to reality in the light of day – a far cry from the uncertainty of night.

In the days to come, the kitchen became central to our activities, the furnace serving as a source of heat, therapy and oven. Between chores, Baba Galya would often clamber on top of it for a short lie-down.

'It's good for warming my back and my arse! It's very kind, my furnace!' she'd say.

After chores we would ask Tatyana about the day's schedule. Every lunch and dinner was booked with a different family. One day we were guests of a local school teacher, on another day we visited a forestry worker. In the week to come we familiarised ourselves with many other families who were keen to spend time with the infamous 'Australians with frozen toes'.

In their company we enjoyed many celebratory rounds of vodka and it occurred to me that the culture of drinking in Russia definitely had its positive side. It was social drinking and far removed from the mentality of 'getting pissed' and drinking to drown one's sorrows.

My wounds continued to dry out without sign of infection. As my worries lessened, I spent more time taking note of life in Babushkina.

The strong community spirit was something that I had only ever read about in children's books. Everyone seemed to help out and we were treated as part of the community. Hardship and lack of money meant that survival depended very much on rallying together.

Everything pointed to a much greater sense of trust and togetherness than I had experienced in the western world. It might have been a hostile climate and an isolated part of the world, but it felt nothing like it.

To suggest that Babushkina was an ideal society would, of course, be going too far. Those who turned to vodka, as Baba Galya pointed out, eventually used up the generosity of the community. When individuals could no longer eat, because they had neglected to grow potatoes, and couldn't make fires because they hadn't collected firewood, the consequences were inevitable. Especially in winter, there was a high incidence of death by hypothermia among the drunks and alcoholics. Nature had its brutally just and merciless way of dealing with laziness.

It occurred to us that it was the women who were stronger, wiser and older. Many men seemed a little shrivelled and devoid of life; there were very few of Galya's age.

Perhaps there was some sense of brutal justice in an abusive drunk dying of hypothermia. But what about the poor teachers who hadn't received their wages for more than twelve months? The unemployed? The elderly without family, and other disadvantaged people? Life must have been incredibly tough.

One day we made a special appearance at the local school. There was a chorus of gasps as we entered the classroom, before the children went supremely quiet. We were the first Westerners many had seen. With the knee-high felt boots and rainbow-coloured stripy thermals under our jackets we probably looked just as weird as they had expected.

The sense of calm didn't last long. A group of about thirty students from another class rushed in and mobbed us with questions, and held out notepads for autographs. 'Please give me something for memory, please something for memory!' they begged.

When we left the school we were followed by a hoard of children running for more autographs. After signing a few, we realised there was nothing for it but to run back to Baba Galya's. Beyond the hype of the visit it was inspiring to see, as Chris put it, 'A little light blink on in their eyes as if they were thinking, Well if they are doing it maybe I could do something like that, too.'

The following day it became apparent that we had become a little too famous. We were paid a visit by a police sergeant. We hadn't registered our passports with the local administration and he seemed to think that we were spies. He demanded to flick through our diaries even though he couldn't understand a word of English, let alone our scrawl. When he left the house Baba Galya said, 'Don't worry, he is just a bit of a fool.'

The next day, however, we were required to visit the police and register our visas and passports. The sergeant seemed a little frustrated that he no longer had the authority to deal with every foreigner as a suspect for espionage.

'You know, boys, during the USSR this would have been illegal! You couldn't have been here freely!' he exclaimed. When asked what we had been spying on, I piped up that we were investigating the ingredients of Baba Galya's pancakes and the way a *banya* worked. The whole event was a scene of great amusement for our hosts and friends.

The last days reached fever pitch levels of celebrations and visits. We barely had a minute to ourselves, and if we did it had to be planned according to Tatyana's gruelling schedule. Much to our embarrassment, Lena and Tatyana decided to handwash our clothes, including our filthy socks and thermals. The job must have been awful, but they simply refused to take no for an answer. Baba Galya stitched up the holes in our clothing and gave us each a new pair of socks. All three got up much earlier than us and went to bed later. It was obvious that they were not only working harder than us but had more energy. It was incredible. We were definitely being spoilt to the core.

It was really quite sad when the tenth day came around and the doctor gave me the all clear to leave; we no longer had an excuse to call Babushkina home.

Our last night was a fitting end. Thirty of our most treasured friends in Babushkina came around for a party. With her collection of old Russian records, Tatyana was DJ and all the babushkas worked together to put on a feast fit for a king. The men supplied the vodka.

We ate on one long table and raised our glasses in toast to Baba Galya, Tatyana, Lena, Babushkina as a whole, and of course the Australians. Our Russian had improved and my attempted thank you speech was greeted with barrels of laughter. They loved the idea that we considered Babushkina 'paradise' and that Baba Galya was our queen. I hoped they understood that we really meant it.

For a few euphoric hours we danced into the night. Chris and I took turns at dancing with all the babushkas, including Galya. The most memorable song had the repetitive lyrics of: 'Babushka! Babushka Babushka! Babushka!'

The next morning we rose to have our last Baba Galya breakfast. Later, we bundled into a Lada for the drive to Vologda. We had long decided that frostbite had ended our cycling for the year. Although we had only covered 900 kilometres (a far cry from the progress Chris had hoped for), the onset of winter made further travel impossible. Our plan was to leave the bikes in Galya's shed and return in three months when spring made cycling feasible. I was more than happy to forget the painful reality of cycling for a while and keep my toes warm.

After repeating final goodbyes and hugging our three hosts, we lurched away and I watched the teary-eyed babushkas through the foggy window.

Within ten minutes we had passed into the forest and left the cluttered collection of houses behind.

A sign that read 'Welcome to Babushkina' caught my eye.

I grinned to myself; it really couldn't have been a more aptly named village.

Fighting the Snow
Babushkina – Kirov
Winter 2000

Chris

I stepped off the St Petersburg–Murmansk express into the freezing gloom of early morning Petrozavodsk. A couple of old ladies wrapped in countless shawls awoke from a standing doze. They were selling sunflower seeds and they raised hopeful eyes to the few passengers. I walked past them, my boots crunching the gritty snow on the platform as I shrugged my heavy backpack into position and made my way into town. I took a deep breath and tried to collect my thoughts.

A lot had happened in the weeks since we'd said goodbye to Baba Galya. Tim and I returned to Finland and spoke at over a dozen schools throughout the country. Afterwards, Tim headed back to Russia to spend Christmas with his mother and sister, who'd come especially to see him. As for me, I hitchhiked to London where I'd booked a cheap return flight back to Australia.

Home! My heart throbbed at the thought of it. Home and Nat.

It was both a reunion and a confirmation. We'd spent two and a half months apart, and proved that our relationship could last.

We got engaged via a sort of mutual proposal. The topic had hovered unstated on the edge of our e-mails and letters ever since we parted in Bucharest and now, oblivious to the world and basking in each other's adoring gaze, the subject had come up with ease. Smiling and without need of words, Nat gave me an engagement ring.

We spent most of the two weeks in each other's arms. I was relishing this new sense of commitment, a new and wonderful top priority in my life. We were both trying to catch up on the months past and to fill our senses and memories with each other to help us survive the year apart.

Inevitably, the clock ticked down and we were finally wrenched apart by the final boarding call for flight 804 at Sydney Airport. It was 29 December, and my departure ruined Nat's twenty-first birthday. Two days later, the new millennium saw me alone and staring wretchedly at a dark ceiling in Stockholm. And two days beyond that, the train spilled me onto the icy platform in Petrozavodsk. Deep down I went over the same endless question I'd been asking myself since the previous year. I was coming back for a stormy, exciting year with Tim. But honestly, I didn't know if I wanted to be there.

In the meantime, there was much to be done. Together with two of Tim's friends from the wilderness guide course we were about to head north on a cross-country skiing trip in the Khibiny Mountains, above the Arctic Circle. We were planning an ambitious twenty-three-day journey through virgin forest and high mountain passes, towing our food and equipment behind us on plastic sleds. The temperature would get down to minus 40 degrees Celsius, and the sun would emerge from below the horizon for less than an hour a day. It would also be my first time on skis.

Four weeks later, I stumbled from the train and surveyed the snowy scene at Petrozavodsk station once again. The skiing trip had been only partially successful. Our cheap wooden skis and spring bindings had broken; one of the tents – a Soviet model – had blown to pieces in a blizzard; and Tim had suffered a mild case of frostbitten toes. On the other hand, I'd learnt to ski; we'd spent two days weathering out a storm in the eerie silence of a snow cave; and we'd experienced the frozen beauty of the Arctic forest under a blanket of winter snow.

I met up with Tim, back from a week of frostbite treatment in Finland, and we started planning our next moves. Originally, we'd been thinking about spending the next month or so travelling into the northern Arctic tundra, where we'd hoped to stay with the Nenets people. The Nenets are nomadic reindeer herders living above the Arctic Circle; spending time with them would have been fascinating. Our experience in Khibiny, however, had made us think twice about living in the extreme cold, and besides, we'd identified a more pressing problem. If we were going to survive for almost another year in this country, we desperately needed to improve our Russian.

We hired a teacher to tutor us in the language and spent six weeks living and studying in Petrozavodsk. Tim rented a flat and I boarded with the Kleshnok family. We spent up to eight hours a day with our tutor, cramming vocabulary and grammar, progressing in leaps and bounds. In the meantime, we were also getting ready to leave.

The plan was to start riding again at the very beginning of spring, when there would still be deep snow in the forest and possibly ice on the roads. We would have to prepare ourselves, properly this time, against the cold and the wet in order to avoid another bout of frostbite. And as we were heading east now, away from the security of Finland and the big Russian cities in the west, we also had to make sure we were self-sufficient for the rest of the year.

We had ridden barely 600 kilometres the previous autumn and had at least 9,000 to go. Every day would take us further towards the vast unknown of Siberia and further away from the civilization of the west. In nine months, almost anything could happen; in fact, I was expecting almost everything *to* happen, both disasters and unexpected, spontaneous joys.

Thus, it was with butterflies in the stomach that I set about getting my things ready for the ride. For me this uncertainty is also central to the addictiveness of this kind of travel. As always, I was hoping for only the wonderful, but experience had taught me that on a journey as long as this, it would be almost impossible to avoid disasters.

I reasoned that a little bit of strategic planning and preparation would help to make disasters enriching challenges, rather than conclusive and irreversible stuff-ups. I quietly packed the most versatile and comprehensive travelling tool kit I could carry before boarding the train for Babushkina.

Baba Galya was looking a little pale and her belly laugh was a little more subdued when we returned to her cottage. She had been in hospital for ten days over winter with a respiratory problem. Usually a picture of robust and bawdy good health, she sat subdued at the table chewing on a piece of smoked pork fat and tut-tutting as we related our experiences of the last months. She was particularly concerned when we revealed our plans to begin riding again at the end of the week.

'There's still two metres of snow in the forest,' she declared, looking pointedly at our toes. 'You'll freeze!'

Nevertheless, we set about preparing our bikes and dropping in on our old friends. Our bikes and gear had spent the past four months huddled in a draughty shed and now the frozen components needed to be stripped, cleaned and reassembled. My luggage rack needed some minor welding and our equipment in general needed a thorough overhaul.

I reached tentatively into one dark pannier and pulled out a heavy jar of peach jam. The contents had frozen in the intense cold and looked like an alchemist's jar of preserved brains. My cycling sneakers had frozen solid as two boards, and Tim's gear and brake cables had completely iced up. We sat rebuilding our bikes in one of the unheated back rooms, rugged up against the minus ten degree Celsius chill and listening to Smashing Pumpkins on Tim's walkman.

We visited our friends and most nights enjoyed a fresh round of enjoyable but less riotous parties. The long, dark winter had taken its toll on the people and I got the impression that our friends were running low on energy reserves. It seemed that everyone was waiting patiently, biding time until the spring sunshine returned to rejuvenate their lives.

One major deliberation we faced was in choosing a suitable present for Baba Galya. Like most pensioners in Russian villages, she lived on a government allowance of only a couple of hundred roubles a month – thirty or forty Australian dollars. In practise this was paid irregularly and never in full. To survive, she had to rely on her own labour: picking and preserving barrels of berries and mushrooms from the forest in summer, growing as many potatoes as she could fit into her plot of land and chopping tons of firewood to see her through the winter. She had put all this on hold to look after us like royalty. We felt we owed more than we could ever possibly hope to repay.

The most precious thing in Baba Galya's life was her daughter, Irina, who lived in the Ukraine on the Black Sea. They hadn't seen each other in years because of the prohibitive price of the train fare – AU$100 for us, yet an almost unattainable fortune for the average Russian. We wanted to give her the fare, but were uncertain as to whether she would accept the money. We decided to offer her half, with explanations on the tip of our tongues in case she refused. But, to our surprise, she accepted the gift straight away. She saw not the cash we were offering but the face of her daughter.

She grabbed the notes at once, bursting into a flood of embarrassed tears.

I went to bed feeling horrible. The sight of the brave face she had put on when she realised that we had not given her enough was still clear in my mind. I waited until I was certain she was asleep then had a hurried discussion with Tim. We found the place where she kept her valuables and added the balance to the little pile of money.

The next day we were ready to depart. Our bikes were as ready as they'd ever be. All of our extra gear was strapped on, and the machines stood heavy and overloaded before us. The road was icy, and it took a couple of practise runs and slippery crashes before we were able to start trundling away.

We waved goodbye to Baba Galya and some of our other friends then turned onto the main street, which was thankfully clear of snow. We headed at snail's pace towards the other side of town and the open highway. We rolled down the hill towards the river and stopped for a crowd that, like most in the village, had heard of us but whom we hadn't yet met. A couple of policemen emerged from the throng, too. They pulled us aside on the pretext of checking our passports, but they were really just itching with curiosity and keen to get a look at our bikes.

We crossed the river and pedalled back up the hill. It was a relatively gentle slope, but such was our podgy condition after the motionless months of winter that it felt like a major mountain range!

I shifted down to my easiest gear then pedalled, heaved and blew. My legs filled with liquid fire and my lungs strained to bursting point. My gulping breaths were threatening to tear apart my chest and my heart pounded crazily inside me. It was below zero, but I was sweating a fountain. Red spots prickled the backs of my eyes and I bit my lip hard, struggling to stay upright.

A toddler from the village watched, fascinated as I veered from one side of the road to the other. She scurried over for a closer look and I gave her a quick grin as she walked beside me. The look on her face seemed to say that she was unsure whether to burst out laughing or to run ahead and tell her friends to come and watch too!

Gasping for breath, I reached the top and let out a cheer. Tim pulled up beside me and we surveyed the open and mercifully flat road ahead. Sure, we'd only come a few hundred metres, and sure we had over 9,000 kilometres to go, but at the top of this slope I felt on top of the world.

We pushed off again and crawled away from the village. Hour by hour, day by day, month by month, we'd make it. Road or no road, come snow or mud. We were finally moving again and it felt great! We were inching our way to China!

An hour or so later, after we'd decided that our pudding bellies had had enough exercise for the day, we realised that the cycling over the next few weeks was going to be the easy part of the journey. The road we were on had been kept clear of snow the entire winter, leaving a two-metre-high pile of muddy ice and snow on either side of the road. We spent an hour hauling our bikes to the top of this formidable barricade, then an hour more bulldozing them across fifty metres of handlebar-deep snow between the road and the treeline.

I slumped exhausted, wet and sweating over the back of my bike. We rested for a few minutes before Tim spent an hour digging a pit for the fire and setting up the shelter. I went off to hunt for firewood. I climbed dead trees and hacked away at the upper branches, then waded through freezing, waist-deep snow, dragging the fruits of my labour back to camp. It was gut-wrenchingly hard work that left us exhausted and it wasn't for weeks – until the snow started to melt and we were getting fitter – that our camp site duties began getting easier.

Later, as the burning wood crackled and the pot of snow slowly melted, we fervently argued our way back to the last meal of our very last day of cycling the previous year.

'What the hell do you mean it's my turn to cook the bloody dinner, you lazy bastard, Chris? I definitely cooked last!' Tim exclaimed.

'What are you talking about, you bludger?' I retorted. 'The last night of riding last year was the night we lost each other just before Babushkina. You're not gonna try and get me to believe that eating a whole bag of biscuits counts as cooking dinner!'

'No.' He paused for a second to regroup. 'But the night before that! Hah! That night it was my turn to cook. So there, it *is* your turn.'

'Sure, mate, you cooked that night, but that means I cooked breakfast two mornings in a row! And in my books, that makes it *your* turn!'

We carried on for a while, until reluctantly I agreed that it was indeed my turn to cook the dinner. A little later, just after realising that I'd left my toothbrush at Baba Galya's, I crawled into my sleeping bag and within seconds fell fast asleep.

The next few days panned out in a familiar pattern. We'd wake before dawn, haul our bikes through the snow to the road, ride all morning, stopping at midday for a hot meal, then pedal on until early afternoon to make camp.

The temperature hovered up and down on either side of zero. During the day, the snow would melt to a wet slush and then freeze at night to form a perilously slippery surface. We were having trouble staying dry and warm. On really cold days, the old spectre of frostbite loomed again. Tim's toes, in particular, were suffering. He took to removing his socks by the snowy roadside and, after making sure there was no traffic in either direction, dunking his feet into cups of hot tea from the thermos.

In the evenings I would hunker down with a candle and write long letters to Nat, while Tim settled down to his diary with a shot of *barmatuki*, tea-infused vodka courtesy of Baba Galya. Before he ran out of this 'bedtime juice' he went through a week of evenings in various states of tipsiness. One evening he described himself as being 'pissed as a newt', a phrase I hadn't heard in years.

After four days we reached our first major milestone. The town of Nikolsk emerged from the trees, first as a few isolated cottages, then as a string of ornate wooden houses. We approached the river at the centre of town and stopped at a rundown *stolovaya*, a uniquely Russian establishment that, depending on the guests and the occasion, serves as a restaurant, café, pub or just a general eating-house for the masses.

The lady behind the counter was unimpressed as we traipsed in with our smelly, dripping clothing and faces smeared with mud and charcoal. Definitely eating-house, I could see her deciding. And hostile service as well.

Outside, a group of local men gathered around our bikes; we could see them poking, prodding and fiddling through the window. I finished quickly and dashed outside – too late to supervise one of the guys who pushed off on my bike and helped himself to a test-ride. He wobbled wildly for a few seconds before slewing heavily into the pavement. The rest of the guys cheered drunkenly while their friend brushed off his ripped pants and grazed elbows, and I went to make sure no damage had been done to my bike.

One of these guys, Igor, was about our age and seemed harmless enough. None, it seemed, really needed to get back to work and within a few minutes we'd been invited to someone's home. Only half an hour after determining that we could probably ride another twenty kilometres for the day, we were wheeling the bikes to Igor's father's house where there was a temptation beyond resistance: another meal!

Igor's father, Yefgeny, turned out to be an old grease-smeared communist. When we came across him, his head was stuck in the bonnet of a huge old Soviet *Kamaz* truck. He greeted us with a grunt from somewhere behind the carburettor, but emerged when he heard our accents. He'd never met a foreigner before but he approved of us instantly. Tim and I were, apparently, everything that foreigners should be: young, Russian speaking and adventurous.

'Such qualities,' Yefgeny said proudly, 'make you just like the fine young comrades of my day!' He looked narrowly at the gathering crowd and added in an undertone, 'They were a big step above listless, lazy young sloths like my son here.'

An impromptu party was thrown. Igor's mother laid the table with platters of boiled potatoes, jars of pickles and slabs of pork fat while her husband gleefully produced the bottles of vodka. Shots were downed quickly – much too quickly – and within minutes my head was buzzing. Yefgeny got rolling drunk and told loud, carousing stories about his good old communist days, while his wife looked on disapprovingly.

It was late at night when the vodka finally dried up. As Igor's guests, we walked across to his flat on the other side of town to be greeted by his extremely unhappy wife. She took one look at us, decided that we were drunk bums and launched into an all-out attack on her husband.

They had a long, loud and almost physical 'domestic'. He was a 'lousy, useless drunk who would lose his job and let her go hungry' and she was a 'stupid cow who should mind her own business'. Their baby daughter screamed unnoticed in another room, and we found our own way quietly into some spare beds. It was a relief to get back onto the road the following morning and head out of town.

We carried on, going a little further and getting a little fitter with every passing day. We went through a cold snap and woke one morning to find that the damp insides of our felt-lined

Russian gumboots had frozen solid. Neither of us wanted to get up, and we each lay silently in our sleeping bags, waiting for the other to make the first move. Finally Tim gave in to hunger pains. But after breakfast, as I was packing up and getting ready to leave, he told me that it was still too cold for his toes, and that we would have to stay put until it was warmer. Selfishly, this annoyed me and we had another fight.

'Come December,' I argued, 'when we're planning on riding into Beijing, it's gunna be heaps colder than now, and if your toes can't take this weather then we're simply going to have to finish up earlier. Like October!'

Actually, this was something that I'd thought about a lot. I was missing Nat terribly – the more so after leaving Petrozavodsk and breaking off the daily contact on the Internet. The thought of being able to knock a single day off the 'exile' was the stuff of my dreams.

'No way,' Tim replied, always the calm one during our arguments. 'We'd have to race the whole way, and we'd miss everything. Besides, there's no way I'm going back to Australia before my birthday.'

Tim's birthday fell on 7 December, and he'd long planned on returning to Australia a twenty-two year old. The seventh, however, was also the anniversary of my relationship with Nat, and a date for which I'd dearly love to be home.

Hard feelings rarely lasted long, the issues mostly dissolving into irrelevance shortly afterwards. We carried on riding, with the weather getting warmer and green patches of grass beginning to emerge on the southern sides of the rolling white hills. We rode through small and large villages and turned off the main highway on to progressively smaller roads. A lot of the locals had never been further from home than the next village and couldn't tell us much about the road ahead. As we travelled further, the warnings became more persistent.

'You won't get through!' people yelled from their windows. 'There's no road up ahead!' We laughed and carried on, feigning incomprehension. We were young and unstoppable, and besides, we had our 'reliable' Russian road atlas that showed us a road carving its way from here all the way to Mongolia.

It was a couple of days later, the morning after we'd pitched camp on our first patch of snow-free grass for the year, that we reached the village of Luptyug and realised what everyone had been talking about.

It was sixteen kilometres to Klyuchee, the next village, and between the two villages ran a provincial border. We turned onto the road, the bitumen ended abruptly, and I crashed painfully. The dirt road was covered in ice and embedded with fist-sized rocks. We were riding on studded ice tyres – the larger rear ones bought in Finland, and the smaller front tyres hand-studded with hundreds of steel screws and glue. These helped to an extent, but the going was perilous and the falls bruising and painful. Within a few kilometres, the road deteriorated again. I waited for Tim to pull up beside me and sat surveying the scene ahead. Nobody, but nobody, it seemed, travelled this way.

The two provincial authorities had obviously not been able to reach any agreement on who would maintain the road across the frontier. The result was that for four months of the year the two villages were cut off from each other by a two-metre-deep tract of snow.

Before us was a trench – a tractor had obviously got through in the past week or two – and we began the arduous task of pushing and hauling our bikes through the slushy snow. It was perhaps more of a moat than a trench – a half-frozen moat interrupted by regular islands of snow. A pattern quickly developed as we made our way through: we would wheel our bikes carefully along the slippery islands then double up to haul them one at a time up and out of the trench and around the moat sections through the waist-deep snow.

It was exhausting, wet work, and after an hour we'd covered only a few hundred metres. We reached the top of a small rise and saw the trench and its string of countless puddles and little islands stretching far ahead. We pushed on, still taking care to keep ourselves and the bikes clear of the water, but as we progressed our standards inevitably relaxed. Before long we were ploughing obliviously through the water.

One of the puddles was deeper than I expected. My bike dived in up to the handlebars, submerging my front pannier bags which contained a loaf of bread, packets of biscuits and my tool kit.

We made seven kilometres before stopping to camp. We quickly lit a fire and set to drying our clothes and sorting through some of the gear. I reached into a pannier and pulled out a bloated roll of toilet paper that had put on almost a kilo during the afternoon. Tim rummaged through his gear and found a bedraggled toy koala that he'd been saving to give as a gift somewhere along the way. Its wet and matted fur seemed so forlorn and the expression on its little synthetic face so homesick and miserable that we couldn't help ourselves. We laughed until our grimy faces were streaked with tears.

It wasn't until much later that we discovered Tim's bike had suffered a serious mishap during the push that afternoon. A submerged stick had caught in the spokes and tangled with his back gear-changer, breaking one of the jockey wheels, a vital component.

Jockey wheels are meant to last forever and I hadn't packed a spare, yet without it, Tim's bike was crippled. It was time, I decided, to improvise.

I cut a section of hardened plastic from the inside support of my front pannier then sat by the fire while Tim took my turn at cooking dinner. I had a traditional, bone-handled knife that had been given to me by a bear hunter we'd met along the road. It was very sharp, and I set to work carving a replacement jockey wheel.

At midnight, with the fire burning low and my eyes glazing over with sleep, my hand slipped and I sliced a deep gouge into the heel of my left hand. I went to bed swearing. Tim could finish the job in the morning.

Amazingly, it worked and after a few hours of pushing through the wet and cold of the trench, it seemed as though we had come through the worst of it. The puddles slowly disappeared and the snow thinned out to be replaced by sloppy, oozing mud. We were able to ride again.

We cruised through Klyuchee exultant. We had conquered the trench. We had made it through; we'd won. The road lay open and snow-free before us and although Siberia was still a thousand kilometres away, the distance seemed like peanuts compared to the past two days. We reached the top of a hill and turned to survey the village and snow – the *frontier* even – behind us. I paused for a minute, smiled and pushed off again.

Watch out Siberia, I thought. I'm on my way Nat.

Tim grinned like a maniac beside me. Then he let out a whooping yell: 'China, look out. Here we come!'

To the Urals
Kirov – Ekaterinburg
Spring 2000

Tim

We inclined along a road that followed a riverbank; soon the forest panned out in a blanket of green. Grey apartment blocks rose from a nearby hilltop like a fortress of civilization. On the river V'atka the reflection of the low sun was shattered into a million glistening shards. Water gushed out in a flurry from widening cracks in the partially frozen surface. The cold was finally losing its grip and it seemed like the corpse of winter was being swept away with the current.

Chris and I pushed harder and harder at the pedals. We were emerging blissfully into the city of Kirov.

Earlier that morning, we had braved the cold to wash in the melt-water of a roadside drain. I gave up after getting an ice-cream headache. Chris, on the other hand, had stripped off and washed all over with soap.

Sixteen days in the cold without a proper wash had taken its toll. Without a mirror to look at my face, it was my hands that worried me. The constant exposure, daily use of an axe and saw, and dealing with pots, had left them stained black and brown with calluses and blisters. In places the skin had dried and cracked, forming painful gashes that refused to heal. When I touched my chin with the sandpaper-surface of my hands, I felt the beginnings of a beard. I had decided to leave my shaver in Babushkina to save weight – and besides, shaving seemed unimportant on the road.

Soon we were in the throng of evening traffic. The driver of a trolley bus stuck his head out the window and yelled out, 'What the hell is that?' The fifty or so passengers that were crammed in the bus stared back at us.

It took several agonising hours to find a hotel with vacancies, and as the light faded, so did Chris's hope of getting to the Internet.

Eventually, we found ourselves outside a twelve-storey building with golden letters emblazoned above the entrance: Hotel V'atka. Several black Mercedes and a Toyota Landcruiser were parked outside, and as we pulled up three men in business suits sauntered out.

Chris darted inside and soon returned with a room key. 'Tim, mate, let's go!' he said. The V'atka was a plush-looking place, but a room for two only cost about AU$15. It was more than our budget allowed but we had little choice; besides, a little bit of luxury wouldn't hurt after what we'd been through.

Moments later we were wheeling the bikes across the polished marble floor of the lobby. There was no hiding our grease-stained panniers, muddy tyres, cracked soft drink bottles, and filthy socks lashed onto my backpack. It took two trips to lug the cumbersome bikes upstairs to our landing on the third floor. As we rolled them down the corridor, the landlady appeared. She stood as tall as possible on her high-heel shoes, accentuating the shortness of her white dress and apron. With her shiny legs bending at the knees and beginning to shake, she let out a deafening scream.

'Aaaahhhhhhh! What are you doing! You are disgusting, you are so dirty! You can't bring motorbikes up here! Get out, get out of here!' Her thick lipstick parted to expose a blur of perfect white teeth; peroxide blonde hair shivered atop her head.

'Oh no, don't worry, it's a bicycle and we have permission from downstairs,' I said.

'Like hell you do! I am going to ring the manager now. This is a clean hotel, we can't have you here. This isn't a garage, you know!'

By the time she made her phone calls, we had already spread our gear across the tiny two-bed room and parked the bicycles close to the window. Sleeping bags were up and drying on a makeshift washing line, bags of food were piled into a corner, and a mountain of dirty clothes sat in the middle of the floor. When she returned we were stripped down to shorts and preparing for a wash. She had no choice: we were foreigners and could be excused for our lack of manners.

When I looked in the mirror, I didn't recognise myself. Black grease stains framed my eyes and my hair was a giant mop that moved as one mass. A rough beard pierced the brown and black muck on my chin.

We divided the washing into two lots. For several hours Chris scrubbed at our socks and pants. It took six or seven bathtubs of black water before any sense of cleanliness was restored.

After a quick dinner of fresh fruit, we slid between the crisp white sheets and fell asleep. It was comforting to know that my legs wouldn't have to face more torture in the morning.

We spent one day in Kirov. It was a relief to be among crowds of people. Our shrunken universe of two had expanded dramatically. Rich 'New Russians', in their slick clothing and polished cars, looked positively shiny in the sunlight. Babushkas waddled around in shoals, selling potatoes along the street. Young women pranced about, straight-backed in stylish dresses, some flaunting long slender legs for the first time since winter. It is said that the end of spring, with the onset of warm weather, is when most car crashes occur in Russia, especially among male drivers.

I have always been fascinated by faces and found the Russians' to be especially expressive. When they are wrapped up in fur hats and coats all that remains is their large dark eyes and infectious smiles. Hours passed as I wandered about, feasting on the sight of such a compact display of life.

However, by the end of the day, I had made no real personal connections. On the empty roads and in the villages we had connected with many people, and I had never felt isolated. I knew that lingering on would only make me feel alone in the crowd.

Apart from the people, I relished the availability of ice-cream, the opportunity to rest my legs, and the chance to give Baba Galya a call; we had promised to keep in touch.

I made the call from a telegraph station in a little wooden booth. 'Hello, Baba Galya!' I boomed down the crackly line.

'Hello ... Tim ... is that you, Tim?' she shrieked.

'Yes, yes, Baba, it's me, we have made it to Kirov!' I said loudly.

'To Kirov! Really, you are already there? How are your toes? You didn't freeze them? How did my toe warmers work? You know I have been worrying about you the whole time. Oh boys, oh boys, my good boys!'

'Everything is fine, just fine, don't worry about us. We will ring again from Perm.'

'Okay, boys, be careful. I will let the rest of the village know. Good luck and thank God!'

Later on, in a small Internet centre, I watched in amazement as Chris leaned over the keyboard to tap furiously at the keys, his eyes gleaming. The points of his mouth rose and fell abruptly, and it looked like he was about to reach out and hug the screen.

As soon as he was done, he would be in a mad rush to get going again. I could see that his mood had lifted, and that he just wanted to get back out there, where he loved it most: on the bike. In light of this, I could understand why he was always frustrated by my meandering. He had a clear idea of what he wanted, while I was more keen on taking it slow and keeping my ear to the ground for unexpected opportunities.

As much as I missed sleeping under the stars it was with some reluctance that I packed up to leave the hotel. After donning shorts for the first time in six months, and baring blinding white legs, I set off after Chris. I cheerily waved at pedestrians and crowds lounging in street cafés until the air filled up my shorts like a parachute. I dared not look back at the spectators; I still didn't own any underwear.

The next destination lay 900 kilometres to the east, just shy of the Ural Mountains. We were heading for the city of Perm. Only by breaking the journey into a series of short goals did the larger aim of reaching Beijing seem remotely achievable.

Thirty kilometres or so out of Kirov we pushed the bikes effortlessly into the forest and camped in snow-free conditions. The following day, I removed my beanie and felt the air rush through my hair. It felt great to ride for hours on end without stopping to warm my toes. Finally, I could use the thermos water for drinking tea and not as a crude way of preventing frostbite.

The increased sunlight brought life back to the forest. Streams glimmered through the trees and we woke to a cacophony of bird song. Several times I saw a v of geese migrating north. The snow was melting by the second and lay in scattered patches like the shredded remains of tissue paper. Plants and rich green mosses reappeared on the forest floor, some still bearing ripe berries from last season.

I felt a part of myself come alive again, as if it had long been in hibernation. The sun caressed my shoulders and face like an old friend. The world was again a three-dimensional picture with millions of shades of colours. By comparison winter had been like a black and white graphic in low resolution. Even

Chris's face underwent a dramatic change. He had often looked pale and sallow in the grey light, but now, almost overnight, his cheeks shone like shiny polished apples.

East of Kirov the forest parted to reveal a series of open fields – green grassy pastures! The transformation had been so quick. A newly arrived tourist from the southern hemisphere would have wondered what all the fuss was over winter. There was absolutely no trace of the cold.

Despite the change we were not yet free of the legacy of winter. Perhaps worse than metres of snow and ice was the viscous mud left over after the snow melted. The unsealed road became more like the path of a mudslide. In some villages stagnant pools had risen above the base of houses, giving the impression that they were sinking.

Once again, we spent more time pushing than actually riding. The mud was so thick in places that trucks had become irretrievably bogged up to the axle. It became obvious why winter is the traditional season for travel in Russia. At least then the earth is hard and the layers of snow and ice render river, forest and swamp navigable.

Not far from the border of the small forested republic of Udmirtskaya the road inexplicably turned into smooth bitumen. The melting snow had drained away leaving a surface that seemed just too good to be true.

'Can you believe this, Chris? That's it, from here on riding is going to be a joy!' I turned to him as he clicked into top gear and shot off down the hill. I followed, roaring down, leaning into the corners. Above the forest, the sky even appeared hazy. We rode abreast, hogging the road and falling in and out of conversation and moments of contemplation.

By the time my senses were reawoken by hunger, we had covered fifty kilometres. And yet I could remember almost nothing of the landscape. Was I finally beginning to understand

Chris's love of cycling? It struck me that the recumbent was perfectly designed to promote thought. With my legs broken in, all we had to do was fill up on food now and then and keep going.

That evening I clambered up a treetrunk with the axe, in pursuit of a dead pine branch. Once among the branches, I decided to drop the axe to the ground and hang off the silvery grey limb until it snapped.

'Look out, Chris!' I shouted, as a loud crack echoed through the forest and I dropped to earth with a thud.

Later, as I was chopping the wood, I happened to stroke my ear in a bid to ease a slight itch. My fingernail came across a hard lump that felt like a scab. I tried to peel the scab away but it stuck hard to my skin. I dug my finger-nails in until it hurt. Finally, it came free with a small gush of blood. Inspecting my finger, I noticed what appeared to be a tiny bug with claw-like legs.

'Chris, what do ticks look like?' I asked, calmly.

'I'm not sure. I think they're small and round with flecks of red,' he replied, not taking much notice.

'You think they look something like this?' I asked.

I was furious. Why the bloody hell did this have to happen to me? Suddenly, everything irritated me. Chris's breathing, the crap firewood and the insect-filled forest. I knew that ticks in Russia were rife with encephalitis and lime disease. How long had the tick been on me? What were the symptoms of tick-borne disease? Worst of all was the thought of revisiting a Russian hospital.

I awoke early in the morning and lay still until the light revealed gaping holes in our *loue* shelter. They must have been freshly burnt by the spitting spruce fire. As I cursed everything under the sun, a peg loosened and the shelter drooped down onto my face.

TO THE URALS

There was no point in panicking. We washed in a stream and prepared to spend a day in the large town of Glazov, only fifty kilometres away.

The town came into view just as the road disintegrated into roughly laid slabs of concrete. Smokestacks and apartment blocks rose above the treeline. Derelict buildings with broken windows lined the road closer to the centre. Piles of garbage had been dumped clear of the residential quarter, forming a charming decoration.

After following vague directions towards the city centre we parked our bikes on the street. As we stepped off the bikes, a short middle-aged man pulled up on a small collapsible bicycle. He had short silvery-grey hair and a subtle moustache that blended almost without trace into his pale, drawn face. He wore an old but clean shirt buttoned up to the neck. His name was Mikhail. 'Wow, look at this thing' he said, eyeing the recumbent. His eyes darted behind slim-lined spectacles. He looked remarkably like a mouse.

We quickly got through the rigmarole of explaining every oddity of the bike, ourselves and about our travels. Then I explained the tick situation.

'I can show you how to get to the hospital if you want,' he offered.

In a second his wiry legs were whizzing around in a blur of speed. A small dust cloud trailed behind his bike and the old cane basket on the back rattled furiously. Locals on bikes always seemed to conclude that because we were long-distance travellers, we were also incredibly fast.

It wasn't long before I was trailing behind, squinting to see which streets Chris and Mikhail were taking. I watched Mikhail's short skinny arms shoot out to indicate direction. With just one hand on the handlebars he almost wobbled out of control before veering out of sight. Inevitably, I lost them.

My legs felt like swollen water balloons and I was puffing heavily when I finally spotted them outside the hospital.

While Chris waited outside, I went into the building with Mikhail. My first mission was to find a toilet. Inside the hospital, a series of dingy corridors were cramped with queues. We approached a woman in a white coat, but she didn't seem to be aware of what a toilet was and just shrugged her shoulders. Then we asked a tall man with a moustache that sprouted as thickly as a hedge from below his nose.

'Excuse me, can you tell me where is a toilet?' Mikhail asked.

The tall man broke into a high-pitched cackle before pulling one of the nurses aside. 'Beautiful woman, hey! Just damn beautiful!' he said, looking her up and down.

Soon the journey from office to office was underway. From the chemist we were sent to the head doctor, then to the registrar and back again. Eventually, we wound up in the office of the Infectionist.

The woman behind the desk was stunned by my presence. 'Are you really Australian?' she asked, over and over again. She prescribed some 'gamma gobulin,' which was to be injected immediately. I was then rushed to the front of a queue and into the Injection Office. 'We have a guest from Australia!' my entourage announced. A nurse in a mask looked up with glee. Her legs rose from the floor like two giant spruce logs, and her elbows rested comfortably on the broad shelf that jutted out from her chest. She was halfway into injecting the withered bum cheek of a babushka.

'Take your pants down!' she demanded, as I lay face down on a bench. Without warning she thrust the needle into my bum. By the time I pulled up my pants she was already injecting an old man who was standing by the bench. 'Are you really from Australia? Good luck to you and getting to China!' she bellowed, as the man winced in pain.

Armed with the knowledge that there was a twenty-day critical period during which I needed to check carefully for symptoms, I thanked her and hobbled out.

When we finally disengaged ourselves from the hospital, Chris was pale with hunger. Mikhail said that he would invite us to his house, except that he no longer had one; he now lived in a rusty garage. Apparently he was a devout Christian who had resigned from his position as a doctor, left his wife and somehow lost all his possessions. The least we could do was buy him a meal.

We should have asked Mikhail to guide us out of Glazov, because it took two hours of circling around the maze of streets to find the road east again. By that time we were irritable and desperate to find the first possible camp site. We knew not to speak before dinner.

For no particular reason we rolled out of the wrong side of bed the next morning. After bickering over whether or not our rolled oats were precooked, I rode off in a stink, relieved not to have Chris in front of me. I stopped only once, when a car pulled up and the driver passed me a litre bottle of vodka. I gladly filled up my empty drink container, knowing it would come in handy at some point.

As I rode, I tried to think of why there was such animosity between Chris and me at times. As tolerant as we were of each other's foibles, we got caught up in petty arguments that could destroy the day. In the scale of things it seemed ridiculous that such insignificant differences could bring about the downfall of our friendship.

It was almost time for camp when we rolled into the village of Igra and stopped outside a shop. Chris handed me the group wallet and I darted inside to find a rare delicacy – *pryaniki* filled with dates! After munching away on two or three biscuits, we looked at each other and laughed.

'Bloody hell, Tim, aren't these just the ultimate!' Chris boomed with crumbs rolling off his chin.

'Bloody oath. They're from heaven!'

The next morning we rolled into a village nestled in the forest. It was a typical northern settlement with greying log houses and unpaved streets.

As we turned into the dusty dirt track that wound through rows of homes, I was overcome with nerves. We had finally decided to pay a visit to a school. Right from the beginning of the journey I had tried to impress on Chris just how important it was to me that we speak to students. After asking a couple of babushkas in the street we headed towards an old two-storey log building. I put on a jacket to hide my dirt-stained white T-shirt and strode into the schoolyard.

I had taken only two paces into the yard when I was surrounded by a growing semi-circle of children, all smiling and whispering. Chris followed and we stood in silence waiting for something to happen. Eventually, a teacher stepped forward. He was an old square-shouldered man with a greying beard, and looked just as eager to ask questions as the kids, only he was a little less impatient. 'So where are you from?' he began.

After a short introduction we told our story and the rest followed. When I produced photos, the 200 or so children broke into wild excitement. Instead of passing the pictures around the semi-circle they rushed forward, wanting the best view. The teachers elbowed their way through the waist-high crowd, also fighting for a look.

The idea of waves, surfing and sunny beaches in Australia seemed beyond imagination. Many of the children had most likely never been much further than the village surrounds. The boys' slicked-back hairstyles, britches with belts and buttoned shirts reminded me of another era.

We chatted for hours, signed autographs and got through the waiting list of those wanting a ride on the bikes. By the time we had signed the last of countless autographs, I could barely stand on my feet. I was starving.

After lunch we watched a dance performance put on by a group of younger students. It was a traditional dance of the Udmirtskaya Republic. The Udmirtskayan people, now a minority, are related to the forest-dwelling cultures that inhabit the north, like the Finns and the Karelians.

Little boys daintily skipped about like gentlemen with straight backs and looks of intense concentration. The girls, with their frilly dresses and large eyes, smiled proudly as if they were conscious of their elegance even at such an early age. Leaning against the ribbed log wall, the bearded teacher strummed away on a balalaika. Beside him a woman played an accordion.

The playfulness and innocence was reminiscent of children anywhere. The purity of the occasion was what affected me most.

When the clanging of the old school bell rang out, it was sadly time to leave. As the children assembled to wave goodbye, we were presented with a wooden-face carving as a gesture of good luck. An inscription on the back read: 'To Tim and Chris – We thank you for your courage and inspiration and hope to see you again one day.'

There was just one nagging issue that had surfaced during the visit. The teachers had been shocked to hear that we were camping in the forest.

'We Russians don't even go near the forest at this time of year. Don't you realise there are ticks everywhere? If you get bitten, there is a high risk of getting infected,' the bearded teacher had told me.

These warnings added another piece to the puzzle that was 'travelling' in Russia. In autumn we had been told to wait until the snows came and the mud froze. During winter we were advised to start cycling in spring. As the snows slowly melted we were politely told that what we were doing was impossible, and that we would have to wait for summer. Now that it was the end of spring, the ticks were reason enough to put off the journey until mid-summer, when the tick season would be over. It was reasonable to expect that mosquitoes would put the remaining summer under a cloud. Yet by the time they were dead, it would be too cold and wet again!

In reality, it seemed there was no easy way to ride across Russia. No matter what, the elements would be unrelenting. It was frightening to think that Russians had to deal with these conditions all year, every year. Even in the three short months of warm weather the insects conspired to make life unpleasant! By comparison, the Australian climate was far more favourable. The very concept that cows could live outside all year round was something the Russians marvelled at. Now I knew why Baba Galya and her friends erupted with laughter when we called Russia *rai*, paradise.

The road east continued through the forest. From above it must have looked like a river meandering through a sea of green. We now considered the narrow strip of gravel a tick-free oasis. For so long the forest had provided a refuge after a hard day's cycling.

Two days after the school visit we found several ticks crawling on our clothing while we sat at a forest camp site. Later, I felt something crawling up my back. I removed my shirt in a panic and Chris flicked away the critter that had been making for my head. We knew that they loved the dark, hard-to-get-to crevices of the body, like the crotch, armpits and hair. We discovered that these are also the hardest places to inspect. As the riding progressed, we found at least four ticks crawling on us a day. Only a miracle would see us through without being bitten again.

I was sad to replace the *loue* with the tent, but under the circumstances there was no choice. Before going to sleep, we'd check each other with a torch just to make sure. And during the day it was common to see us slide a hand into our pants and after a bit of reconnaissance retrieve it with a look of relief.

As we neared the city of Perm the landscape transformed from the pancake-flat forest plains into undulating hills. Rarely was there a time when we weren't rising up steep slopes or rushing down the other side. It was a sign that we were finally nearing the fabled Ural Mountains. This range, which is a mere wrinkle in the earth's surface, forms the geological divide between Europe and Asia. More significantly for us, it represented the border separating western Russia from Siberia, which roughly includes all land east of the Urals as far as the Bering Strait, and as far south as the semi-steppe land on the borders of Kazakhstan, Mongolia and China. Our planned route through Siberia ran roughly along the southern fringe of the taiga forest. From Lake Baikal it left the northern environment altogether and passed over the high, arid steppe of Mongolia.

For the first time in ages, we had a string of uneventful days. Besides tick sightings, the only scare happened one afternoon when I discovered that my urine had turned a fluorescent, glow-in-the-dark yellow. I was drinking a lot, so it couldn't have been due to dehydration. Over lunch, I told Chris.

'What? You too!' he exclaimed. For the rest of the day we discussed the possible causes; the most frightening being that we had been eating radio-active *pryaniki*. If that was the case, we were sure to have a high radiation reading. We also recalled the many times we had collected water from drains, and chewed over the prospect that we were destined to become mutants by journey's end. What with the Soviet Union's terrible waste management record, heavy-metal pollution and chemically enhanced crops, it didn't seem that far-fetched. Not to mention the widespread nuclear testing program and the fallout from disasters like Chernobyl.

A couple of days later, after some simple tests, we were relieved to discover that our extraordinary urine was due to the vitamin-B tablets that we were taking to supplement our diet!

According to Chris I looked especially dishevelled and dirty as we rode into the city of Perm. Judging from the looks I got, he was probably right. Once again it was a shock to be in civilization. Perm was the largest city we had been in to date; it positively bustled with activity. We passed a square in which scantily clad girls walked hand in hand with their partners. Drunkards sat on park benches and boys on roller-blades circled around a statue of Lenin. Outdoor cafés emblazoned with the Coca-Cola trademark were an unavoidable eyesore.

We were both looking forward to a well-earned rest. Unfortunately, we discovered that the only hotels with free rooms were going to blow our budget of AU$4 a day. The Kirov hotel and the cost of the gamma gobulin for my injection in Glazov had set us back substantially.

On my return from another fruitless hunt for cheap accommodation, Chris was talking to a couple of guys and a girl. They were probably in their early twenties. They greeted me with vigorous handshakes, and it wasn't long before we took up their invitation to stay with them.

Our living quarters for the night turned out to be a rust-bucket cabin surrounded by a tall, barbed security fence. Squeezed between our cabin and the security fence were hundreds of lockers where workers at a nearby market kept all of their goods overnight. There were no taps, so we washed our faces with the scummy water from a rusty metal drum.

Of the three hosts, one seemed to be making all the decisions and looking after us. He was a short and stocky man with a crewcut and a remarkable scar that ran down his forehead to below his left eye. His dark skin and bushy eyebrows were distinctive among the mostly Caucasian Russians. He said he was of Indian descent and that his name was Sergei.

While Chris dumped his gear and took off, I sat on the doorstep and talked with Sergei. He told me that he had spent six years in a Russian jail, and had first been locked away at the age of sixteen. He recounted his experience with pride and explained that his family and siblings had all done their time as well. Apparently, he had been arrested for smoking and dealing marijuana. Nowadays, he was a sports trainer at a school.

There was something about the way he spoke that suggested he respected our journey, and even envied us. I thought that he was about to open up when he shook my hand and took off.

Later in the evening I realised something wasn't right. Two men burst through the door, changed their clothes, washed their hands, placed a pair of scissors under a cushion and ran off again.

When Chris returned with a loaf of bread and some jam for dinner, Sergei came running in with the girl we had met earlier. They hassled us for a spoon and minutes later I watched the girl inject something into her arm with a syringe.

In the early hours of the morning, we were woken from our sleep by an erratic banging at the steel door.

'Who is it?' I yelled, trying to sound infuriated.

'It's me!' came the crazed voice of a woman, followed by a sickly giggle.

I let her in and for ten minutes she traipsed around the cabin shrieking unintelligibly before disappearing into the night.

Obviously, it was not going to be a night for sleep. When I did manage to close my eyes, I was plagued by a familiar dream. I was sitting on the couch at home in Australia. I tried to move but couldn't. I felt powerless, hopeless, mute. My family and friends milled around, looking on with growing concern. They seemed happy that I was home, but somehow surprised, as if my return was unexpected. I sensed that they assumed I had plans for the future, and wanted to know what they were.

All I could say to them was, 'Let's see what is next.' Suddenly, I was left alone, waiting for eternity, as if I had stepped off into a great swamp of grey nothing. The future was a blank. It dawned on me that by returning home I had cut off my ties with the life I had built in Russia and Finland.

I didn't need any help to work out what the dream meant. Here in Russia, I knew who I was, what I wanted and had found freedom. And yet day by day, as we cycled east towards Beijing, we were nearing the end of the experience and moving away from the place that I loved. I imagined the flight home would be like spiralling back to earth, completing the process of self-administered exile.

The following afternoon I was browsing through a market stall when someone shouted from behind. I turned to see Sergei and his friend running towards me in a sweat. They looked panic-stricken.

'Tim, c'mon, let's go back and have a chat with Chris. Where have you been?' Sergei shouted.

Back at the cabin he looked grave. 'Tim, understand, I have already told Chris. My grandmother died today, and I desperately need three hundred roubles for the funeral.' Three hundred roubles was the equivalent of AU$18.

I reached into my pocket and handed over thirty-five roubles in change. He snatched it without a word of thanks.

'No, Tim, you don't understand. Thirty-five is nothing; I need three hundred. I will pay you back tomorrow.' He clenched his fist and looked away for a moment before glaring back at me. His eyes had turned a darker shade. 'Tim, I just can't imagine what will happen if I don't get the money.'

He was pretty small and between Chris and I, he didn't pose much of a threat. But then again his experience in jail had probably toughened him up. Hoping to get some breathing space, and stave off coming to blows, I thought of a temporary solution. 'Well, we haven't got money. But maybe I can get some using my credit card.' I had been speaking in Russian and Chris looked at me in confusion. He knew that I didn't have a credit card. What he didn't know was that I did have an expired card. I produced the card and asked Sergei if he knew the whereabouts of an automatic teller machine.

'Be careful, Tim, be careful. There are criminals everywhere. I will help you protect it. You can trust me. Don't show it to anyone,' Sergei said, his eyes glued to the card.

With Sergei in the lead, we went in search of a bank. We spoke only in Russian. Fearing that Sergei would sense something was afoot, I did not tell Chris my plan.

'Let's see, if I withdraw five hundred roubles, when you pay me back tomorrow I will have just enough money to get us on the road to Ekaterinburg,' I said.

'Yes, of course. I will pay you back tomorrow morning,' he replied.

'Please send my deepest sympathies to your family.'

'Yeah, I know it's just awful. I rang her this morning and she was fine. This afternoon she passed away. Now they are digging her grave,' he said. He shook his head sorrowfully.

Eventually, we came to a teller machine. It was enclosed in a special room that could only be opened with a swipe of a card.

My mind raced. Sergei glared impatiently through the glass door. I knew that the card wouldn't work. It dawned on me that if I typed an incorrect PIN number it would cause the machine to eat the card. To my dismay the card was spat straight back out. 'Card expired, call your bank' read the message on the screen.

I eyed the disposal slot, but the card was too thick. 'All right then, it looks like you are going into the receipt slot,' I muttered. Frantically, I pushed the card into the slot.

'Tim what are you doing in there? Where is the money?' shouted Sergei, banging on the glass. Halfway in, the card jammed. I pushed harder but it wouldn't budge, and now it wouldn't come out either.

The banging came again. I pushed the card harder and it disappeared from sight. Then I stepped through the door looking bewildered and upset. Under the circumstances it came pretty naturally. 'The machine ate my card!'

Sergei fell for it. Unfortunately, so did Chris. Before I knew it there was a crackle over an intercom on the wall. 'What's the problem?' a voice enquired.

'Tim, tell the lady what happened!' Chris shouted, angrily.

'Chris, Chris, mate, it didn't really eat my card,' I whispered.

'The machine ate this man's card. What are you going to do about it?' Sergei demanded.

Meanwhile, Chris stormed through the door and withdrew money with his own card. When he emerged, Sergei grabbed the money, waved down a car and disappeared.

Chris and I walked back to the cabin, agreeing that we should leave the city as soon as possible. We'd barely had time to reflect on the journey from Kirov, let alone take in Perm and rest our bodies. Worst of all, we'd been hoodwinked out of a substantial sum of money – more than the hotel would have cost. And we hadn't even had a decent wash!

I felt jaded. How could someone spoil the perfect lifestyle we had been leading to this point? For days, as we rode east, the image of Sergei's steely eyes was branded into my head. The worst thing was that I had seen the caring and genuine side of him. How could he lie so blatantly and not be ashamed? I put it down to the drugs, but really there was no excuse. In hindsight it wasn't a lot of money, but it meant a great deal to us – five days of living costs and a further depleted budget.

It wasn't just Sergei we were escaping, but the city itself. Perm had felt like an island of unhappiness cast like a stone into the paradise that was Russia. Come to think of it, all cities had the same effect. It usually took an hour or so of riding to get through a city, from one end to the other, before we were back among the solitude of lonely roads. In that hour we encountered more problems than in weeks of riding.

For hours we rode in silence. The landscape seemed to have irrevocably changed; the northern forests were a thing of the past. Fields stretched to every horizon, ploughed by old Soviet machinery. Rusty signs proclaimed each former collective farm a 'paradise'. The phrase *Slava Trudu* was forged in steel along the roadside and painted onto the rooftops of houses. Roughly translated it means 'hail labour'. Most of the old propaganda was peeling off and rusting.

With the dry earth and hint of summer growth, I was suddenly overcome with chronic hayfever. This seemed to be a substitute for the ticks that we encountered in the forest. I wondered if there would ever be a time when the environment gave an ounce of mercy.

We found some comic relief from our problems by discussing the super-human strength that overcomes a person when they desperately need to find a toilet. We had both been in such situations, in the midst of considerable traffic and with no private place to relieve oneself. When you could no longer hold out, you would dump the bike on the roadside and make a desperate dash for the nearest bushes or cluster of trees. When it was all over, you would turn around to find that in the process of getting there, you had jumped two-metre ditches, pushed through brambles, even squeezed through narrow gaps between trees, which, under normal circumstances, would have been physically impossible to fit through. Getting back to the road was often near impossible. It reminded us of stories about people who had suddenly found the strength to lift up a tractor or car to rescue someone trapped underneath.

A refreshing wind brought relief as we finally hit the Urals. The small rounded hills were a welcome change from the treeless plains. Once again the road carved a path through the forest. The birch had begun to sprout fresh translucent leaves. Several lakes dotted the valleys like blue gems and on their shores sleepy little villages looked as timeless as the hills themselves.

Two hundred kilometres from Ekaterinburg, we awoke to the patter of light snowflakes falling onto the tent, as soft as ash from a distant forest fire. It had gone from thirty degrees Celsius to below zero overnight. It was like the good old times, warming the toes by the fire and shivering violently as we rolled down the first hill. I wondered whether this unseasonal weather was a sign of things to come in Siberia.

Later that day, I found myself lagging far behind Chris. The return of cold weather had sapped my energy and the *pryaniki* had disappeared at a frightening rate. Chris was having a good day and for some reason decided to stop for lunch fifteen kilometres further than our agreed location. I suspected that it was the usual build-up of energy that boosted him as he neared Internet access. By the time we met again, I was ready to strangle him but didn't have the strength.

In the afternoon I stopped at a village for a good feed. The evenings were my strong point and often, when Chris stopped for camp, I felt that I could keep going for another couple of hours. With ample energy, I pushed on. My legs felt strong and they were finally losing their skinny chicken look.

After about fifty kilometres, I began to look out for the flag that indicated where we would be camping for the night. I still felt strongly that rather than flagging the location, it would be prudent if the person in front waited; usually the second person wasn't more than fifteen minutes behind. When I was in front it was my preferred method. It boiled down to this: what I called caution, Chris called pessimism.

After I had covered sixty kilometres, Chris was still nowhere to be seen. I must have taken my eyes off the road for a while, because when I looked up, there was a bearded man waving me down. I hadn't even seen his car stop. I thought fleetingly about riding straight past him but he seemed harmless enough.

'Hello, where are you coming from!' he boomed, as two more men stepped from the car. His name was Sergei, too.

It wasn't long before they invited me to their holiday house on a nearby lake. The words *banya*, vodka and 'lots of fish' were enough to raise my spirits to the point of near ecstasy. 'Great! It's just that I have to ask my friend Chris. He is riding somewhere ahead,' I said.

They took off to look for him in a fluster of excitement. Not far down the road, I stopped at a police checkpoint to ask whether they had seen a traveller on a similar bike. The answer was no.

I doubled back and rode a good five kilometres but still there was no sign of Chris. He must have somehow gone further ahead. Eventually, Sergei and his mates came back. They too had seen nothing of Chris.

With simmering frustration I had to turn down the offer of a *banya*. The fury renewed my energy and I rode ahead blindly, venting my feelings.

'It's typical. Anything that remotely breaks up his routine or disturbs his train of thought is a distraction!' That included having to wait for me on the roadside. It was the same in regards to filming. Whenever I wanted to do some filming, Chris would say, 'Not now, let's do it later.'

For me, filming enhanced the experience; for Chris it detracted.

Bloody hell, he probably considers offers of hospitality a distraction as well, I thought.

Fuming, I eventually pushed the bike into the forest and set up the *loue* shelter. As I lay down to the crackle of the fire it occurred to me that it was just as well Chris wasn't there.

Into Siberia
Ekaterinburg – Omsk

Late Spring 2000

Chris

I woke to a glorious sense of space and freedom. The dawn sunlight filtered down through low branches and around gnarled trunks to dance orange on the cover of my sleeping bag. I gazed lazily from one side of the tent to the other. On a sudden impulse, I stretched my hands and feet to the corners of the tent.

I laughed like a kid – all this space for me! I sat up and looked out through the mosquito mesh of the window. Propped up against a tree stood my bike – alone – and nearby, a small fireplace with a few leftover bits of wood from the night before. No Tim! Not a sign of him. Not anywhere! I stuffed my sleeping bag into its nylon shell and climbed out of bed.

There were, for the moment, both good and bad points about his absence. Good: well, all this room for me; and a welcome break, probably for both of us, from the growing frustrations. Bad: we'd been planning to ride into Ekaterinburg today; and finding each other might now take up a good part of the morning. More than likely, he'd simply missed my flag by the roadside and ended up making camp further along.

Of course, it was always possible that something bad had happened to him: an accident, kidnapping, or maybe even the elusive Mafia that everyone kept warning us about. But then, these were dangers that we had to live with and as long as they didn't happen, they didn't bear worrying about.

I surveyed the space around me once again and felt the stirring of a temptation to prolong the time alone. On the other hand, we were in this together, for better or for worse, and it wouldn't do to seriously lose each other.

Besides, I thought, as I pulled down the tent, I'm hungry and he has all the breakfast supplies.

Yesterday had been an all-day slog into a freezing wet wind. Tim had struggled, but late in the afternoon I'd had a burst of energy and had left him at a roadside café while I pedalled on to look for a spot to camp. As we often did, I left a signal by the roadside to mark the place where I turned off. Then I wheeled my bike into the forest and started collecting firewood, expecting Tim to join me within half an hour.

Now, as I pushed my bike back to the road, I noticed that my fluorescent orange flag was still there, wedged into a section of aluminium crash barrier. It was hanging near the edge of the road at what would have been Tim's head height.

I retrieved the flag and pushed off, expecting to find his camp a little way down the road. But twenty kilometres further, there was no sign of him. I waved down a few cars but no one had seen him. I got worried. There was no way he could have come this far last night. I turned back to scan the road more carefully around the potential turnoffs and camp sites.

I'd cycled halfway back to my original camp site when I finally spotted him riding towards me. He'd had warning from a driver that I was coming and we met up in good spirits, joking and catching up on the night's adventures. The good feelings didn't last long, however. He had decided that the mix-up was my fault.

'You have to put your flag somewhere where I can't miss it, Chris!' he said, stonily. 'This is the second time this has happened and it's a bloody big pain in the arse!'

He was referring, of course, to the night when we'd lost each other outside of Babushkina the previous year. That, admittedly, had been my fault. But this time I felt things were a little different.

We both spent the morning simmering but, by the afternoon, tensions subsided below the surface. Later that day, we reached the very top of the Ural mountain range. A small marker by the roadside told us that geographically, if not politically, we were on the verge of crossing from Europe into the subcontinent of Asia. That, we decided, was something to feel proud of.

I sat on the divide and surveyed the scene before us. The lights of Ekaterinburg twinkled in the half dark and the forested plains stretched to the horizon beyond. We pushed off and sped down the long hill – out of the mountains and into Siberia.

I looked through the window in the guard tower and saw Tim gesticulating from the other side of a high, razor-wire security fence. With me were two guards. They have jobs for everything in Russia, and these two guys were the official guards of the local high-security carpark. They were at work – strictly no alcohol – so rather than the usual bottle of vodka, we were sharing a pot of tea – from shot glasses! We drained our cups, said goodbye and I hurried down the steps to find Tim waiting with Sergei. They'd met the night before, whereupon Sergei had invited us to stay with his family.

Sergei didn't have a car, and had decided that the route to his flat, buried deep within a suburb of identical Soviet apartment blocks, was too difficult to explain. We walked to a busy intersection looking for a taxi and ended up flagging down an empty city bus for an on-the-spot charter ride.

Sergei was an enterprising engineer who, among other things, worked in the design department of a local munitions factory. We arrived late, but sat up for a long time, drinking, eating and making merry with his friends and family. We watched a long, wobbly and drawn-out home video shot the year before when Sergei had taken a barge 3,000 kilometres up the Ob River. He'd been selling crates of alcohol, cigarettes and other such 'vital provisions' to the isolated villages along its banks and had made a huge profit. But by the time they'd sailed back home, all of the money had been completely swallowed up by the bribes and 'protection' payments that he'd been obliged to make to various armed representatives of the vodka and tobacco industries, as well as to regional mobsters. The moral, he explained, was not to get involved in anything big enough to attract the attention of the Mafia.

He spent a day escorting us around the city, showing us the sights. It was interesting but frustrating. My first priority on reaching a city had always been to find some place where I could log on to the Internet and sate my longing for contact with Nat. Today, however, we were guests, and our hosts were spending a lot of time and effort entertaining us. We wandered round the city eating ice-cream in the cold wind and straining to understand information boards in local museums. My need to get in touch with Nat had to wait until the next day, and somehow I managed to divert all of my pent-up frustration squarely onto Tim.

We spent several days in Ekaterinburg. Sergei and his family were wonderful hosts who made us feel at home in their flat. One of Sergei's friends took us to see the local lake and nature reserve, still snowy and cold, then drove around the slushy suburban streets filming from the car window as we pedalled along.

On the third night of our stay, we had dinner with another young couple that we'd met on the road the previous week. They picked us up in a brand new car then took us shopping in an exclusive western-style supermarket that had a limited range of imported goods at double and triple western prices. They were small-time 'New Russians', a euphemism for crooked business people who were making their way in the world by exploiting the new democracy and quietly embezzling in some field related to computers. They were nice people, though, and interesting. They'd done a lot of cycling in their younger days and had once run a business importing Shimano bike components. When Sergei picked us up later, we heard him describing our new friends as *gopniki*. We quizzed him for a translation and he laughed. Apparently it was a new term meaning something like 'Russians striving to become American'.

The day before our departure, I quickly ducked into the city to the Internet café. Walking fast on my way back through the metro station I was hauled aside by a policeman of the type that we regularly saw occupying little cubicles all over Russian cities.

This guy was big, broad, muscular and angry: typical military. His crewcut, square jaw, cauliflower ears and beady eyes all stared menacingly down at me and I realised, with a horrible, sickening, soiled-pants-type of feeling, that I'd forgotten my passport. We quickly established that I was both a foreigner and that I had no ID. He dragged me into his cubicle and sat me roughly on a wooden stool.

His teeth were brown and coated in phlegm. A smell like rotting carrion wafted from his mouth, threatening to overwhelm me. Quickly I glanced away, only to see a set of thick, calloused fingers lovingly caressing the handle of the big black nightstick. I dug my nails into my palms to stop my body from shaking. He lowered his crooked nose till it almost touched mine, took a deep, powerful breath and let out a roar. 'WHY DON'T YOU HAVE A PASSPORT?'

My skull throbbed and resounded like a church bell. 'Ah, ah, I left it at my, ah, friends' ...'

'WHERE ARE YOUR FRIENDS?'

'Ah, *oni zhivyot,* ah, ah ...' Shit! This monster was only just beginning to build up steam and already my Russian was leaving me! I tried again. 'Ah, I don't know the address but they live, um, not far from here.'

'WHERE ARE YOU FROM?' A look of murderous insanity had started to creep across his face and his cauliflower ears were turning beetroot red.

'Um, ... *Avstraliya,*' I stammered, weakly.

'Australia! HARGH!' He threw back his head and let out a half-strangled snarling snort. He lowered his head towards mine. His bloodshot eyes held me transfixed.

'You are a foreigner,' he growled, laying the facts slowly and deliberately on the table. 'You have no documents and you have a strong accent, a strong *southern* accent.' I trembled as he paused, eyes gleaming, moving in for the kill. 'YOU ARE A CHECHEN TERRORIST!'

He yelled this last at such close range that my face was plastered with flecks of spittle. He's fucking crazy, I thought, desperately trying to think of something that would keep him from patriotically ripping my head off.

'I'm just a boy,' I began to beg, feebly, with my lower lip trembling. But just as I was about to break down completely, the door opened and another policeman stepped in through a ray of golden sunshine. I was saved.

This guy was just as big and burly as his partner, but he wore a kinder expression. He looked at me briefly, taking in the spag in my hair and the tears in my eyes, then wrinkled his nose thoughtfully – probably trying to sniff the air and see whether he'd come in time to save me from letting go in my pants. He looked at my executioner, standing now and puffed up like a strutting peacock, then back at me.

'Boris?' he asked slowly.

'HE'S A TERRORIST!' The reply was still thunderous but less certain. My saviour looked back at me, eyebrows raised. 'Are you a terrorist?' he asked. I shook my head, unable to speak. 'Right,' he decided. 'Boris, I think you'd better go do your round of the station. I'll handle this one from here.'

The new policeman had a much firmer grip on reality. He was aware that Stalin had been dead these past forty-five years, and was also aware that the KGB was an obsolete institution. He even believed that I was from Australia (by some amazing coincidence I happened to have a few Aussie coins in my pocket to add credibility). But let me know, nonetheless, that I was in pretty serious trouble.

I had not a scrap of ID and worse, didn't know Sergei's surname, his phone number or his address. I watched as the policeman filled out the necessary forms, made a phone call then placed me in a tiny lockup in the corner of the room while he catalogued my personal belongings. I'd just been to the bank and he sheafed through notes that were probably the equal of two months of his salary. He seemed more resigned than jealous, however, and we chatted amicably through the bars until a van came to take me away.

The duty sergeant at district HQ was a harassed and busy man. A few vagrants who'd rolled drunkenly out of the van before me were processed first, then I was prodded toward the counter and told to hold out my hands. The sergeant skimmed quickly over my arrest report as he removed my handcuffs.

'You know how to get to where you're staying?' he barked. I nodded. 'But you don't know the address?'

'No.'

'Could you show an officer the way if he was to drive you there?'

I replied eagerly in the affirmative.

'Right, we'll do that then,' he decided. 'But you'll have to wait a while.'

I was put in a large, communal lockup. It was 5 p.m. and I waited till midnight. I'd been due to meet Tim and Sergei for a party at eight. A few other prisoners came and went. They stayed an hour or two, pacing and swearing until their friends came to bail them out, but I sat by myself and avoided talking. Finally, I was collected and put in a van full of officers on their way home from work. They did a long lap of the city (just to disorientate me!), dropped the officers off first, then headed in the general direction of Sergei's flat. Halfway there the radio crackled into life. 'Have you got that Australian?' The driver looked at me and I beamed. Good old Sergei. He'd managed to track me down.

When we arrived, the policeman took a cursory look at my passport and visa. He left and Sergei gave me a walloping angry whack on the backside. Then, at 3 a.m., after briefly explaining my story, I collapsed into bed.

We left the next morning. I was feeling tired, drained and subdued. Sergei and one of his friends drove ahead of us with their hazard lights flashing, leading us out through the suburbs and back onto the highway. We said goodbye and promised to keep in touch. Then we pushed off and pedalled, without looking back, away from Ekaterinburg.

I slept long into the next morning and awoke feeling uninspired. It was 300 kilometres to the next city of Tyumen, and we'd decided the night before that it would be a good idea to split up and ride most of that distance alone.

We rode together for half a day until I spotted a nice camp site in the forest among a copse of old pines. We had lunch together then Tim packed up to leave.

We divided our equipment without saying much, then we shook hands and wished each other well. I'd be only half a day behind with the tool kit if he were to suffer any serious breakdown, and he assured me that he'd set up camp and wait twenty kilometres from Tyumen. We agreed on a contingency plan (we'd leave a telephone message with Sergei if anything went wrong), then he cycled off and I realised with mixed feelings that this would be the first time in four months – the first time since I'd been torn apart from Nat back in Sydney – that I would be completely on my own.

Stopping in cities always complicated things for me, and our break in Ekaterinburg had really affected my mood. After one or sometimes two weeks of settling into a simple life of cycling we'd reach another major city and dive into a hectic world of shops, crowds, parties and people. Our basic lifestyle of cycling and camping went straight out the window, and after a few days of living the 'civilized life' I always ended up feeling emotionally drained and exhausted.

We'd stayed in Ekaterinburg for four days and we'd had a great time. Physically, the break had done us good. Our bodies had had a chance to recover from the strains and stresses of riding heavy bikes day after day. I was feeling fresh and ready to go but mentally, when it came down to it, I was completely stuffed.

The near escape from horrible death at the hands of the maniac policeman had shaken me and the effort of being an interesting and agreeable guest in a foreign language had also taken its toll.

I climbed onto my bike the next morning and set off feeling tired and fuzzy headed. I pedalled constantly towards a distant horizon, paying barely any attention to the hills, forests and villages that I passed. My thoughts were dull and repetitive. What should I eat for dinner? How far do I have to go today? When can I be bothered to fix that niggling squeak in my hub? A flash of unexpected perception hit: I could suddenly understand what it must feel like to be a car. I pushed on, the spark of romance gone from cycling, just trying to cover the miles. Finally, I judged that I'd gone far enough for the day and made camp. In the morning, after another long night of dreamless sleep, I was feeling more alive and ready to go.

As I rode, I pondered what seemed like a strangely circular contradiction. We needed to stop in a city every few weeks or so to recharge our bodies, but after a few days of resting in a city, I needed a few weeks of riding to recharge my brain! It didn't seem to affect Tim in the same way, and as the miles passed I wondered why.

One of the beauties of cycling is that pedalling alone on a long, empty road allows a lot of time for protracted and uninterrupted trains of thought. After the first few thousand kilometres, the riding becomes second nature and the body can cruise along on autopilot, leaving the mind free to drift and roam. And even if such thoughts are mostly just a mixture of unimportant, irrelevant jumble and are less profound than I always hope they might be, they do inevitably reveal the odd titbit of wisdom. The reason that cities screw me up so much, I decided in the end, has got a lot to do with my being away from Nat.

Away from the towns, I'd go for long stretches without any contact with her. Starving for details, I'd spend hours trying to imagine what she was up to, and creating faces and personalities for the new friends that she mentioned in her letters. This would go on for weeks, until all in one burst I'd be hearing her voice through the phone and spending hours chatting to her over the Net. A lot of love and energy went into those exchanges and more still into the anguished partings. I left every city feeling like I'd severed a connection just as we were starting to get to know each other again.

On the other hand, as much as these stops meant to me, I always felt a kind of impotent frustration while stationary in a city. I'd come over here to ride. To ride, to meet Russians and to experience life in the villages and countryside. The cities were good in that they let us stock up on supplies, but for me they never held much fascination. It was only on the bikes that I was really in my element and I think that Tim felt the same way too.

As the days passed, my mood improved immensely. By the time I got close to Tyumen, I was feeling inspired and ready to get into the next leg of our journey with new gusto. The time apart from Tim had been a boon. I'd gotten over many of my petty frustrations and although I hadn't exactly been lonely, I was looking forward to having a friend with whom I could share thoughts over the campfire.

I pulled over by a dusty embankment exactly twenty kilometres from Tyumen and found a scribbled note in a plastic snap-lock bag tied to the base of a road sign.

Chris, mate, it read, *got here last night and got bitten by another fucking tick. Trying to hitch into Tyumen to go to the hospital this morning and will hopefully be back tonight or tomorrow morning. Left my bike on the other side of this embankment, hope it's still there.*
When will this shit end?
Tim

I pushed my bike over the embankment to find Tim's bike in a heap on the other side. There was another note attached.

This one told the story again, in case I hadn't found the first message, and also told me how to find the spot where he'd camped the previous night.

About ten o'clock, I was on the verge of brushing my teeth and hopping into bed, when Tim strode down the slope against the sunset-painted sky. He looked tired but successful. I quickly stoked the fire and warmed some soup and macaroni while he told me of another day of adventures in the Russian hospital system.

We pedalled into Tyumen the next day and left our bikes in a private carpark under the care of a bemused-looking security guard, before taking a bus into the centre. It was a public holiday and the crowds were out in force. The day was meant to be a celebration of the Allied victory in the Second World War – a good couple of months before similar celebrations in the west – but the people in the cafés and on the streets seemed more interested in celebrating the eternal glory of the vodka bottle.

We found an Internet café and visited the post office before making our way to a central park to have a bite to eat. There was a paved area and a fountain nearby and we watched in horror as an argument between teenagers developed into a brutal bashing. A group of young thugs wearing Reeboks and gold chains stole a Discman from a guy on roller-blades then pulled him to the ground and savagely kicked his head until he managed to get to his feet and skate away. This was not what we'd come to expect from Russia. Although the news bulletins on the television invariably showed gruesome corpses and graphic war footage, we'd never encountered any hint of such public demonstrations of violence. These teenagers were the younger generation of the *gopniki*. Everything, from their dress to the roller-blades, was lifted straight from MTV, and the shocking violence was chillingly reminiscent of a Bruce Willis movie.

We bussed back to the outskirts, picked up some groceries from the market, collected our bikes and gratefully pedalled away from town.

Ahead, the road stretched over 1,000 kilometres to our next destination, the city of Omsk. We rode through areas of undulating hills and low, cleared grazing land. The weather closed in and for three days it alternatively rained and hailed. At one stage, we passed over a huge, recently flooded plain. Dead trees stood in metre-deep water with their lowest branches tugging violently in the swirling current. In other places, the tips of old fence posts protruded above the surface, choppy wind-driven waves lapping incessantly against them.

The road ran straight through the centre of this unexpected lake, on top of a massive, banked-up causeway that stretched to the horizon. A roaring gale whipped horizontal sheets of rain and hail over the road and we struggled right into the teeth of it. Stinging streaks of water and ice lashed my arms and legs, forcing me to pull my cap down hard to shield my face from the barrage. I was being rained on from underneath too! Eventually, I realised that it was the bizarre wind currents created by the causeway that was tearing water from the surface of the lake and hurling it vertically up at me.

I struggled along, pedalling in my smallest gears and wobbling dangerously around the road. Tim was somewhere behind me, no doubt finding it tough going, too.

The countryside changed but the weather remained uncertain. Day after day, we travelled south-east. Soon we'd passed through the southern extremes of the taiga forest and into the vegetation region known as the semi-steppe. Fields of long wild grass replaced the endless expanse of pines and spruce trees and all around stood small and medium-sized forests of white-barked birch trees. There were no fences and the spring leaves were a glorious, fresh bottle-green. We would leave the road after our day's ride and bounce, often for miles across the open plains to find the perfect camp site on the edge of a forest. Sometimes, a curious stockboy on horseback would drive his herd of lazy cattle towards our campfire for a chat. Often, we saw thin tendrils of smoke rising skyward from a village on the horizon.

We were woken at dawn on one such morning by the sound of a horse's hooves outside the tent door. I looked out to see a young guy who'd visited our camp the evening before. One of the cows from the village herd had wandered off and he wanted to know if we'd seen it. We hadn't, but it didn't take him long to find out where it was.

The cow had been killed by a truck on the road during the night, and as we wheeled our bikes out of the forest, we saw that an old woman was already busy gutting and skinning the carcass. She was anxious to get the meat preserved before it went to waste. Helping her was a man who'd brought a tractor to haul away the remains. Our young friend, the cowherd, was standing nearby in tears. He told us that he'd have to work for six months without wages to repay the owner. We gave him a bottle of vodka that had been given to us by an overexcited driver a few days before. Maybe he'd be able to sell it and start raising the sum that way, or maybe he'd just try to find a solution at the far end of the bottle.

As the skies finally started to clear, we met a great number of people drawn to the outdoors by the warmer weather; they were all amazed by the spectacle of our weird recumbent bicycles. Kids who'd never even heard of Australia pedalled frantically beside us on ancient, oversized bicycles, firing breathless questions. Middle-aged men in sturdy grey clothing waved us down to share a quick shot of vodka, or a pocketful of unshelled sunflower seeds.

There was an art to eating these sunflower seeds – *semichki*, as they are called – that I never quite mastered. The little black seed is popped into the mouth and a clever nip with the teeth opens the shell so that the tongue can extract the kernel.

Then, all in one fluid action, the husk is spat out onto the ground – or the floor, or the bus seat, wherever the person happens to be.

Eating *semichki* is something of a national pastime. There are little weather-beaten babushkas standing on virtually every street corner selling them for a pittance. Almost everyone we met had a stash and was willing to share but it took months before I came close to getting the technique right. During that time, I threw countless crowds into roaring fits of laughter as they watched the Australian splutter and choke on his bloody *semichki*. Usually, I'd get fed up and simply swallow the darned things whole until, months later, I learnt that the husks are carcinogenic. On the other hand, I'd also read that due to the potent fertilisers used during Soviet times, the average middle-aged Russian would have consumed 60 per cent of their bodyweight in heavy metals and toxins. With the huge appetites brought on by riding we were probably eating at least three times as much as the average Russian and, doing the maths, that meant we'd had up to 1.5 kilograms of lethal chemicals each over the year! With all that inside me, the sunflower seeds were hardly going to make any difference.

With the warmer weather and our improving fitness, we were soon covering up to 100 kilometres a day. Just to add spice, a few days before reaching Omsk, I caught a stomach bug that had me regularly sprinting to hide behind the first available tree, with my pants down and retching at the same time. I spent a day groaning in the tent and cut my diet to bread and water before I improved enough to ride again. All the same, during the final days into Omsk, Tim would often come across my bike hastily dumped by the roadside, with me nowhere to be seen. We covered the distance steadily and reached the city in the nick of time. I'd just used my last square of toilet paper.

Bruce

Omsk – Scotland

Late Spring 2000

Tim

The apartment blocks were coming to life. Windows glittered like golden gems embedded into concrete monoliths. I paced along the banks of the Irtys River, growing tired with each slap of my boots on the pavement. We had only been in Omsk for two days but I felt the need to escape. There was just too much to digest. The streetscape was a constantly spinning kaleidoscope of people and events, traffic and shop-fronts. I found it easier to cope in the countryside where each village scene was vivid but not cluttered.

For a while I almost gave up hope; the river appeared to be all but strangled by a network of bridges, buildings and outdoor cafés. It was with relief that I eyed a narrow beach below the embankment and out of sight of the traffic. I scurried down a flight of stairs, took off my shoes and collapsed on the sand.

There I lay listening to my heart calm down. The sand gave way to the contours of my sore body and I felt the tension begin to drain. I always began these moments of therapy with the most basic observation that came to mind, feeling that this would be the foundation for making sense of a complex world.

When I sat up, resting my elbows in the sand, I found myself engrossed by the river. The same breeze that tugged gently at my hair ruffled the open, murky water. The riverbanks were steep and rose ten or fifteen metres to the base of buildings perched close to the edge. This steep terrain was the only stronghold of nature; scraggy bushes and trees clung on for a shot at life. Carried along in the current I noticed some driftwood and tried to imagine its journey; passing through the city would be a fleeting moment as it wound its way north for thousands of kilometres, joining the Ob River, one of the longest in Siberia, and journeying through forest and tundra, to eventually drift into the Arctic Ocean. I sympathised with the bushes and envied the driftwood.

Then the words came back to me as bluntly as I had read them half an hour earlier on e-mail: 'Basically, bouncers and an undercover policeman beat me up. My nose and cheekbone were broken and my teeth knocked severely. My nose was put back into place but is now permanently bent. My teeth are still numb.'

It came from my nineteen-year-old brother, Jonathan. Jon has always been like a best friend to me. He has the muscular body of an athletic hero. As we were growing up, his build highlighted my weedy figure, typified by my kneecaps that are wider than my thigh muscles. Yet behind Jon's broad shoulders and beefy chest, I knew him to be a soft and caring person.

I pictured the bewildered look on his face as some brute mistook him for a thug and smashed his face, knocking him unconscious. It brought back flashes of the incident in Tyumen when we had watched a boy on roller-blades being attacked.

I thought of my mother. She had probably been more hysterical than Jon about it all.

When the air began to chill I made my way back to the hotel room where Chris was still lying in bed. His bouts of diarrhoea had worsened in Omsk and he couldn't keep food down. I had spent two days trying to find a tent for the solo journey to Novosibirsk. Failing that, I bought some material and befriended a family that owned an old manual sewing machine. I was quite proud of the fly netting I had subsequently made, which would hang inside my *loue* shelter and protect me from ticks and mosquitoes.

'Hey, Chris, mate, what do you reckon about this?' I asked, unravelling the netting.

He rolled onto his back and groaned. 'God, I feel like crap,' he said. 'But I think I am getting better, and there is no way we can spend more time in the city. It's hell watching you munch down ice-creams and greasy pies when I can barely stomach bread!'

'Yeah, it must be. But check out this fresh batch of potato pies. They're steaming hot, came straight out of a babushka's handbag. Divine!' I replied, provoking a grin across his pale face.

We agreed that we would leave the following day and split up for the 800 kilometres or so to Novosibirsk. We had been talking about going our separate ways for months. Not only would it be a chance to clear the air between us, but it would also give us the chance to experience Russia alone.

At midday the next day we were in a parking lot making final arrangements. Dusty Ladas rattled over the bumpy tarmac on the nearby street. The parking lot was boxed in with rusty old lockers and portable garages. The manager wandered about in the sweltering heat, grazing on an ice-cream.

There was just one more thing to do, and then we could leave the wretched city behind. We only had the one road atlas between us and needed to make a photocopy so that we could each have a map.

Feeling a little irritated, I made my way to a crooked watchtower where a bored security worker sat brooding over his desk. He responded blankly to my questions. In the meantime a short bearded man shouldered up beside me. 'What do we have here, a traveller?'

His name was Misha. Minutes later I was in his car, roaring from one commercial centre to the next. In a city of more than a million people, it was possible to find top-of-the-line luxury cars and hi-fi equipment, but not a single bike-tube repair kit or photocopier.

Unexpectedly, Misha pulled a mobile phone from his pocket. 'Go on, ring home to Australia!' he insisted, as he swerved and overtook another Lada.

'No, do you realise how expensive it is? I can't,' I pleaded.

'Go on, just do it!'

I dialled home. 'Hello, Dad. This is Tim, just calling from Omsk,' I said.

'Tim, have you heard the sad news?' he asked almost immediately.

'No.'

'Your Scottish friend Bruce Cooper, he passed away on Thursday night. He committed suicide.'

At 5.30 a.m. the next morning I slid my putrid travel clothes on, flipped a small rucksack over my shoulder and left for Omsk Airport.

'Chris, I have never been so frightened in my life,' I whispered.

The Lada that took me to the airport broke down and I left the driver cursing and kicking the tyres in the morning greyness. By the time I stumbled into the airport, I was dripping wet from heavy rain.

Within twenty-four hours, I was in London waiting for a bus ride to Scotland. Bruce's funeral was to be in a week.

From Victoria bus station, I called some friends who I hadn't spoken to in a year or two. I hoped to find some comfort in a familiar voice, but midway through my first call I felt something peculiar in my pocket. As the money began to run out on the phone, I felt for more change only to realise that someone had stolen my electronic address organiser. I had no other records and couldn't ring my friend back to finish the call. Three years of accumulated contacts and friends disappeared. I had AU$100 left, no credit card, and no phone numbers. I spent the evening in a police station filing a report. At 12 a.m. I boarded a bus for the twelve-hour journey to northern Scotland.

An eternity later, the bus wound and jerked its way through the Highlands. I crouched over the toilet bowl in the tiny cubicle at the back of the bus, being thrown from side to side against the flimsy plastic walls. My body felt limp and battered. I hadn't eaten in fifteen hours or so, and watched without expression as the bile dribbled out my nose, down my hairy chin and into the discoloured bowl.

At 10.30 a.m. the bus pulled into the small town of Aviemore. Neil, Bruce's twin brother, had come to meet me. 'Bruce!' I almost cried out.

Later, as we sat in a café, he broke the uneasy silence. 'Last Thursday evening,' he said, 'Bruce and I planned a trip for this coming weekend. We told each other that, yes, we have to get out and spend more time in the mountains and stay away from the pubs. The mountains, that's where he really enjoyed life.'

From Aviemore we drove across the empty wind-beaten moors to Elgin, Bruce's hometown. Peering out at the bleak landscape, I recalled battling along this road with Bruce. We'd been cycling and the rains had come, drenching us to the skin.

BRUCE

When the car came to a halt in Duff Avenue, I approached the house feeling numb and tired. In the past I had savoured every moment spent with the Coopers. My arrivals had always been greeted with warm hugs and a celebratory shot of whiskey. Being around Bruce, no matter what was happening in life, was an uplifting experience.

Bruce's father Sandy greeted us at the door. Almost instantly he broke down and I went pale.

Inside, Bruce's three-year-old niece, Alexa, giggled and played about in the lounge room.

Bruce's room stood empty. I walked in and read the famous words of Martin Luther King stuck to the wall. A pen sat idly next to a notepad with the lid off, still waiting for Bruce.

'Bruce had fought such a long battle ... and he lost,' Neil said softly. It was a relief to finally give in to tears.

I'd met Bruce while working in a children's adventure camp in England. We had been working for a lousy forty pounds a week and sleeping on beds made out of stolen bread crates. Bruce lived in a leaky canvas tent, and I was crammed into a small room with three other young Australians.

He was a tall, athletically built Scot with bright ginger hair and a cheeky smile. We often spent our spare time discussing things over a beer, dreaming about places we'd rather be. On one of our days off, he introduced me to the mountains of Snowdonia, in northern Wales. As we made for the cloud-drenched distant peaks, the extraneous matter of life evaporated and we shared moments of pure joy. Over the following two years there were countless cycling, hiking and mountain trips. At one stage, I lived with the Coopers for three months while working in a shortbread factory in northern Scotland. Our last journey together had been eighteen months ago in the Cairngorm mountains during winter.

Over all this time, Bruce set an example for me. He demonstrated that there was a greater risk at stake than safety when climbing mountains: the risk of not trying something uncomfortable. That feeling of reaching the top and knowing that you had earned the view wasn't worth throwing away in the face of fear.

But more than anything else, I admired Bruce's humility, generosity, humour and ability to connect with people. His many years of working with the blind and the disadvantaged had given him a rare insight into people and society.

In the lounge room, Rita, Bruce's mother, broke down. 'We are just so bewildered, Tim,' she sobbed. Neil moved over and held her in his arms; he was putting on a brave face. In a corner of the room, I saw a photo of two cheeky-looking, red-haired twins. A squeal of delight came from a far room as Alexa played with a soft toy.

When Bruce came home the next day he was in a coffin.

He'd spent his last evening in a local pub with Neil and a long-time friend, Robin. Around midnight Neil and Robin left, leaving Bruce with a school friend he hadn't seen in years.

He had been suffering from Seasonal Affective Disorder, a condition that often results in depression during the dark winter months in northerly latitudes. After receiving light therapy he seemed to be on the mend.

Perhaps the alcohol mixed with his anti-depressant tablets on that final night had been his undoing. At some point he would have come to Duff Avenue, perhaps even walked past his house, but the decision must have already been made. In any case, he didn't make it home. There was no note when he was found in the morning, hanging from a tree in the front yard of a retirement home.

Was it a spur-of-the-moment thing, triggered by the mix of medication and alcohol? Or was it premeditated? We will never know. Some people may picture a frail, quietly spoken person who was driven to suicide by self-pity, as if he was predestined for such an end. But that wasn't Bruce. He was strong, outgoing and had a zest for life and a humour that few are graced with.

'There was just no fear in him when he did it. There can't have been,' Neil said. 'He would have been feeling so alone. He knew how much it would hurt Mum and Dad. He knew it ... We've just got to respect his decision. It's selfish for us to think otherwise. He is gone now, released from the world that probably tormented him.'

Two days before the funeral I sat motionless in the car. Beside me, Neil's face was expressionless, eyes staring blankly through the windscreen. He turned off the engine and there was only the rain drumming on the roof. A gusty wind whistled through tiny cracks and rocked the car violently. Outside, a cloud had all but enveloped the mountain before us. It was Ben Rinnes, Bruce's favourite local peak.

'I just can't believe he did it, Tim ... I'm going to miss him so much.' Neil's words were almost inaudible.

'C'mon, Neil, you take my coat. We have to climb this mountain. That's where Bruce will be, not moping around that coffin,' I urged.

The car doors slammed shut and the raindrops pelted down hard. Leaning into the howling wind, we began to push upwards along a rough path. The horizontal rain lacerated the open wedges of rock and threatened to pulverise bracken and other plant life close to the ground. It cut into my body, but I felt nothing. After half an hour or so we stopped.

'Bruce loved it up here. This is what he lived for,' Neil said. 'I don't know about you but I am absolutely soaked.

We can turn back now, but I guess it doesn't make much difference anymore.'

I was shivering, but it wasn't from the cold. Silently, we turned and trudged on.

Further on I removed my beanie. The wind caught the raindrops from my hair and sent them flying. For no particular reason, we stopped again and turned to face the direction we had come from.

'Neil ... Neil! Look!' I shouted. But he was already transfixed.

Far below in the valley, the brilliant glow of a rainbow rose. It arched gracefully over our path and descended into the misty valley on the far side. The colours seemed to pulsate as they grew in intensity until they were viscous, almost solid.

Above, the clouds parted to reveal a misty blue sky. The rain cleared. I felt a warm sensation on my shoulder, like a hand, and the shivering ceased. The mist rolled away in great billowing swirls to reveal the rocky mountainside, which glistened like dew on a clear winter's morning. In the distance, myriad peaks rose like emerald-green islands from a white sea.

'It's Bruce, Tim. It's really Bruce!' Neil cried, a smile erupting across his face. Tears flowed and I broke into a croaky, relentless laugh.

It was the most beautiful thing I had ever seen. And what's more ... I believed it. Bruce was far from gone. I am not religious or a believer in mysticism, but what I saw, whether contrived by our minds or not, will remain with me for the rest of my life. I promised myself in that moment that I would never view the world without the magical and enchanting perspective that Bruce had graced us with.

We turned to climb further up the slope and into a light veil of mist that curled over the ridge. The sun burnt through and appeared as a silvery disc in the sky above the peak. The wet rocks on the ridge reflected the glow like a series of glittering quartz.

'This is it, Tim. The light, the walking up to greater things. Only that bugger Bruce up there, as usual, is striding ahead!' Neil shouted.

The mist felt warm for a few minutes. Neil walked ahead and his silhouette melted into the glowing white. Now and then a thick plume of vapour rushed over the ridge and he was temporarily erased from sight. The sun had retreated behind thick cloud by the time we arrived on the summit, and the rocks appeared dull and lifeless.

'Even though he has died, I can feel him trying to make me happy,' I said, after a long silence.

'I know, Tim. I feel the same. Everyone is so sad, but it's crazy. It's not the end ... it's just the beginning. I just have to wait until it's my turn and we are reunited,' Neil replied.

The funeral passed like a celebration. Rita commented that it felt as if it should have been a wedding. When it was all over I sat up the back of a National Express bus as it pulled out of Glasgow. It was an overcast day and rain fell in light, random showers.

What will it be like as everyone trickled out of Elgin and back to their normal lives? Soon there would be just Rita, Sandy, Neil and an empty room. Today was the seventh day without Bruce.

One thought hit me before I sank into long-needed sleep. I hadn't seen my family in more than two years. There was, after all, a very good reason to look forward to returning to Australia.

Bruce Gordon Cooper ended his life at the age of twenty-six.

Finding Our Way
Omsk – Ishimka
Late Spring 2000

Chris

I kicked a stone along the pavement then hurried after it on my by now familiar path through the city. I passed tiny street-side booths overflowing with newspapers and swerved to avoid a crowd of well-dressed young people milling around the locked door of a student caféteria. I glanced at the sign on the door as I passed. It was supposed to have opened for lunch twenty-five minutes ago.

Two blocks on, I reached the glitzy electronics store where I would turn left off the main road and head towards the Internet café. On the steps outside sat what looked to be a pile of rags but, as I came closer, I realised that it was actually an old woman. She was wrapped from head to toe in ragged strips of dirty fabric and her head was down, sinking towards the gutter. The only sign of life that I could see was a shaking hand extended to the passers-by. Behind her, through the store window and through an unimaginable divide, an overweight, middle-aged Russian businessman with a red face and an imported suit negotiated with a shop assistant over the sale of what appeared to be a DVD player.

How could things have come to this? Like every other elderly Russian, this old woman was entitled to a pension, but looking at her, it was painfully obvious that she wasn't receiving one.

I paused to drop a few roubles into her hand. It was enough, at least, to buy a loaf of bread, and she raised her head to thank me with a faint smile. She was clearly not a drug addict or an alcoholic, the most common excuse doled out about Russia's homeless. I wrenched my gaze away from her watery eyes and looked through the window to see the man paying for his DVD from a thick wad of American bills. I clenched my teeth and walked away.

I quickened my step and soon reached the Internet café where I had come every day for the past week. I found a space next to some more newly rich citizens and logged on to spend a couple of calm and blissful hours chatting to Nat. As much as I lived for this contact, however, it was no longer enough to brighten my day.

As soon as I walked out the door, a familiar frustration returned. I kicked a stone and accidentally sent it whizzing into the gutter past yet another slick New-Russian. He turned and looked angrily at me from the door of his black Landcruiser and I scowled right back at him.

Tim was not due to return from Scotland for another three days, and I spent them waiting. My life was stagnating and I was repeating myself to Nat in ever-gloomier circles. I had nothing new to add and although I tried to be upbeat, I could tell that I wasn't really succeeding. I knew that Nat loved me, but she was studying for exams and I was beginning to get the feeling that she could better spend her time elsewhere.

I hadn't moved in ten days and the lack of exercise combined with a diet of greasy, unhealthy food had left me feeling unfit and sleeping badly. I couldn't remember what it was like to have a clear thought and I'd forgotten the enjoyment of the simple cycling lifestyle that I loved. In ten days, I'd hardly learnt a thing about Russia or its people. The waiting was killing me. It was a waste, not only of time, but also of the life that was waiting for me back in Australia.

The day before Tim returned, I hit rock bottom. I seriously considered chucking it all in and flying home but in the end decided to delay the decision. As much as I wanted to be back with Nat, I knew that it would be hard for me to return to her knowing that I'd failed. Besides, Tim and I had long ago decided that we'd ride the next leg – 800 kilometres to Novosibirsk – alone. I'd decide whether to continue or not when we got there.

I thought about Tim and what he would have gone through in Scotland. How would he be dealing with the death of a close friend? I tried to empathise but found it hard. The friends I'd had in high school had mostly drifted away. And what about facing up to the idea that it was suicide? Did that change everything, too?

When Tim returned I could see immediately that his thoughts were far away. We went through the greetings and catching up, but his replies were stilted and automatic. He was looking blank, tired and uninspired.

He told us about the experience of Bruce's funeral while Misha helped himself to a large bottle of expensive whiskey that Tim had bought in Scotland. It was only eight in the morning, but he got rolling drunk and soon lost interest in listening to Tim. He turned his attention to his wife and started abusing her, instead.

We decided that we'd leave early the next day and that we'd think about splitting up later on. But early, when it came around, turned out to be 4.30 p.m. Tim, who was easily distracted at the best of times, was in another world and he could only do one thing at a time. If he was drawn into a conversation during a meal, even as a listener, he would hold a forkful of food hovering in mid-air until the talk stopped. Then he would return his attention to eating. I knew that I should be tolerant and understanding; I wanted to be, but after half an hour my best efforts were exhausted and I was back to being pissed off with him.

Finally, we said goodbye. I was grateful to my hosts, Natasha and Dima, for their hospitality and sorry that I'd probably been a less-than-ideal guest, but I had no regrets whatsoever about leaving Omsk. Once we made it out onto the road, I pedalled faster and faster. Tim was somewhere behind and I knew he was going to be angry that I'd raced ahead, but somehow I couldn't help myself. I felt a desperate need to get away from the city. It was a place where I'd felt more trapped and frustrated than ever before in my life, and I didn't stop to wait for Tim until the last of the tall apartment blocks had passed and I was well and truly into the countryside.

Away from the city, the black cloud that had been hovering over me lifted a little, but there was still no room for enthusiasm. Tim was dragging a chain of low morale too; and after riding in silence for an hour, he tried to explain how he was feeling.

'Bruce's death ... it was so pointless and he threw so much away. But somehow I can feel that he's still there and that he's telling me to cheer up and enjoy it because there's just so much here to live for. It's what he's always said, that's how he lived life himself. And now ...'

I could understand up to a point, but as I'd never known Bruce I could only dredge a little bit of consolation from my own dispirited gloom.

We camped late in a small birch forest and the sky, which had been grey and threatening all day, now let forth a steady downpour of soaking, humid rain. Tim wasn't interested in food, and I decided that I couldn't be stuffed cooking dinner just for myself. Instead, we lay in the tent, sweating and exhausted. We were way too close and well inside each other's personal space when, ideally, we should have been alone. I mentioned my thoughts about chucking it in and flying home and Tim, after thinking about it for a minute, told me what I should have known all along.

'You're here, mate, so you're obviously riding this next stage. And I'm sorry, but just at the moment I've got too much else on my mind to really get my head around that sort of thing and talk sensibly about it. Can't we talk about it later?'

Our conversation rambled. Inevitably, we found something about which we could disagree. We began a drawn-out argument, but neither of us had the energy to put much passion into it. Soon it had turned into more of a rambling discussion of each other's failings. As our anger gradually subsided into exhaustion, we became completely blunt with each other.

'I hate it that you always disagree with just about everything I bloody say!' Tim told me.

I conceded that he had a point, but explained that this was because I felt that most of his opinions were couched in sweeping generalisations and were said in a tone that really offended me.

Tim told me he understood that my regular stormy moods were a result of missing Nat, but criticised me for almost always letting them spill over onto him. There was something to that and it worried me. I knew it really wasn't fair on Tim and I tried to explain.

'I really am sorry that it seems like that, mate, but it's when I constantly have to stuff around waiting for you that I miss Nat the most. And that's when I wish like hell that I was back home!'

We carried on, until the early hours of the morning, when we simply ran out of things to say. We agreed to work on things and to try to compromise, then slumped into bed. After two emotionally draining weeks, things had come to a definite head. The argument had been civilized, but the personal criticisms we'd levelled at each other had been honest and we'd covered topics that had previously been taboo. The steady disintegration of our friendship had been checked. Hopefully, the journey could still be rescued.

We slept late the next day and didn't get going till the middle of the afternoon. Tim was subdued and I was still feeling brain dead, but at the same time I was more enthusiastic about the journey than I had been for a long time. We struggled back onto the road, then set off along the bitumen under a clear summer sky.

We were taking the back route to Novosibirsk, which meant over two weeks of cycling along minor roads from one out-of-the-way village to the next. The map showed a myriad of place names and connecting lanes scattered evenly across a vast flat plain. It soon became obvious that the author of the map (which screamed 'reliable' in big red letters) had never set foot in the region and had been indulging in a bit of make-believe. Occasionally, we tried to follow roads that were marked but had never been built, and sometimes vice versa. Mostly, we were simply baffled by villages either inaccurately named or marked. This, together with the fact that none of the minor roads were signposted, made navigating a frustrating challenge.

We both needed space and mostly travelled several kilometres apart, catching up only when we stopped for meal breaks and at uncertain-looking intersections. We also made a habit of cycling into villages together. This gave us extra kicking power in the likely event of a dog attack. It also helped when asking directions from locals.

We rode into a village on the first of June, the first day of summer and three days after leaving Omsk. It was called Chistovo, but our map located it almost twenty kilometres away. The main street was a continuation of the road we had arrived on – a single lane of worn bitumen with wide, potholed dirt shoulders for overtaking. It stretched only a few hundred metres through the village with a dozen or so log houses scattered on either side.

Fields dotted with workers and heavy machinery reached for miles around, but the only signs of life from within the village were a few barking dogs and a very old man sitting on an uneven bench outside his house. We pedalled up to him. He half struggled to his feet and half tried to wave his stick at us. We left the bikes and walked cautiously over to him, map in hand.

'Um, could you please tell us the way to Yaminka?' Tim began.

'Eh!' he said sharply, peering with bright eyes. He'd obviously noticed the accent. 'Where are you from?'

'*Avstraliya*,' I replied, reluctantly. This was going to be another one of *those* conversations.

'Eh!' he said again, looking us slowly up and down. We waited uncomfortably for almost a full minute while he considered this information. Then he finally smiled. 'Austria! Well I never.'

'Ah ... Yes.' Tim let it pass and tried again. 'Do you, by any chance, know the way to Yaminka?'

'Eh!' He turned his head slightly and thrust a wrinkled ear towards us. 'Where?'

'YAMINKA!'

'Eh!' He settled back down, looking puzzled and shaking his head slowly for a good few minutes, before he finally looked up with a cunning smile, as though he'd caught on to our game. 'There's no Yaminka here. Where are you really from?'

Now it was our turn to be confused. 'We've got to get to Yaminka,' I tried again, showing him the map. 'It's supposed to be only twenty kilometres from here. Do you know which of the roads we should take out of this village?'

He studied the page closely for several minutes then handed it back to me. I got the distinct feeling that he'd never seen a map in his life.

'Very good then.' He smiled confidently. 'Have a good journey. Goodbye.'

We said goodbye and retreated on our bikes, totally unenlightened. We looked around for somebody else and saw, in a nearby paddock, a gigantic ploughing machine.

The metal monster rumbled along parallel to the road, leaving a vast swath of chewed-up earth and a billowing cloud of dust in its wake. We braked to a halt and waved at the driver. The driver's arm protruded from a tiny window and waved back vigorously. We waved harder, and so did he. In a final effort, we waved as though we were trying to flag down a passing plane and finally got the desired result. The roar of the motor slackened and the machine grumbled to a ponderous halt. The door opened and the man scrambled several metres down a ladder. He extended his hand with a smile. He was short and skinny but he had a vice-grip handshake. We went through the preliminaries then got down to business.

'Could you tell us how to get to Yaminka, please?'

'Hey?' He shook his head. 'There's no Yaminka around here. Do you have a map? Show me where you're trying to go.'

We handed him our tattered map and pointed out the road we were looking for. He scratched his head and muttered for a minute then flipped a quick glance at the front cover before looking at us. 'Where the hell did you get this map?'

We told him and he snorted derisively. He turned back to the map. 'The roads are all marked wrong,' he announced.

'But I think you're looking for Ishimka. It's across the border and you *can* get there ...' He paused for a moment, as though trying to weigh up our competence. 'No one from around here does though because there's not really a road.'

Tim and I looked at each other and laughed. 'Oh well, at least there won't be any snow this time.'

He went on to explain directions. 'Take that road there, about four kilometres to Ribinsk,' he said, pointing. We looked at the road then back at the map. The village was unmarked, of course. 'Then take a left, then a right, then go about two kilometres around the village until you see a little track going off to the right past an old shed.' I nodded and Tim looked at me to make sure I'd got it. 'Then you just head east for about fifteen kilometres. The track doesn't continue, but there's quite a few other tracks out there on the steppe, so good luck!' We shook hands and began to move off. 'Oh, by the way,' the man said, 'where are you going?'

'To China!' Tim replied, brightly.

The man snorted derisively again, checked himself and laughed. He walked back towards his huge machine muttering to himself. Probably evil things about stupid, crazy Australians.

Halfway to Ribinsk a huge cloudbank appeared on the horizon. By the time we'd reached the turnoff it was pouring. The hard clay track had become perilously slippery and to make matters worse, there were a dozen people sheltering from the downpour under the old shed that we'd been instructed to keep an eye out for.

I slipped in the mud and fell first, rather than Tim, for a change. The onlookers who had been staring at us agape cracked up laughing. Tim looked round to see what they were laughing at and he came down, too. The laughter doubled, then it doubled again as we struggled to our feet, smeared in red, claggy muck. The shed was about seventy metres away, just too close to comfortably ignore the audience. I slipped over again and swore. I looked over at Tim and noticed that he was actually having fun.

'We should go over and charge them five roubles a head for the show!' he suggested, happily. My foul mood gave way in the face of Tim's good spirits and I laughed, too. That'd be about right, I thought ruefully. Tim's always more comfortable being covered in dirt and muck than I am ...

We slipped over a dozen more times before the audience started getting bored. The road was now sticking to our tyres, and our mudguards and brakes were so jammed with gunk that the wheels wouldn't turn. We made slow progress, stopping every five minutes to scrape away the mud with sticks but, luckily, the rain didn't last long and the road eventually dried out.

The next day the real fun started. The track we'd been following petered out completely and left us facing a broad, flat plain. We followed a cattle pad through some long grass for a few hundred metres then climbed a low ridge and took a good look out over the surrounds.

The view was the most expansive we'd seen for months. Looking north, I could still make out regular clumps of birch forest scattering the plain. Looking south, pale brown grass merged into pastel blue sky on the shimmering horizon. There was not a tree to be seen all the way to Kazakhstan.

We were on the border of the endless grassy steppe, and precisely ... I looked at the map for a moment. We were precisely ... I handed the map to Tim. 'Which way do you reckon it is to this Ishimka place?'

He studied the map for a few moments then handed it back to me with a grin. 'Yep, I definitely agree, mate. You're spot on. Amazing view, isn't it? And by the way, which way did you say we go from here?'

We fiddled with our compasses for a while, then set our sights on a distant patch of forest. We followed another cattle pad that became increasingly substantial until we decided that it might have been a vehicle track at some stage in the past. Where there'd been vehicles, there must have been people, and maybe a nearby village, too!

The first track joined another, and although it wound round a fair bit, it seemed to be heading generally north-east. I peered at the map while Tim had a better look around.

'Just thought you might want to know that the forest we were aiming for has completely disappeared,' he told me, amused.

'That's okay, I guess,' I replied, measuring distances on the map. 'Even if we don't find Ishimka we just have to keep on heading vaguely east and we'll bump into a real road somewhere in the next hundred kays or so.'

We pedalled along until an intersection left us choosing north or south. We flipped a coin and rode south. At the next intersection we turned east, then north and then south again. It was great fun and we had it all to ourselves. Besides the long forgotten tracks, there was not a trace of civilization to be seen. We'd both lightened up immensely since leaving Omsk, and I wondered whether Tim's laughter was a sign that he was starting to come to terms with the loss of his friend.

Eventually, we saw a boiler-shaped water tower rising above the treetops in the distance. With all our turns and diversions we must have cycled at least thirty kilometres but we had no idea how far we'd come in a straight line, or exactly which direction we'd been heading in. We might have found Ishimka, but then again we might be somewhere different altogether. As long as we hadn't inadvertently crossed the border into Kazakhstan, everything would be fine.

We rode towards the tower. Soon a few houses and buildings came into view. We were approaching the village from behind, and I guessed that this was definitely not the main route into town. We saw a group of kids playing soccer on the street nearby and managed to hide behind a fence before they saw us. Tim stayed put and set up the video camera while I prepared to ride over to them.

They didn't see me until I was quite close. One little girl, seeing the look of amazement on an older boy's face, turned around to see me riding straight towards her. She screamed and ran away. I pulled up, and the rest of the group stood stock still, looking at me in astonishment. Their ball rolled into a puddle, unnoticed. I cleared my throat, a little self-consciously, and prepared to break the silence. 'Um ... I wonder, can you tell me what village this is?'

They all took a shocked step backwards: It talks! Then a few of the older kids held a brief, whispered conference. The younger kids stared even harder, some starting to look a little afraid. It talks *funny* too, they must have been thinking. I had to remind myself that my bike was probably the weirdest thing that any of them had ever seen. It was almost certain that none of them would have encountered a westerner before, either. I wondered for a moment whether their reaction would have been much different if I'd landed in a UFO.

The whispering ceased and one of the boys stepped cautiously forward. 'This is Ishimka,' he said slowly, an urgent question burning in his eyes. 'Where are you from?'

'Oh,' I answered happily, 'we're from Australia but we've cycled here from Petrozavodsk in Karelia.' Another silence. Some of the kids would not have heard of these other places.

'Tim, come here,' I yelled back over my shoulder. Tim trundled up, and the kids seemed to forget me as they surged forward to see him riding. I overheard some of their excited whispers as they scrambled past me.

'It's amazing. Where do you think the motor is?'

It didn't take long before most of the kids had overcome their nervousness and were swamping us with questions. The crowd was growing too. In less than ten minutes, the group had swelled from ten to about thirty – every kid in the village must have come running, it seemed.

We grabbed a couple of the braver-looking of our new friends and plonked them on the bike seats. Ten-year-old legs strained hopelessly in an effort to reach the pedals until the kids were lying horizontally, clutching the handlebars and staring with excited eyes at the sky. We asked them to take us to the village shop and jogged along, pushing the bikes and holding them upright while the two thrilled little drivers zigzagged crazily down the road.

We quickly finished our shopping and stepped outside to find that the crowd had grown larger still. There were big kids now, too. The local teenagers had pulled up, packed onto the back of two ancient motorbikes. They were trying their best to remain aloof while quizzing the crowd of animated littlies as to what was going on. One of the village men had come down as well. He'd been briefed by his son, and now thrust his way through the crowd to invite us back for a cup of tea. His name was Vladimir, and as he walked us to his house we asked him whether Ishimka got many travellers.

'We did have one once,' he replied, scratching his beard thoughtfully. 'About seven years ago, I think it was. A Russian, of course. He was walking from Omsk to Lake Baikal.' Tim and I looked at each other, amazed by such a feat, and by the fact that so few people had ever passed through. 'Nobody here has ever met a real westerner before, though,' he added with a grin.

We were ushered through the gate into a clean-swept courtyard. Most of the kids who tried to swarm in around us were pushed firmly back out again. One who did get through was Ilya, the boy who'd steered my bike to the shop and who'd firmly manoeuvred himself into position as my new best friend. He was small for his age but a bundle of energy. He bounced around all over the place, firing off questions then changing the topic before I had a hope of answering.

Another kid who joined us was Tolya, Vladimir's son, who'd had the foresight to get his dad before we could be whisked off elsewhere.

We sat for an hour drinking tea and talking with Vladimir, his wife Tatyana and a few of their friends. All the while there was an excited buzz coming from outside. Through a small window by the table, I could see rows of little fingers curled over the top of the high front fence, straining to lift heads up and over for another glance at the mysterious *Avstralitzi* and their weird travelling machines. Several other adults arrived, bringing small gifts for our hosts, then pulling them aside for whispered conversations. I realised that negotiations were taking place as to who would put us up for the night. I conferred quickly with Tim. We hadn't really planned on staying, but Ishimka was shaping up to be an amazing experience and the chance to stay seemed too good an opportunity to miss. Besides, it didn't seem as though we had much of a say in the matter.

Vladimir helped wheel our bikes into his shed, then reluctantly handed us over to the crowd of kids waiting impatiently outside the gate. They were disappointed to see us reappear without our bikes, but we assured them that we'd bring them out again in the morning. Tim took his camera and was hauled off somewhere by one group of kids, while Ilya and half a dozen of his buddies grabbed me and we all headed off to the village lake. It was a couple of kilometres away but the kids with worn out shoes, grubby clothes and bright white smiles possessed incredible energy. They never walked anywhere, it seemed. If they were going somewhere, they ran.

We reached the lake in no time. The children gathered to point out a family of beautiful swans floating gracefully among olive-green waterlilies about 200 metres from the shore. I admired the perfect image for a moment, then looked down to find that each eager little kid had produced a slingshot and was racing to load it up, anxious to be the first to show off their sharp-shooting skills. The first stone – Ilya's I think it was – landed with a splash about ten metres short of the nearest swan. Appreciative Oos and Aahs came from the rest of the kids and I realised with relief that the swans were probably just out of range. A dozen more stones splashed near the centre of the lake and the swans disdainfully cruised away.

Then it was my turn to have a go. I pulled back carefully, only half as far as the experts around me had done, then released the sling with a whoosh. The elastic smacked painfully into my thumb and the rock bounced away on the ground. I swore in English and sucked my thumb. All the kids laughed and wanted to learn the word I'd used. My incompetence with the slingshot meant that it was time for an impromptu coaching session.

We jogged in fits and bursts back to the village and held a dozen sprint races along the way. By virtue of my longer legs, I won the first few, but the days of riding hadn't prepared me for speed, and when they started imposing handicaps I was well and truly outdone. Someone suggested arm-wrestling and we all hunkered down in the dust outside the village to test our manly mettle. It was two of them against one of me. With a spark of inspiration, I introduced them to the art of thumb-wrestling. The game had never been seen before in this part of Russia and they battled fiercely against each other for an hour, enjoying the novelty and giving me a well-earned rest.

We returned to the village as the herd of village cows was brought home from the plains by a boy on horseback. He drove them towards the main street, flicked his whip a couple of times, then left. I watched in amazement as fifty cows ambled along the village streets, each animal heading back to its own house for milking.

My gang allowed me to return home for dinner, but only for a little while. No sooner had I finished eating and started to think of settling down for a relaxed evening of conversation and vodka than they started banging at the door. This time both Tim and I were enlisted to spend the evening hours on a bumpy, muddy field playing a sprawling game of no-rules soccer.

We returned to our hosts after dark and learned a little about life in the village and how it had changed for the worse since the days of communism. In turn, we told them of our lives: on the bikes, and back home, half a world away in Australia.

We finally made it to bed at around 3 a.m. I smiled as I thought back over the events of the day. It made me realise how privileged and lucky we were to be here experiencing a life and a culture that few westerners even knew existed. Yet, at the same time, how easy would it really be to get here? With a few thousand dollars to spare, I could get a visa in Australia and reach Ishimka within a few weeks, at most.

No, what made our being here so special was that we'd come the hard way. We'd arrived on bikes, living a basic lifestyle that the locals could relate to, even if they did think we were crazy. More than that, we'd taken the trouble to learn Russian and could talk freely to everyone we met. Perhaps the most significant thing was that we were young.

Twenty-one, I thought, is an ideal age to be. We were young enough to have fun with the kids and young enough that the majority of babushkas got all fired up to feed and look after us. But we were also old enough to converse meaningfully with adults.

I made the choice about continuing the trip as I was drifting off to sleep. I loved Nat dearly, but this opportunity to live in Russia and to get to know its people and culture was unique. Tomorrow we'd be riding again, and the day after that we had decided to split up and spend the next week riding alone. What chance encounters and fantastic opportunities were waiting along that road? What about Lake Baikal? And Mongolia? And China? One thing was for certain: unless I continued the adventure to the end, I would never know.

Alone
Ishimka – Novosibirsk
Early Summer 2000

Tim

'See you in a week!' Chris said as he pedalled off.

From inside the shelter, I strained to hear his bike down to the last sound. I could just make out his tyres, crunching the fine gravel and mud. Then came a breeze. Then silence.

As reluctant as I had been to split up, I knew it was important to do so. Our planned route was along the semi-steppe lands close to the Kazakhstan border. It was agreed that one person would ride twenty-four hours ahead, and then wait twenty kilometres from Novosibirsk. From where we were, it was a further 600 kilometres to Novosibirsk; so we approximated that it would take six days. The crux of the decision for me was who would ride ahead and who would follow.

Although I had become more confident at bike repairs, I feared a breakdown. I depended on Chris for back-up and knew that if he rode ahead, depending on him wouldn't be an option. To add to my worries, my solitary experiences in the past year, perhaps due to bad luck, had all turned into mini-disasters. The worst had been in the Arctic during a solo trip in spring the previous year. I had fallen through river ice, become lost and trudged on for three days almost without sleep, close to delirium and hypothermia. Now, I feared that everything would start going wrong the minute I was left alone.

I asked Chris what he preferred and he confirmed my suspicion. He wasn't going to let me out the easy way. 'This could be my last ever trip alone, Tim. Once I get back to Australia it will be the beginning of a completely different life. I think it's important that we do this alone, and that I ride in front.' I was amazed by his courage and resilience. He would never be fazed by the child-like fears that haunted me.

For a long time after Chris had gone I lay in the shelter, waiting for something to go wrong. It was as if I had personal ghosts that taunted me during my most vulnerable moments. One way to beat the ghosts was to remain active and positive. After a failed nap, I filmed myself crawling in and out of my fly-net, and reflected on the hellish night that I had spent.

Chris had taken the tent with him, leaving me with this 'mosquito-tick protector' that I had made in Omsk. The ground sheet of the contraption was made of a lightweight silk material to which I had sewn a fly-net and attached a zip. It was like a big fly-netting sleeping bag that hung inside the *loue* shelter.

It was only when I crawled into it that I realised it was too small. The fly-netting collapsed, which meant that mosquitoes could bite me. In the stifling heat, I had no choice but to use my sleeping bag as a barrier. The moment I turned onto my side, the mosquitoes pounced on my bare face. Worst of all, the holes in the netting were wide enough for mosquitoes to crawl through, turning the system into an insect trap.

I dreaded another night in the netting, let alone a further six or seven.

In the afternoon I made a fire and sat staring into the flaring birchwood. Despite my fears, it was a relief to be alone. I needed to work out who I was, as a separate identity from Chris and the whole cycling Siberia thing. How much of what annoyed me about Chris was just a reflection of myself?

It wasn't long before a cold change rushed across the plains, engulfing my camp site. The leaves fluttered furiously, as if fighting to break free of the branches. The light dimmed and a drizzle began to fall from dark, burly clouds. Contentedly, I slipped into my sleeping bag for a cosy session of diary writing.

By late evening, the rain became heavier and distant rumbles whispered rumours of a storm. After eating a generous slice of *sala* with garlic cloves, I put my head down. There was just one thought in my mind as I drifted off: the road was dirt.

In the gloom of the overcast morning, I shovelled down some Siberian muesli which consisted of rolled oats, sultanas, powdered milk and bananas doused in water from the nearest puddle. The sour taste that was typical of Russian oats was unbearable; and I threw most of it into the forest. Then I pushed the bike onto the road, lay back and fitted my runners into the toe clips.

The tyres pressed deep into the sticky clay surface, making a sickly sucking noise. Two metres later, the back wheel slid out. Narrowly avoiding a fall, I stamped my foot down and felt the tendons in my right knee draw tight until it felt like they would snap.

Once again I pushed forward. Feeling sure of my balance, I lifted my sight to the panorama ahead and knew instantly that I had made a foolish mistake. The front wheel lodged into thick mud and the bike crashed. Unable to leap free, I was thrown down with my legs pinned beneath the frame and heavy load. A nauseating pain shot up my leg as my shin copped a gash from the front cog teeth. Leaving the bike in the middle of the road, I stormed off, swearing.

Upon inspection, the bike was undamaged but clogged with the viscous red mud. There was no point even trying to ride, so after picking up the bike, I leaned over and began to push. The surface was so saturated that with every step my feet slid backwards. My runners felt like heavy clogs. Every twenty metres or so I had to tip the bike over and scrape out the mud from the guards and wheels.

Ahead, the road cut a relatively wide swath of dark red above the swampy landscape. I peered into the distance in the hope that there was improvement in sight. I thought of Chris, who was probably on a nice bitumen road somewhere, gliding across the landscape. What worried me was that if I didn't make it to Chris on time, he would continue alone into Novosibirsk. If only I could tell him that I was probably going to be late.

After an hour or so I became curious about the deep grassy drain that ran along the side of the road. Surely it would be easier to push down there. I clambered down into the five-metre-deep drain to discover a sea of stinging nettles, long grass and ankle-breaking holes.

It took what seemed an eternity to push the bike back up the near vertical incline. By the time I dumped the bike back on the road I was trembling with hunger. Ever since Bruce's death, hunger, along with many other sensations, seemed irrelevant; when I ate, everything tasted indifferent. Even physical pain was dulled and happened somewhere beneath my thoughts. I didn't feel refreshed by sleep and yet didn't feel the complete sensation of exhaustion, either. Making fires, collecting wood, riding huge distances: what was the point? I knew that it was an unhealthy situation, and somewhere I missed the sensation of experiencing the highs in balance with the lows.

Munching into a thick *pryaniki*, I looked back along the road. To my astonishment the camp site was still in view. In two hours, I had covered less than two kilometres. In the midst of all this, thoughts of Bruce kept coming.

I thought of a conversation that I had with Bruce's father, Sandy, one night. I had just returned from a cycling journey to the Isle of Skye and was planning to get work on the broccoli farms in southern Scotland. Before hitchhiking back to Bruce's home early one morning, I had been feeling ravenous and decided to swipe a pint of milk from the doorstep of a small hotel. When I mentioned the broccoli farm work to Sandy, he replied, 'Oh, Tim, ye don't wunt to werk down there. Down there are the kind of people who would steal milk off your front doorstep!'

I burst into laughter and the truth came out. The event only added credibility to my tag as a 'thieving Australian convict'. From there on Bruce joked that he warned Sandy to hide all the valuables, including the knives, forks, toilet paper and milk, in a safe.

I had no idea how long I had been sitting there, but the bag of *pryaniki* was just about empty. With some composure restored, I set myself to the task of pushing. Somehow I found a rhythm and took pleasure in the way my muscles stretched. As I peered down I couldn't help but feel proud of my tattered runners that now openly displayed two rows of toes. The repetition and sense of getting somewhere, however slow, was satisfying.

The sun finally thinned out the low cloud and brought with it a warm ambience. Before me lay a metre-wide band of road that was clearly solid enough for riding.

Finally, I began to make ground. The further I went, the better the road became. Eventually, I found myself gliding along carelessly. I rode as if I was experiencing one protracted moment. The crunch of gritty sand beneath the wheels and the constant pushing of my legs didn't feel like a timeline of events, but a state of mind and body. The road meandered over such flat ground that for what must have been hours I didn't need to touch the gears. Was that the land passing me, or me passing over the land? The horizon gradually came into focus through the rippling heat and passed again into the haze. When hunger threatened, my arm reached automatically beneath the seat to find more *pryaniki*. I was the passenger of this journey, not the driver. I let my mind fall into an abyss of merciful blankness; I wanted for the thoughts to come, not to think them.

In the distance there appeared the shimmer of a lake. The skyline was engulfed in a mirage of gin-coloured flames. A familiar scent in the air, the harsh light, and the rippling horizon told me it was the sea. It occurred to me that this was an estuary, like the one near my home in South Gippsland – a shelter where gulls and seals came for refuge from the wild waters of Bass Strait.

Then the waters changed. Far out on the horizon I saw great clouds dropping bending columns of rain. The squawking of a lone gull cut through the air, thick with menace.

'There it is, the Moray Firth,' Bruce said, pointing to the north. It was Scotland, on the coast near Elgin. And yet it wasn't.

'Why, Bruce? You stupid bastard,' I whispered. 'Now that I have the chance to live life, how do I do it best?'

The sky opened up into a hazy blue, adulterated by a few wafer-thin clouds. All there was, was sky. There was no bike, no road, no lake. I couldn't even feel my hands on the handlebars or my back against the seat. And I was positive that if I could only launch myself upwards, I would once again be with him.

If he was up there, drifting with the clouds, then there was solace in that. I remembered the pale blue lips and his body lying in the coffin, his boots powdered in Cairngorm Mountain dust. He didn't look sad, or in pain. He looked like he had found the freedom he had dreamed about.

ALONE

It was a village, nestled into a slight curvature of the land, that brought me back. Faded log houses were embedded into the landscape like weathered lumps of silver-grey granite. A horse and cart rattled along the single street, rising and falling over the potholes.

The sight of civilization reminded me of how isolated the road had been. Just the wind, trees and passing birds.

I approached the village as if it were some kind of homecoming, excited by the prospect of talking to someone for the first time in more than a day.

Several men were milling about a particularly dilapidated house. The spine of the roof curved in an s shape in line with the uneven ground. The fence was a collection of twisted birch branches and other bits and pieces of timber. Three of the men wore buttoned vests and beret-type hats. All wore a kind of cut-off gumboot bottoms as a crude style of summer footwear.

As I neared, two of the men turned with a drawn-out, fluid movement. One man stumbled backwards and reached out for support. He fell onto a pointy ridge in the road that bent his back into a painful arch. I only caught a glimpse of their darkened faces and vacant stares. The empty bottles lying near their feet confirmed my suspicion. I gave a tentative wave, and put foot to pedal.

'Hey you, come here!' someone yelled, as I took off down the other side of the hill. As hospitable as Russians were, I'd had enough of drunkards.

The orange glow shrank to a strip on the horizon, and I knew with a sense of dread that it was time to make camp. It was in the dark that I was most taunted by my fears. It must have been around 11 p.m. Now that we were nearing the start of summer, the daylight hours had increased dramatically.

After finding some muddy water in a roadside puddle, I pedalled to an island of birch trees. I hadn't stopped for lunch,

159

and in a pathetic gesture to my stomach, I gulped down a bit of pig fat before crawling into my tangled fly-net.

The following morning I greeted the sunrise with a sigh of relief. Throughout the night I had been keen and alert. Now, in the bright morning sunshine, even the darkest corners of the land seemed friendly. After breakfast I was back on the bike. There was pleasure in the certainty that there was a whole day's riding ahead of me.

Another village came into sight just as my legs were warming up. My *pryaniki* biscuits and bread supplies desperately needed restocking. Water from a village well would also make a nice change.

The village ran along the track, with two single rows of wooden homes. Although it boasted a population of less than 300, it was probably half a kilometre long. The main street was just as rough as the one I had seen the day before. Water had gathered in stagnant pools at the bottom of deep trenches, forming a river between the rows of houses.

I rode until I spied a hand-painted sign with *magazin*, shop, written across it. It seemed that my arrival had gone unnoticed but for a couple of boys who were riding at a safe distance behind me, whispering excitedly. Perhaps the heat that fell heavy and damp had lulled everyone into a doze. Certainly the few dogs I passed barely bothered to glance up. By the time I rested the bike against a fence, the boys were taking turns to show off with skids, before racing off again.

The shop was stacked with canned fish, vodka, biscuits and confectionery. Other than that, a few enormous sacks of sugar, macaroni and flour were plonked on the floor behind the counter. In one glass cabinet you could choose between a toothbrush, bra and a tin of shoe polish. The shop owner, a short middle-aged woman, came rushing out wearing the standard blue, white-bordered apron. 'Yes, what would you like, young man?' I could tell she was trying to suppress a giggle. Her hair sprang up in tight bushy curls, and thick pink lipstick contrasted starkly with the blue of her apron, which barely fitted around her bulging waist. 'I was wondering if you had any bread?' I asked.

'Sorry, no bread here. Everyone in this place makes their own.' She seemed almost proud of the fact.

'Okay, well then can I have a kilo of *pryaniki* biscuits?' I asked, after a pause.

With lightning fast swipes she whipped a couple of beads across an abacus and shuffled over to the shelf. 'Do you mind if I ask where you are from?' she asked.

'Australia.'

As I left, she was almost shaking with excitement.

Outside, the boys were waiting. 'Hey, boys, do you know where I can fill up my water bottles?' I asked.

Their freckled noses began bobbing up and down and they tore off on their old single-geared bikes, expecting me to ride at the same speed. They were probably no older than nine or ten, with the crewcuts that were the standard for Russian boys at the beginning of summer. Their faces were already an earthy brown and darker than their translucent blond hair and eyebrows.

As I filled my water bottles I smiled, and a split second of eye contact gave them all the confidence to start asking questions.

'So where is the motor?' one boy asked.

'No motor on this bike. This is the motor!' I said, pointing at my legs.

'So, how far do you ride a day?' the other boy asked.

'Oh, it depends, between seventy and a hundred kilometres. It depends on the roads,' I replied.

'Really!' The boy's eyes lit up. The other boy nodded slowly, accepting my response with the indifference of an older man.

Questions ranged from what I carried on the bike, to what kind of food I ate, and whether I liked vodka. Like most children, they had a simple, uncomplicated view of the journey. To them it was a matter of riding, eating, sleeping, and now and then stopping in villages. In many ways, this was accurate. It contrasted with the reactions of adults, who were more inclined to disbelieve, or to talk up all the obstacles that made such a journey too dangerous, too expensive and too difficult. I wondered at what age the attitudes began to change.

Now for bread. I pushed the bike along the path until I came across a woman pottering in her front garden. Like all yard space in the village, every inch was being dug over for planting the staple vegetables of the Russian diet.

'Hi, excuse me. I was just wondering if you had any bread that I could buy?' I asked.

'Oh well ... sure. I haven't got that much but you can have half a loaf or so. Where are you riding to?' She looked at me, her initial stiffness melting to a friendly smile.

'Actually, I am from Australia, but I'm trying to ride to Beijing. I don't know if you have heard of Petrozavodsk, but we started from there,' I replied.

'Really! Gee, you are a good boy, aren't you? Well done! Gee, you are a good boy!' she exclaimed, shaking her head. The woman, like the shopkeeper, was in her middle years. Blonde lengths of hair fell from beneath a blue scarf and her eyes glistened as she smiled. Her kindness seemed to flow from the heart and come to rest on her hips. Her full figure, with a pronounced behind and bosom, was typical of Russian women between the gracefulness of youth and the stout strength of babushka age.

I offered to show her my photo album. Within minutes we were sitting on the porch with her eighteen-year-old son Mikhail and her sixteen-year-old daughter Anna. More than anything, they were interested to see photos of my family. 'What does your mother think about this trip?' the woman asked.

'Well, I don't know. I guess she is used to it, and she is definitely supportive, but she probably misses me and worries a little.'

I always found it hard to answer this question, especially since travel had long become the norm for me. Many people suspected that my mother would be worried sick. In fact, Mum told me on many occasions that her intuition told her that I was in no great danger. It was a special connection that I shared with her, and if the day ever came that she feared for me, I figured that I should be very cautious. Of course, worrying about someone was different to missing them. I tried to imagine what it would be like to have a child on the other side of the world for such a long time.

Inevitably the family invited me to lunch. The glee with which they stared at the photos and their warm company had distracted me from my lone journey. I found myself smiling and giggling along with the children. There was no option but to accept their invitation.

We ate a meal of fresh yoghurt, followed by borsch, steamed potatoes and meat. The meal was served in a small shack separate to the house, which was used as a 'summer room'. The woman proudly showed me the enormous jars of preserved cabbage and cucumber that she still had from the previous summer.

Anna wore a white dress and stared with wide curious eyes, unsure what to make of this greasy-haired, unwashed westerner. How could she keep such clean, long-flowing hair and a spotless dress in these trying conditions?

After the meal I asked where the toilet was. Visibly embarrassed, they pointed me in the direction of the barn.

Inside the barn, I looked for a long drop. Then I realised that there wasn't one. A terrible stench rose from the floor that was covered in food scraps, cow manure and human faeces. It made Anna's cleanliness even more staggering. It seemed a contradiction for such a petite, well-groomed girl to pick her way through the mud and cow manure to go to the toilet. No doubt, on special occasions, she and her mother even wore high heels for such forays!

With bread stuffed into my panniers, I prepared to leave. Mikhail held up one side of the bike and began to push it backwards towards the front gate. Immediately, a grating, clicking sound came from the back wheel. I stopped pushing and bent over to inspect before going any further. As I did so, Mikhail must have thought it was his turn to push. By the time I thought to shout, 'Stop!' it was too late.

There was a loud snapping noise, like a breaking bone. The gear-changer had snapped clean off and was hanging limp in the chain. The last thing I wanted was to worry the family. If they exaggerated the gravity of the situation, it would only make things worse for me. I put the gear-changer back where it should be. Even at a glance I could tell it was beyond repair.

A wave of blood rushed to my head as I recalled the near-empty shop and the rusty one-geared bikes the boys had been using. There wouldn't be specialised Japanese-made parts for thousands of kilometres!

'Mikhail! Mikhail! What have you done!' the woman called out.

'Oh, nothing, everything is fine. I just have to make some small repairs,' I said calmly, trying to douse the hysteria.

Now, she too was bent over the bike, inspecting the damage. 'You can fix it, can't you, Mikhail, can't you, Mikhail?' she said, a series of lines cutting across her forehead.

Suddenly the village wasn't a homely break, but a trap. I had to get out of there before something else happened.

After wheeling the bike into the backyard, I realised that there was one way of saving the situation. If I removed the gear-changer, then I could change the chain length and ride in one gear. I hoped it would be enough to get me out of sight of the village.

With the work done, all three came out to wave goodbye and give me a push start. Miraculously, the first couple of cranks were smooth and the bike began to move. Twenty metres later a clunking sound was followed by the sensation of jammed pedals. The chain had come off and become stuck. Not daring to look back, I pulled out the chain.

'C'mon, c'mon, bloody work!' I muttered, my hands trembling. Again, I waved at the family, this time noticing their forced smiles.

It took four stops before I was back on the road; it felt like greeting an old friend. I continued pedalling frantically, stopping again and again until the village was a blemish on the horizon. There I sat on the roadside fiddling with the chain. It didn't matter to me whether it was fixed properly or not. The priority was to keep moving. The longer I sat there, the more the ghosts gathered around, taunting. When I was riding, every little pothole avoided, every tree passed, was a victory.

For hours I rode, stopping frequently. I heard the clunks beneath the bike but ignored them until the pedals would no longer turn. Eventually, I tinkered with the chain to find a reasonable fit. The road became a series of enormous holes and dry, cracking ridges.

As the sky began to glow peach in the evening light, the heat and struggle of the day faded. Although progress was much slower with one gear, I had probably covered around ninety kilometres. I would need to cover an average of 100 a day to meet Chris, but I was quietly pleased with my progress and happy to call it a day. For the first time since the village ten hours earlier, I had time to take in the view.

The trees had almost thinned out altogether, leaving a bare and empty landscape. With the sun sinking below the clear black edge of the earth, my sweat cooled. The wind had abruptly stopped, leaving me sharply aware of the calm. A flock of small birds darted across the sky not far ahead. Silhouetted against the molten colours of sunset they appeared like pepper sprinkling down from the heavens.

I recalled advice from a friend just before leaving Omsk: 'In your contemplation, listen to what whispers from across the wild, open steppe, and not from what man has done to damage it. Perhaps this will help in your grieving for Bruce.' It suddenly struck me that I had not even thought about him all day.

By the time I found a patch of trees, the glow had all but vanished. The few wispy bands of cloud looked like cobwebs. After falling up to my waist into a watery ditch, I was forced to put on a beanie and full-length clothing, the mosquitoes having reached an intolerable level.

When sleep finally claimed me, I was plagued with nightmares about my solo trip in Arctic Lapland over a year ago.

I had undertaken the solo journey in spring, as part of the wilderness guide course. At night, the temperature in Lapland drops below zero, while during the day it is high enough to melt the snow and ice. The traditional way of travelling in these conditions is to sleep during the day and ski across the frozen crust at night. I had planned a long and arduous route that relied on good conditions. As a precaution, I was required to visit a checkpoint on a certain date, otherwise a search party would come looking for me.

Unfortunately, I struck unusual weather. The temperature didn't drop low enough during the night, and I found myself sinking into melting waist-deep snow. My pace was slowed to less than one kilometre an hour, and for four days I didn't see a soul. For three days, I was forced to travel non-stop for twenty-two hours. I fell through river ice and only by chance managed to scramble out. Sheer exhaustion left me dangerously close to hypothermia. I made it close enough to the checkpoint to be found before the alarm was raised for a rescue party.

The unfortunate experience had well and truly crushed my confidence in doing things alone. I thought I saw a pattern emerging: when I was part of a group, even if I was leading it, things tended to go right. Alone, even the fires didn't seem to burn as well.

Now, as I reflected on my dream, I realised that my bad luck had nothing to do with a curse. Problems were a part of all journeys and an integral part of life. If I could confront my fears head on, then maybe I could regain the confidence to deal with things by myself.

Casting a look down the road, I reflected that there was another day ahead. It was an opportunity to overcome my self-taunts. There would be no more hiding.

As I pedalled on, it was easy to lose track of time. My daze was broken now and then by a passing horse and cart, and children on mushroom hunts. In villages, and from brief conversations with fishermen on the road-sides, I began to hear stories about Chris. Occasionally, children raced up to ask how many there were in the race. In some of the smaller settlements, word had spread about the Australian riding an armchair on wheels. When I arrived the villagers mistook me for Chris and shouted, 'The Australian has returned!'

Later, Chris said that all he had done was ride through without stopping. It made me wonder about the stories and rumours we had left in our wake since beginning at Petrozavodsk.

Gradually, the forest began to encroach again. I rode until darkness without lunch breaks, and met my goal of 100 kilometres a day.

I slept no more than one or two hours a night. I thought a lot about Bruce and my family, and felt uninspired to write in my diary. Yet I knew that the experiences of the past few days would last as some of the most memorable of the journey.

At one stage I came across a detour sign on a section of the road that had been closed for repairs. Ignoring the sign I rode over the rough gravel and was soon confronted by the hulking shape of a steam-roller edging closer and closer. It stopped twenty metres from the bike and the driver stepped out. As he approached, you could see that his enormous stomach stuck out so far that any attempt to make his tracksuit pants and shirt meet was in vain. His arms angled out, following the - contours of his torso.

'*Privet!*' he boomed, before falling silent. He was well over six feet tall and although his face was thrown into shadow by a weathered cap, it was obvious that he only had a couple of teeth remaining.

'*Privet!*' I replied. And another silence ensued. 'Um, I am from Australia, I am riding a bike,' I started.

But before I could even finish the sentence, he lunged forward, double chins wagging, and grasped my hand. The handshake was so vigorous it felt as if he was going to pluck my arm from the socket.

'Australia! Wow! Do you realise that you are the first foreigner that I have ever met? I have seen them on television, and even from a distance. But to meet an Australian! I would have thought that I would meet a Chinese person or a European before someone from your end of the world!'

'Yes ... Actually I am trying to ride to Novosibirsk at the moment,' I replied.

'Well, why don't you take a photo of me before you leave? You can show it to everyone, and tell them that I am the fat man of Siberia. I've been working these roads for thirty years!'

Despite his bulk, he seemed a gentle man. And the way he spoke of his children and job indicated a rare kind of integrity. After signing a photograph for his children, I went on my way.

Three days later the road became smooth bitumen. There remained just 130 kilometres to Novosibirsk, and it seemed that meeting with Chris on time wasn't going to be an issue.

As I pedalled along, a creaking noise from the bike nagged like a child demanding attention. Over the last few hours it had become louder, as if, somewhere, a screw was loosening; yet every time I checked, there was nothing out of place.

'All right, all right!' I muttered, coming to a halt. Rolling the bike over, I checked the bolts and screws; everything seemed to be fine. But as I put the bike upright I noticed a strange quality to the frame. It seemed to be bending. Moving the pannier from under the seat, I inspected further and, as I did so, my grimace turned to a look of terror. The thick tubing of the main frame had completely fractured, with just a thread of metal joining the two halves. In fact, the bike seat was the only thing attaching the front half of the bike to the back. The bike had snapped in half.

The sight crippled me. More than anything, I wanted to believe that if I kept riding I could still make it to Novosibirsk. As the full extent of the damage dawned on me, I was left wondering why the bike hadn't already given way beneath me.

After some time I was able to break free from my mood and roll down the hill to where bridge repairs were underway. I found the workmen laying a grid of wire on the embankment. They were covered in dust and sweat, and most wore a red worker's vest over a tanned bare chest. I looked closely at their tools and at the slow, shaky actions of their work. How many years had they been doing these repairs?

'Men, hey, men!' I yelled.

'What?' someone shouted.

'You wouldn't happen to know where the next village is? Or the next garage?' I asked.

They paused before pointing in the direction of Novosibirsk. 'Where are you from?' came another cry.

'Australia!' I yelled.

'Well, bugger me!' Everyone put down their tools and stared at me with hands on hips.

There was a quick discussion before they made their way up to me. When I showed them the bike they were adamant I stay the night. 'C'mon, we will get it fixed!'

The bike was hurled into the tray of a van and I squeezed into the cabin with four men. It took some time to rouse the drunken driver from a deep sleep, but when he came to, he started the engine and swung the van onto the road. The van lurched forward at frightening speed; the driver's head rolled loosely on his neck and slammed down on the dashboard.

Hunching over, he clasped the steering wheel tightly and leaned towards the windscreen, eyes narrowed. Although the window was clean, he peered out as if through heavy fog. After a few hundred metres, we turned down a dirt track. The motor revved violently as the vehicle bounded into the air over a series of potholes. I hadn't been in a vehicle for weeks, and the speed alone was terrifying. I could only imagine how the rest of the workers and my bike were being tossed around in the back.

'Slow down!' I screamed at the wobbling head of the driver. 'The bike is going to be completely broken if you don't slow down! Do you understand?' I had to repeat myself twice before his foot came ever so slightly off the accelerator.

The village consisted of a collection of run-down wooden houses built into the hillside. Nearby, white concrete buildings lay in decay; they were the remnants of milking sheds and barns for collective farms. At one time they would have housed several hundred head of animals. Now they were empty.

At a glance I could tell that it was one of the more dilapidated villages. Many of the houses were in disrepair, with rotten logs and missing planks. A group of men stumbled past with bloodshot eyes. The place filled me with dread. I wondered if anyone was sober.

'Look, just over there we live,' one of the workmen said, pointing to a small concrete building that stood among a garden choked with weeds and grass. Most of the windows were broken or missing, and what remained of the white paint was a scattering of loose flakes. Rusty play equipment cut a stark silhouette against the grey sky. The building was an abandoned kindergarten.

The men dragged me in, proudly showing off their home. What must have been the main classroom had been turned into a dorm, the musty air heavy with the stench of alcohol and rotting produce. On one wall I could just make out the smiling face of a cartoon character.

'Here is our boss. Get to know him,' the men said, thrusting me forward like an offering to their chief.

A man rose with difficulty from a sunken mattress. He wore a blue singlet and tracksuit pants, and his eyes were unnaturally wide and vacant. A dark tufted beard set hard with dried tomato sauce grew around his chin. His bare, pale shoulders were straight and seemed to be too close together, as if he had been wedged into a tight space for most his life. A terrible wheeze came with each fragile breath, and a potbelly that spread out far wider than his shoulders heaved up and down. He stared straight past me, drunk to the point of incapacitation.

'I ...' he slurred. 'I am an engineer ... I have a high, the highest of education ... Here are my simple workers, but me, I am a man of education! Of interest! I myself build bridges!' He pronounced the last words with a triumphant clenched fist, before collapsing back on his filthy mattress.

I felt on edge and unwilling to take part in the drunken stupor that I would, no doubt, be invited to join. Somehow, I had to keep alive the original purpose of getting the bike fixed.

One man, Misha, seemed the most alert. Not long after our arrival, he ushered in a local who had agreed to weld the bike.

The welder wore handmade clothing with colourful patches in the places where seams had come apart. A cap sat over a short crop of hair that curled around the ears. The grin on his face and his straight posture indicated a certain pride in his work. His name was Sasha and he was twenty-one years old, the same age as myself. The fact that he was sober was enough to convince me that he could be relied on.

Out on the muddy street, Sasha was impatient to show off his skills. He charged at the bike with his welder, damaging the frame further. Misha inspected the damage before grabbing Sasha by the arm. 'We need a gas welder. Sasha, where can we find a gas welder?' he asked.

The miracle came in the form of an old man who had been roused from sleep. His silvery-grey hair was set off by his gold teeth, his hands appeared to be permanently black, and although he walked straight backed, he had a subtle limp. At over six foot he had the wiry figure of a man who has spent his life doing physical labour. 'Russian, Polish, Chinese, it doesn't matter! I weld tractors, bikes, cars, cemetery fences for anyone at any hour,' he shouted.

For an hour, between violent and extended bouts of welding, he screamed obscenities at the bike. Eventually, he screamed out, 'What kind of bloody metal is this! I have only dealt with this once before. It's very strange.'

I turned to look at what seemed to be a burnt molten mess. As the metal cooled, however, it turned dark silver in colour and I realised that the frame was in one piece.

'It's all done,' he remarked, shrugging.

'Is it strong?' I asked.

'Is it strong? Of course it is. I guarantee that you will be able to ride another ten thousand kilometres at the very least. You can even jump up and down on the frame and it won't break!'

One of the drunks took the challenge literally. He stood on the frame and began to jump up and down. I pushed and sent him toppling to the floor. The welder laughed.

I felt indebted to this tall stranger, yet when I offered him thanks and some money he refused. 'No, it's I who thank you for giving me the chance to meet such a traveller. There is one condition – that is, you must come to have a glass of vodka with me.'

With the bike fixed, being merry was tolerable again! Back in his cottage, we toasted the meeting. I never knew his name, but he was of Polish descent. He and his father had been sent to Siberia during Stalin's reign. Briefly, he spoke of relatives he had never met in Poland. Unlike most men who swore at the mere sight of my bike, he congratulated me for having the will to do the trip.

'I was also a sportsman once,' he remarked, with nostalgia.

As abruptly as he had opened up, he slid the bottle back into its niche in the wall and shook my hand. Our brief crossing of paths was over.

Back in the kindergarten, the workmen were warming up for a heavy night. They sat around a table dishing out a mix of stale bread, tomato paste, salt and cold, stodgy macaroni.

'Sit down! Come and sit down!' The master engineer beckoned. My presence heralded the opening of a four-litre jar of *samagonka*, which is homemade vodka, but usually with a higher alcohol content.

The men raised their glasses in excitement. It was difficult to guess their age. With greasy stubble and leathery complexions, they wore their dank clothing like a second skin. Apart from the boss, most appeared slim and square-shouldered.

A plate of tomato paste and macaroni and a glass of *samagonka* were shoved before me as the feast got under way. While the others starting slurping, one man was struggling to focus through a pair of crooked, cracked glasses. You could tell that he was mulling over a question.

'There in Australia, the capital is Sydney, right? And you have a lot of deserts and in some parts some mountains?' he asked solemnly, as if wanting to confirm that his education was correct.

Before I could answer, the others butted in with a volley of questions.

'Do you have potatoes in Australia?'

'Don't be stupid; potatoes are Russian!'

'What do you drink in Australia? Have you tried vodka?'

'What do you think about Russian girls? Are they the best in the world?'

'Have you tried *samagonka*?'

'What kind of money do you have there?'

The best I could do was nod and shake my head as everyone demanded an answer at once. This went on until the master engineer slammed his fist down on the table. 'You know my workmen. You are my comrades, my simple workmen. We today have here an Australian. Do you know, men, that in the forty-five years of my life, including my high education in Moscow, I have never met or talked with a real foreigner. Comrades, this is a great event. You know we must give him pork fat, potatoes and milk to go on his way.'

The men were silent, awed. Then: 'Eat, eat, as if you were at home!' They demanded, breaking the silence. They felt proud to be sharing their wealth, and I could see that beyond the slops in front of me there was a heartfelt generosity.

As the drinking continued I blended into the group, asking my own questions. Misha, who had stayed by me from the start, was a short man with a long wispy moustache. When he smiled, lines forged deep channels from his eyes like the splayed rays of the sun.

'Misha, how long have you been working on the bridge?' I asked.

'Oh, about three months, but I will probably work here for another four or five,' he replied.

'And have you been paid for it?' I probed.

He looked as if I had asked a stupid question. 'No, I haven't been paid anything, but the boss says we might get paid soon.'

Misha had two children and a wife in a village a couple of hundred kilometres to the south. I had the feeling that he was too proud to go home without payment, and yet disillusioned with the work. Typically, like the other men, he had turned to vodka.

'Well, you know, I get angry sometimes because I should be back home cutting the hay, working the potatoes. I mean, how is my family supposed to survive?' he exclaimed, departing from his quiet tone. He pointed around the room. 'Yes, him over there, he has three children, and that one over there too.'

It felt as if I was seeing a desecration of life. Here were grown men drinking themselves to death in what was once the playhouse of children; children that they themselves had at home.

I knew that the men would drink all night and eventually pass out. At around midday there would probably be some rousing of heads. After some more *samagonka* to lessen the hangover, they would stumble to the bridge and achieve almost nothing. It was true that they were still working unpaid, but there was no honour in that. In fact the work they were doing, largely in a drunken, apathetic daze, was so unproductive that it didn't warrant payment. They were achieving absolutely nothing; not successfully repairing the bridge, not earning money, not helping their families. If this scenario was typical of life in the thousands upon thousands of villages in Russia, it shed some light on the extent of the country's economic and social woes. Alcohol obviously had a crippling effect. The typical Russian man drinks a pint of pure alcohol every two days, compared with less than two pints a month for the average American. Approximately 40,000 Russians a year die of alcohol poisoning, not to mention the huge number of alcohol-related deaths. Outside of Africa, the male mortality rate in Russia in 1999 was worse than any country, except Haiti. This could be attributed mainly to alcohol and tobacco abuse, little exercise and a poor diet. The mortality rate has been increasing ever since 1965, but particularly since perestroika when the old Soviet systems and institutions were thrown into disarray.

I stared contemplatively into my glass, and then decided to down it.

Sasha eventually arrived to announce that the *banya* and dinner were ready. I slipped out without the men noticing. It was still raining as we made for his home.

'What is your occupation here?' I asked.

'Well, at the moment I weld and drive a tractor in the fields,' he replied.

'And how much do you earn?'

'One hundred roubles a month.' Three dollars fifty, US.

'But how can that be possible? People in the north get one thousand roubles a month on the pension!' I cried.

He shrugged his shoulders. 'Well, I am not on the pension yet,' he finally replied.

His home was a tiny wooden cottage that stood on a small plot of land. Its foundations were giving way, leaving a bent and twisted structure. The small square windows were contorted so that there were gaps between the glass and the windowsill. Above the windows, intricate woodcarvings added life and character.

'So come in. Welcome to our home,' he said, opening the door. 'I'm afraid that I don't have tea, but I have some leftover cocoa if you would like.'

Inside, the soft patter of rain on the wooden roof made the three-room house feel cosy. It was quiet compared to the endless chattering in the kindergarten. A cat lay stretched out on a bed, purring. On the walls hung some stained carpets. One depicted paradise – a white castle rising above a forest where beautiful people rode horses.

'Here, have some soap, and get changed while I fetch some water,' he said.

I sat looking around the main room. Like everything else, the electrical wiring was self-made. The stove was a coiled wire set into a brick. When Sasha hooked it up by twisting wires over the power terminal, it turned a glowing red. Other than a chipped cabinet and a small Chinese-made radio, his possessions were negligible. As in most Russian homes, his glassware consisted of a couple of old jars.

Sasha was like many friends of my own age in Australia: he had just moved out of home and was trying to build an independent life. His girlfriend had fallen pregnant, but complications forced her to have an abortion. She was yet to arrive home from hospital.

But it wasn't just independence that had brought Sasha here. In the city he had been unable to survive. At least here there was enough milk, meat and crops to live on, even if the wages were pitiful and irregular.

Sasha returned and I headed for the *banya*. One of the reasons I enjoy *banya* so much is that it is a chance to get close to the surroundings. There is nothing like sitting in the yard naked, watching horses and carts go by and observing the houses while steam pours from your body.

While I stood outside, cooling off, Sasha was in the vegetable garden collecting ingredients for the borsch soup. Nothing around me hinted at modern life as we know it in the western world. Probably thousands of villages like this one lay neglected and out of sight from the main roads.

I imagined leaving the village behind and riding to Novosibirsk. In the city, this place would be just a memory. For some reason I felt guilty that I could just arrive, experience the place and leave again. And yet, although I sympathised with the workmen, I was partly baffled. Why in their kindness and maturity did they drink so much? Did the hardship that contributed to their generosity and joviality also drive them into depression and death?

After my experience of the past day, it was no wonder that life expectancy for Russian males is just fifty-nine years. This is shorter than men in three quarters of the world's countries, many of which are much poorer. In fact, against the trend of most countries, the life expectancy for men in Russia has been declining since 1965 when it peaked at sixty-seven.

After a while I returned to the *banya*. I placed a large scoop of water on the stones and the small room filled with heavy steam. Sweat quickly built up on my body and I washed away the dead skin, grime and dirt that had built up over seven days on the bike. It was a deeply cleansing feeling and induced a sense of calm. I took in deep breaths and let the urgency and adrenaline of the past week dispel.

For the first time since separating from Chris, everything was in one piece. The broken bike was now irrelevant; it had led me to a far greater insight than success on the tarmac could ever have given me. As I peered out the small square *banya* window, I saw Sasha return with a bundle of carrots and onions; he was soaked to the skin. My problems were nothing.

Most of the men were still passed out when I gathered my bike in the morning. Misha came out to wave goodbye as I rode out of the village. I stopped only once to take note of its name: Filipimovo.

Later that day I rolled down a grassy hill into a patch of birch trees. It was still light and I could see across to the plains. Here and there, clumps of trees formed a scattered archipelago. It wouldn't be long before the sun began to dip and the mosquitoes came out.

I pushed the bike slowly, bottling in triumphant laughter. I felt no urge to rush and the threat of disaster didn't worry me.

Almost there.

I knew that Bruce was gone, and although I would never know why, I could only learn from it. The smiles of children and Sasha's struggle to construct a life was enough to spark my reaffirmation of life. And what better way to live than by an armchair on wheels across Russia?

As for Chris, well hadn't I been overly introspective in the past week, craving the freedom to ride uninterrupted? What if, just what if, that was the way he'd been feeling the whole time?

As Chris's tent came into sight, I wasn't overcome with relief. I felt proud of the way I had managed the week alone.

Off the Rails

Novosibirsk – Bratsk

Mid-Summer 2000

Chris

I sat in the bum-shaped curve of a fallen tree at the bottom of a grassy slope and chewed at the end of a pen. On my knees, I held a notebook full of Russian words that I was trying to learn, and resting on the log beside me was a long letter to Nat that I'd been trying to finish. I was only twenty kilometres from Novosibirsk, and as long as Tim arrived sometime that afternoon, I'd be talking to Nat on the phone in the morning. Somehow, I couldn't put my energy and my thoughts into a letter that wouldn't reach her for another month.

I gave up and looked around for something else to do. The headset that connected my handlebars to the bike frame had come a little loose over the previous week and it needed adjusting, but I didn't feel like hauling out my tool kit and getting all greasy. I went for a stroll along the grassy bank and eyed off a few prospective pieces of firewood instead, but the pile by the tent was already more than big enough to last the evening. In the end, I turned back towards camp and did what I'd wanted to do all afternoon. I grabbed a water bottle and set off up the hill to find a stakeout spot where I could watch for Tim.

No sooner had I reached the top, than I saw a familiar, smudgy white and brown blob on the horizon. I did a double take and looked again. The blob wobbled its way into focus and became Tim on the bike. I raced back down the hill feeling ridiculous and settled on my log just in time to see Tim ride over the top of the hill. He came hurtling down with a huge grin and braked to a squealing halt beside me.

'Long time no see, mate. How'd you go?' I asked, smiling.

'Yeah, not too bad,' he replied, casually. 'Had a few problems with the bike, but other than that ...'

'Oh, yeah. What happened?'

'Well, just let me think.' He scratched his head and glanced at me with a twinkle in his eye. 'That's right, the gear changer snapped off a few days ago, then yesterday I had a little problem when the entire bike snapped in half, but nothing too serious. How about you?'

'Wow!' I said, impressed. 'I had a couple of flats and my handlebars came a bit loose a few days ago, but ...' I paused for a moment. Tim was struggling to keep from laughing, but it was useless. A grin erupted from somewhere beneath his beard and a moment later we both cracked up laughing.

After a week apart, it really was great to see Tim again. I'd missed his company more than I thought I would. I'd enjoyed the freedom to ride in uninterrupted contemplation, to think and ponder the world for hours on end. And I'd also needed to get away from everything about him that annoyed me, but I'd missed his company all the same. I'd missed sitting under the stars by the campfire and chatting about the world and our respective futures. I'd missed hearing his unique comments and ideas, some of which irritated me to distraction, but most of which intrigued me as a very different way of seeing the world.

I got the fire going and put some water on the boil. Then Tim showed me the jagged, brutal-looking weld line across the frame of his bike and the way that he'd rigged up his broken gear changer. I was impressed at how well he'd managed to pull through in the face of such disasters; and I could see that as casual as he was being about it all, he was proud of himself.

We sat by the campfire well into the evening, catching up and laughing at the confusion we'd caused in the villages as we passed through a day apart. One group of kids I'd met in the village of Kotchki had got it into their heads that I was involved in a long-distance bicycle race from Moscow to China. When they saw Tim roll in the next day they had urged him to pedal faster: 'C'mon, hurry up! The first guy's only a day ahead of you!'

The next day we rolled into Novosibirsk to meet Nina Koptyug, the lady who was to be our host for the week. Nina and her husband Ivan were academics. She was a professor of English and Ivan a physicist. They lived with their daughters in the suburb of Akademgorodok, or 'Academy Township', which in its heyday had been a driving force behind Soviet science and technology. At its peak, the township housed up to 65,000 of the USSR's top scientists and their families; Nina and Ivan were children of the very cream of this intellectual stock. Nina's father had been the director of one of the institutions and had moved on to become a member of an elite think-tank advising Mikhail Gorbachev. Ivan's father had been chair of the board of academic directors of the entire academy. Although Nina and Ivan had established their own lives independent of their families, and while much had changed in Akademgorodok since the fall of the Soviet Union, the week we spent there gave us a glimpse into the astonishing world of power and privilege that had been the domain of the Soviet elite.

We had come into contact with Nina through the Internet; she was one of the handful of people who had responded to the thousands of e-mails Tim had sent to Russian schools from Finland. Dismayed at the quality of primary and secondary language education in Novosibirsk, she had thrown in her university post to teach English at her daughters' school and had become a well-known local activist and advocate for education reform. She'd invited us to stay at her flat and had arranged for us to speak to as many English students as she could schedule into a week. We were, of course, more than happy to do so.

We had arrived late. Due to Bruce's funeral and the delay in Omsk, we had reached Novosibirsk after the end of school term. Despite her best efforts, Nina had only managed to arrange for a few groups of students to meet with us. We visited several schools in different corners of the city and spent a fascinating morning talking to bright-eyed kids in a public orphanage, but apart from that, the rest of the week was our own.

Every day we'd take the bus thirty kilometres through the suburbs then ride the subway into the bustling heart of the city. The days were hot and sunny and people were out in force. I spent many hours on the Net, catching up with Nat, while Tim searched the city's many sports shops, in vain, for a replacement gear changer.

With nearly two million people, Novosibirsk is the biggest city in Siberia. Tim saw thousands of imported western bikes, but did not manage to find anyone who stocked spare parts. In the end, we resorted to removing the three-speed gear-changer from Ivan's old racing bike and bolting it onto Tim's.

It wasn't much, but with mountainous terrain ahead, at least he had a few gears.

We left Novosibirsk after a week; we were both glad to get back on the road. As we slipped back into our familiar routine, I realised that I'd actually been missing some of the things that Tim loved about the journey.

At first, I'd felt indifferent to Tim's beloved taiga forest. The tall, pencil-straight pines, spruces and birches looked sickeningly monotonous. One camp site seemed to be as good as another. As reluctant as I'd been, Tim had finally taught me a little about my surroundings. Slowly, I had come to appreciate the subtle beauty of the northern forest. My subconscious no longer compared it to the Australian bush and I found myself looking forward to nights spent by glowing fires of resinous pine stumps. More than anything, though, I began to appreciate the sheer size of this ancient wild forest. I found it sobering to look out the tent door and realise that the trees, the fallen branches and the rolling, needle-strewn ground continued north, unbroken by road, track or any other mark of humankind, for thousands of kilometres.

We followed the highway north and east, away from the flat grassy steppe of the south, and back into the taiga forest of what I'd come to consider the 'real' Siberia. The full heat of summer had arrived during our stay in Novosibirsk. With the heat came the first real armies of Siberian mosquitoes. These were not your normal, slap, slap, backyard-barbecue, repellent-fearing bugs stupid enough to melt themselves on a zapper when there was good fresh flesh around. These were serious mozzie mercenaries and although not quite as terrifying as the fist-sized, blood-sucking 'mosquitobirds' about which we'd been warned, we figured that they must be juveniles. To escape from the hordes, we were forced to wear full-length clothing, mosquito-net hats and stay out of the shade.

We took back roads for several days, heading east. The baking sun had dried the road to a fine, powdery dust, which managed to find its way into all our gear and every crevice of skin. Each car or truck that passed threw up a billowing cloud that first left us coughing and spluttering, then settled down on our sweating limbs to form a thin coating of muddy grime. Tim was philosophical about this extra dirt. He thought that having an additional coating on our exposed skin might deter the mosquitoes but I wasn't so sure. I found it hard to cope with the constant feeling of having abrasive, grimy skin. My dirt tolerance had naturally gone up since starting the trip, but seeing beads of sweat turn to mud the instant they oozed from my skin was starting to drive me insane.

We crossed hundreds of creeks and rivers as we rode up and over undulating hills, from one valley to the next, and we stripped off to swim in most of them. The heat of the midday sun made riding almost too much to bear, and we'd have long, extended breaks at lunchtime. Before climbing back on my bike to pedal off again, I'd drench my shirt in the cool water and for a while I'd enjoy the sensation of cold shivers under the blasting sun as icy droplets trickled down my spine.

I pulled off the road one evening to find a camp along a little sidetrack. The mosquitoes were particularly bad for some reason, and every minute I waited for Tim, the worse they became. It was as if every mozzie within a range of several kilometres had smelt the blood of a fresh young Australian and come tearing over to get some.

Tim was only a few minutes behind, but by the time he came into view I'd managed to quickly pull on my waterproof pants, fleece jacket and mozzie-net hat – my insect armour – and set up the video camera. I was ready and waiting for what I figured would be a good show.

I zoomed in first on Tim's face. Framed by matted hair and a bushy beard, it was a picture of consternation verging on panic. All around him a buzzing, moving cloud darkened the air and I had to zoom out quickly as he raced towards me, his legs whirring in a blur of speed. He'd come 100 metres in less than fifteen seconds and almost reached me when it became clear that the onslaught was too much for him. He dismounted quickly, foregoing the usual routine of applying the brakes and simply vaulted off the seat and over the handlebars. The bike crashed behind him, and he hit the ground running.

Tim raced towards me. 'FUUUUUuuucckkk!' His wail switched in tone like the siren of a passing ambulance as I panned around with the camera, and his flailing legs sent him shooting up the road. *'HELP CHRIS!'*

It was a plea of desperation and I stood uncertainly for a moment wondering if he was expecting me to go tearing after him. But, in the next instant everything became clear. Tim performed a sliding turn at full sprint, then sidestepped quickly to dodge the cloud of mosquitoes that were zooming after him. He sprinted back towards me – a good five metres clear of the bulk of his attackers now – and barged a rapid path down the hill through the stragglers. I quickly ripped his pants and jacket out from underneath the lid of his pack and we performed a neat relay handover as he streaked past me once again. His head was back, his arms pumping, determination showing in the whites of his eyes.

I ran back to the camera just in time to see Tim leap nimbly into the air. His body crouched over and his knees rose to his chest to gain plenty of vertical elevation. I realised that he was going to try to pull on his trousers in mid-air. He got one leg through then leapt again. His second leg was through now too, but I cringed as I saw that he was about to land at full tilt with his pants round his ankles.

He sprawled face first onto the ground as I'd feared, but even as I was focusing the camera, I could see that he was still working to a plan. Harnessing his momentum, Tim flipped deftly over onto his back. Still sliding, he hitched his pants up to his waist before performing an agile back-flip to land on his feet – all within an instant of going down!

He was facing in the opposite direction, but his legs were still pumping. He sprinted triumphantly back to pick up his jacket and hat and the rest, from there, was a piece of cake.

We cycled steadily eastwards. We did our shopping in small towns and met a broad mix of people along the way. We met a convoy of lively central Asian truck drivers transporting tons of fresh produce from Turkmenistan to Krasnojarsk. They pulled us over for an impromptu feast of vodka and juicy tomatoes while showing us bullet holes in their trailer covers that were the result of a run-in with armed highwaymen in Uzbekistan. We stopped for lunch on the banks of a lonely creek and shared the freshly cooked catch of a silent but smiling boy who'd cycled an ancient bike fifteen kilometres from his village to spend the day fishing with a homemade rod. I stopped by the roadside one day and listened for an hour as an old man who was selling potatoes from a bucket explained his philosophy on the limits of personal responsibility. Tim, the lucky guy, was invited on the spur of the moment to be the guest of honour at a wedding reception.

The most amazing encounter we had was with a lone Russian traveller by the name of Gregory. Gregory was a remarkable-looking man. He was tall and skinny with a clean-shaven scalp, deep, furrowed smile lines around his eyes and a gigantic, ruddy brown bush of a beard that extended halfway down his chest. He was wearing a deeply stained shirt, heavy trousers and a pair of shoes held together with old scraps of leather and bits of string.

Like us, he was travelling by bike, a typical single-gear Soviet machine with a cracked and pointy-looking leather saddle.

The bike was laden with bulging white potato sacks that hung behind the seat and over the handlebars. Gregory introduced himself to me with a twitch of his demonstrative moustache. 'Hello! My name's Gregory. I've just been talking to your friend here and admiring his bike.'

'Hi, I'm Chris.' We shook hands. 'You've probably already told Tim, but where are you heading to? You're the first traveller we've met in five months!'

'Yeah,' he chuckled. 'I've been on the road for most of the last fifteen years and I've only met a few, too.'

'Wow.' I gaped.

'I'm going that way for now,' he continued, pointing in the direction from which we'd come. 'But apart from that I'm not really heading anywhere in particular.' He noticed my eyes straying back to his bike and chuckled amicably. 'I'm just sort of going to continue along until the bike stops going, then I'll probably start walking.'

He agreed to make camp with us for the night and we rolled down the hill to a little river in the valley. Automatically I pulled the tent out from my pack and slung my sleeping bag over a nearby branch to air, as I'd done every night for most of the past year, but then stopped to watch in amazement as Gregory untied one of his potato sacks and rummaged around inside. He produced a few bits of clothing, but it appeared that a large part of what he was carrying consisted of books.

'Ah, them,' he said, when I asked him about the books. 'This and that mostly. Russian authors and a few translated texts, too. Orwell. You know him?' I did, but what I really wanted to know was why he had them all weighing down his bike.

'Well,' he started, reflectively, 'books are the only things I've ever really bothered to hang on to, and I don't have a home where I can leave them, so I just sort of bring them along, I suppose.'

Gregory pulled a shortened axe from his bag and trudged off into the forest to find wood. He emerged a while later dragging a large tree stump behind him. After exchanging a surprised look with Tim, I set off to find more manageable pieces of firewood. Gregory trudged off into the forest once again, and Tim took the opportunity to quickly get a fire going.

This was an area in which Tim excelled. He'd studied under expert fire-lighting tutors during his year in Finland – he could bring a pot of water to the boil using only one match, his pocket knife, and a soaking tree-stump pulled from a creek! After building two to three campfires a day for most of the past five months, he'd become a consummate one-match magician. No paper, only wood.

Gregory returned bearing an armful of mushrooms and a bag of berries. He looked at Tim's compact cooking fire in dismay. 'Tut, tut, tut, boys.' He shook his head and clicked his tongue. 'That's no way to make a fire. Come, I'll show you how to make one properly. I'll show you the Russian way.'

Tim and I rolled our eyes. This was something we'd come across many times before. The locals always had a better way of doing things. 'Russians,' we murmured under our breaths. Then, as Gregory began to hack into his log and lay out a bonfire, we burst out laughing.

We shared a meal of macaroni, tinned herring and the rest of a bag of Turkmeni tomatoes, then sat at a respectable distance from Gregory's bonfire and talked into the evening.

Gregory was an eternal wanderer. He'd worked in various jobs at different times, but it didn't really suit him, and so he'd spent most of his adult life making his way in the wild. He lived on wild wheat and barley and on what he could find in the forest or in the rivers: berries and mushrooms, fish and the occasional small animal. In winter, he stayed in abandoned huts in the forest and hunted game. He'd walked extensively through many parts of Siberia's wilderness, but had never travelled by bike before. Basic as his bike was, he had minimal tools to repair it. The single gear and heavy load meant that he had to walk up any hill steeper than a dead-flat plain. He wasn't expecting it to carry him far.

He looked at our bikes and gear with what could have been a faint twinge of envy. We thought that we'd been doing it tough, but compared to Gregory, I could now see that we were living a life of relative luxury. We were strangers too – foreign curiosities – and we received gifts and hospitality almost every day, whereas Gregory mostly received none. A great deal of our curiosity value stemmed from the fact that most Russians we met couldn't understand why we chose to live a life that they regarded as harder than their own. We were bums with a difference whereas Gregory was just a bum.

The fire burned low. Gregory manoeuvred the glowing coals into position between two thick logs laid out together on the ground. 'It will smoulder all night this way,' he explained. 'I'll sleep right up alongside these logs, and the coals will keep me warm. Hopefully the smoke will help keep some of the bloody mosquitoes away.' He looked at us and offered a downcast explanation. 'I don't have a tent or a sleeping bag you see.'

Tim and I looked at each other and then at Gregory, who sat there swatting mozzies away from the inflamed red bite-marks on his neck and exposed scalp. Tim reached into one of his packs and pulled out the zip-up mosquito net he had used on the solo ride to Novosibirsk; we weren't planning to split up again.

We rose early the next morning and invited Gregory to join us for breakfast. With the warm weather we'd stopped cooking our porridge in the mornings and had started eating the raw oats as muesli, instead. The greenish oats with clumpy milk powder tasted sour and metallic, but usually they were all we had. This morning, however, we had extra luxuries.

I handed Gregory a bowlful of first-class muesli complete with sugar, sultanas and a fresh chopped banana. A full-blooded Russian used to savoury foods for breakfast probably would have tipped the mixture out in disgust, but Gregory was something of a philosopher and took the bowl with an open mind. Tim and I sat nearby, munching heartily and watching as Gregory looked into his bowl dubiously. He tried a tentative spoonful and considered it for a moment before breaking into a beaming smile. 'This really is good soup!' he said, earnestly.

All of a sudden he was dodging a spluttered mouthful of flying oats and shaking his head uncomprehendingly. He'd caught us unprepared. I'd been in mid-mouthful and Tim was halfway through swallowing. Gregory could only watch with bemusement as we rolled around on the ground, choking and spluttering, struggling to laugh and breathe at the same time.

When the time came, Gregory rode off to the west, leaving us with a newfound sense of just how comfortably we were living. We continued east, and after a few days of cycling along dirt roads, we reached the next big city along our route. We climbed to the top of a gradual hill, and suddenly found ourselves looking down at the long, narrow city of Krasnojarsk, snaking along the Yenisey River valley far below.

We left our bikes at a guarded car lot then headed to a comfortable hotel near the city centre. Our room didn't have a shower so we washed away a fortnight's road dust in the little basin, turning the nice white hotel towels a festering dark brown. The next morning the cleaning lady came screaming down to the foyer and blocked us from leaving.

She flicked at us with the filthy, wet towels and yelled abuse until the manager and a security man came to drag her away.

We spent several days in the city, going through our usual routine of getting in touch with home, relaxing and eating lots of good fresh food. The weld in Tim's bike frame had started to crack again, and he spent an adventurous day getting it fixed. I spent a day unsuccessfully scouring a city of a million people searching for much needed tyre patches.

'No one's got them,' I was told. 'The city's been out for months.'

We went to the cinema, restocked our supplies at a bustling market and then, after three enjoyable days, wheeled our bikes onto the road and cycled happily out of town.

Civilization became sparse; we found ourselves pedalling for endless miles along eternal stretches of bitumen. The sun was up for twenty hours at a time and we adapted our routine accordingly. Often we'd ride until midnight and then sleep till early afternoon. We averaged over 100 kilometres a day on roads that, for a whole week, were inexplicably covered by billions of butterflies.

I was on top of the world. I loved the long uninterrupted hours under the sun, watching the scenery glide slowly by, but Tim was struggling. He was still using the old gear changer we'd picked up in Novosibirsk, which would have made riding harder for him. It seemed to me, though, that at least some of Tim's disenchantment had to do with food.

In the month since we'd left Omsk, Tim had recovered – physically, at least – from the shock of Bruce's death. His appetite had come back with a vengeance and he was eating more than ever before. I'd only just come out of an endless appetite myself, so I thought I'd seen most of what there was to see in terms of pigging out. But Tim's capacity was something else again. I watched amazed as Tim casually downed kilogram bags of *pryaniki*, and was left bewildered at lunchtimes when he swallowed loaves of bread as though they were snack food.

The problem was that Tim hadn't realised any of this. He bought provisions according to his usual appetite and as a result he was almost constantly starving. This placed him in a vicious circle. The hungrier he got, the more absent-minded he became, and the more absent-minded, the less likely he was to remember to eat!

Our petty arguments had started up again, and ballooned out one evening into a rowdy yelling match. I can't remember how it ended up, but the whole thing started with a disagreement over a plan I'd had since the beginning of the trip. I wanted to modify our bikes to ride along the tracks of the BAM railway.

The BAM is a major railway that branches off the main trans-Siberian line at the town of Taishet – a few hundred kilometres further on – and continued for another 5,000 kilometres through northern Siberia, to the eastern coastal city of Komsomol'sk On Amur. We were planning to follow the line for just over 1,000 kilometres to the northern tip of the gargantuan Lake Baikal: the deepest in the world, and known locally as the 'Jewel of Siberia'.

Our map had roads marked only along the first part of the railway, and Tim wanted to follow the road until it ran out. I had only a vague idea about how I'd go about turning a bicycle into a rail-rider, but I was excited about the prospect of cruising along a smooth metal track for as long as possible.

It was this railway that had sparked my first dreams of Russia. The BAM was fundamental to the journey for me, and I wanted to make the most of it.

We rolled into Taishet in the middle of the morning a few days later and, as usual, we caused a bit of a stir. Cars veered onto the opposite side of the road as drivers turned to gawk over their shoulders. Kids yelled and pointed and the elderly stopped to shake their heads in disbelief as we pedalled by.

We rolled down the main street until we found a park sporting a rusty but imposing Soviet tank with the nozzle of its cannon pointing high into the air. We investigated the tank for a time while a group of teenage cyclists on well-loved and heavily-patched bikes spied on us from a distance. All around the tank lay shattered glass and litter. The sides were streaked with crude graffiti and white bird crap. From inside came a concoction of very nasty smells. It seemed strange that a people who lusted so strongly for the 'good old days' of communism had let an icon of Soviet power decline so drastically. I wondered if the defacement of the tank had occurred only in the past decade or whether, isolated so many thousands of kilometres from Moscow, the people here had never paid much attention to the grandeur of the Soviet war machine.

We turned our attention to the group of kids circling us at a distance. They were moving gradually closer, and one of them looked as though he was plucking up the courage to come over and find out who and what we were. Their hesitation disappeared once they realised that we could speak Russian. The usual questions progressed to general questions about the bikes and a good deal of awestruck pointing at our racks of Shimano gears.

A few kids escorted Tim to the market, while I found a slab of wood and sat, minding our bikes and chatting to two boys. They were both mad-keen cyclists and spent every minute, when they weren't at school, riding. They offered to escort us out of town later that day and we willingly followed them along a rough, bouncy track that served as a shortcut. We stopped in a village to fill up at a hand-pumped well, and as we headed back onto the road, I begun to hear an ominous clicking coming from somewhere underneath me.

I investigated and was surprised to discover that my rear hub had come loose. I'd checked and tightened it only a few days before. The clicking noise was probably the sound of the ball bearings and the inside of the hub starting to disintegrate.

This was a lesson that I'd learned well on my trip around Australia – ignore the sound of a self-destructing hub at your peril. So, I dragged out my tool kit to put it right. A few twists of a spanner and we were back on our way again, but five kilometres later the sound returned. I started to worry. The noise was definitely that of a hub in the process of devouring itself, but having tightened it, I couldn't guess what the problem could be. Dismantling the hub for a full service was a process of at least an hour, and our friends, who had stuck with us for most of the afternoon, were getting impatient. I rode with them for another few kilometres, wincing at each grinding metallic crack. Finally, they turned back to Taishet and I found a shady corner where I could settle down and fix my machine.

An hour later, I was getting worried and Tim was getting bored. I'd dismantled the hub, cleaned out all the ground-up little flakes of steel and iron filings, replaced the worn ball bearings and reassembled the whole arrangement. But I couldn't tighten the hub sufficiently. It took me another hour to pinpoint what was wrong. The internal cone of my hub – one of the two surfaces which sandwich the ring of ball bearings that allow the wheel to roll – had developed a hairline fracture and had slowly cracked away from its position. As I tightened the hub, I was simply pushing this broken surface backwards a fraction into the hollow interior. Before long, the two rings of ball bearings would be pressed up against each other and the axle would snap.

My bike was fatally wounded and I feared the worst. The closest replacement hub that would fit my bike was the one on Tim's bike (I eyed it longingly for a second), and the nearest one after that was probably at least another 5,000 kilometres away. It was time for desperate measures.

Carefully, I sawed off one of the aluminium legs of my camera tripod. I shortened it and used it to brace the inside of my hub against any further collapse. It was definitely only a temporary measure. Even if the brace did work, the cracked surface of the cone would spin around like a grinding machine and slowly decimate any ball bearing in its path. I carefully reassembled the axle, stood the bike upright and realised that I was scared.

I explained the gravity of the situation to Tim, who summed it up neatly. 'Looks like we're stuck in the shit then, doesn't it, mate!'

We wheeled our bikes back onto the road the next morning and I hopped on cautiously. The brace held. Tim and I let out great whooping yells of jubilation. But after ten kilometres I had to stop again and dig out my tools. The brace I'd made wasn't broad enough to keep the bearings stable and my back wheel was wobbling dangerously.

After some readjustments, we pressed on. I was testing fate and counting on luck. We were in the middle of nowhere with a mortally wounded bicycle. The only sensible option would have been to turn tail, hop on a train and buy a replacement part in Moscow. But I didn't want to waste that much time and Tim certainly didn't want to hang around for a fortnight until I returned. While there was still even a glimmer of hope, we decided that it would be best just to keep on riding.

'And besides,' Tim said, 'even if you can't fix it, even if it dies completely in another two hundred kilometres, at least we will have gone two hundred further. And we'll *still* be in the middle of bloody nowhere. There's not really much to lose.'

I spent an hour modifying the brace and made it to the top of the next hill before it needed adjusting again. I was so absorbed in the impending disaster that I hadn't been paying much attention to the scenery, but Tim had.

We'd finally branched off the main route through southern Siberia. We'd left the trans-Siberian railway and adjacent highway behind, and with it we'd left the main logging corridor. Our new route along the BAM was relatively new, and had only recently been set upon by the mechanical teeth of the timber industry. The result was that although wagon after wagon of ancient pine logs rumbled past, we were able to fully immerse ourselves in the taiga forest for the first time since we'd entered Siberia.

I looked up from the greasy, troubled mess of my bike hub and let my gaze float towards the northern horizon. Before me, the familiar trio of pine, spruce and birch stretched out in a mottled green sea, interspersed with their native Siberian counterparts: fir, larch and what the Siberians call cedar but is actually a variety of pine. The whole expanse extended over one and a half thousand kilometres northwards in a vast undulating continuum, broken only by secret river valleys and rocky ridges, until finally, it merged with the empty rolling tundra and then the Arctic Ocean.

We set off again and I suffered two successive flat tyres. After a day and a half of non-stop bike repairs, this was enough to test the limits of my patience. It was getting late so Tim rode on, out of range of my curses, to wait in the next village, Kvitok. I patched my tyre and limped on to find him waiting for me outside a shop, in the middle of a seething throng of sidecar motorbikes, Ladas and kids on bicycles. He'd managed to completely snarl the main intersection of the village.

I rode up unnoticed and stood up to catch a glimpse of Tim over the heads of barefoot kids straining to see the excitement. In Tim's hand was a bulging bag of pink *pryaniki* and on his face was the broad, totally-immersed-in-the-moment grin that I'd grown to know and like so well.

I worked my way to the centre of the crowd and quickly learned that our accommodation and meals for the night had already been arranged. First up we were to visit Vladimir, whose wife was already at home cooking up a feast, and who'd be angry if we didn't get over there *right now*. After that, we'd been invited to spend the night with the family of a pleasant, but serious-looking man called Andrei.

We were escorted to Vladimir's house by a cavalcade of onlookers who cheered as we got our ungainly bikes going. Once inside, a beaming Vladimir introduced us to the other guest of honour. Seated proudly at the head of the table was his favourite thing in the whole world – a huge twenty-litre jar of double-strength *samagonka*. In the Russian tradition, he poured everyone a liberal shot, while explaining that he made it to sell to the village.

'Yeah! And he's his own best customer,' an old woman squawked from the corner, receiving a rowdy burst of laughter before we all drained the shots. 'Bottoms up.'

Two more rounds of firewater preceded the first course, and the meagre helping of food was quickly followed by more rounds again. With an empty stomach full of potent alcohol, my impressions of the evening soon became a blur. There must have been over twenty people in the room, but to save my life I couldn't remember more than two or three. The only distinct memories after those initial rounds were of everyone dancing to loud music from a tinny gramophone, and of a teary Vladimir holding me in a tight, slobbering embrace, slurring drunkenly in my ear. He'd forgotten our names.

'I have to thank you and praise you and Tom like the gods, Kosta. You have made this into the best day of my entire life!'

Thanks to a healthy cyclist's metabolism, I was starting to sober up by the time we moved a few doors down the road to Andrei's home. Most of the crowd had dispersed by this stage but a twisted handlebar and a bounced-off pannier bag told us that a few intrepid souls had obviously taken the bikes for a ride.

We pushed our bikes along the muddy road, past high paling fences and sturdy solid log walls punctuated with warm, friendly windows. Vladimir – still devastatingly drunk – escorted us to Andrei's front gate and bid us a slurred and incomprehensible farewell before wandering slowly back home. We pushed open the gate and wheeled our bikes into what seemed another world.

Andrei and his family were immediately different to any Russians I had met. True to form, they fed us a second dinner (it was midnight by this stage), but incredibly, and to our immense relief, there was no vodka. They asked us intelligent questions and listened to our replies. The conversation ranged and as they slowly became more comfortable with us, they started to crack jokes, laughing uproariously, then patiently explaining the naughty punchlines and puns that we'd completely failed to understand.

They told us briefly of their religion. They were devout Jehovah's Witnesses. It became very clear that their religion pervaded their entire way of living and thinking. We talked, laughed and listened into the small hours of the morning before finally being ushered towards the beds that had already been made up for us. I lay there in a happy, exhausted daze, staring at the ceiling, still softly illuminated by the faint moonlight creeping gently around the curtains.

That morning I'd woken in a dirty tent with a broken bike. I'd spent the day fighting to keep hope alive against the growing realisation that my hub was fundamentally stuffed and now, twenty hours later, I was lying in a bed in a wooden cottage nestled in a clearing somewhere in the middle of the Siberian taiga forest.

What a day! This is what it's all about – the basic addictiveness of travel. Wake up with a broken bike, go to sleep with new friends and a whole village to get to know. Our journey had opened wide the wildly unpredictable door of surprise. The hub was still busted, but as I drifted off to sleep, I was quietly confident that somehow, a solution would be found in the morning.

Miraculously, it was! Andrei, his two brothers and his brother-in-law were all tradesmen – welders, woodworkers and mechanics. The next morning they took a quick look at my hub, held a brief conference, then loaded the wheel into the back of Andrei's little car. Together, we drove to the other side of the town to the workshop of the village school. Inside stood a home-built lathe, made out of an old diesel-powered truck engine. Pasha was the expert on this machine, and after making a few precise measurements, he was able to slot a chunk of old steel into the lathe. Half an hour later, he handed me a piece of engineering that was perfect. I stripped out the broken cone, hammered in the new device, and the whole thing was as good as new.

We returned to the house for a sumptuous lunch prepared by Andrei's mother, Clara. Afterwards, they hitched up their stately old horse to a wooden cart, and we all trundled off to a nearby field. The village tractor had broken down irreparably a few years before, and so they were slashing hay with scythes. We spent the afternoon raking up all the dried hay and loading it onto the cart with long-handled pitchforks. They sang religious songs and hymns as they worked, and talked of their lives as we pitched in by their sides. The whole extended family worked hard all through the summer, gathering hay and growing potatoes. They did not drink or smoke, and by growing more than they needed for the winter, they were able to sell their leftover produce in the village market. At twenty-six, Andrei was also a highly skilled welder; he worked long hours to bring in regular commissions. The family and all of their devout relations in the village were prospering while other villagers seemed to wilt with bitterness. We asked them about this at dinner, and after a moment of consideration, Andrei explained. 'Most Russians were better off under the old regime. They had jobs and security. Their pensions were always paid.' He looked at us and we nodded. We had heard that many times before.

'But for us and people of our faith, things were different. We were prisoners under communism. My father, Slavic, spent fifteen years in a gulag labour camp because he refused to deny God!'

I looked towards Andrei's parents with a profound new respect and understanding. Their eyes were filled with tears that told of the anguish of their lives, filled with unimaginable hardship and suffering, as well as the newfound peace and tranquillity of their old age. Clara looked lovingly at Andrei, himself choked up with tears. Her gaze held the quiet, loving pride of a parent, watching her son grow to live in a new world, taking advantage of opportunities and chances that she had never known.

'Our country has changed,' Slavic continued gently. 'Our lives are hard but now they are free.' He smiled and gestured at a heavy, leather-bound bible in the centre of the table. 'Before, we kept this book of God's word in our house at the risk of our lives. Now it lies there for all to see. People yearn for the return of communism, but all they really wish for is a return to the days where they lived easily because they were not free. People want the riches and the benefits of capitalism, but they want to keep the security and safety of old times. They wish to earn like westerners, but they also want to work lazily and without risks, as they did during the communist times. That is why their lives have become harder. We have always lived by God's laws. We have always been free in spirit. And so you see, it is easy for us in the new system. Now we can live freely too.'

We sat up talking late into the evening. After working a summer of eighteen-hour days, Andrei had been able to buy a video camera and television. He showed us hours of wobbly footage: the extended family singing hymns and slashing hay in a field many times larger than the one we had seen that afternoon; the local river in flood, and a trip by train to Lake Baikal.

We asked about their singing and they joyfully produced an array of instruments, from an electric guitar to a balalaika, and they played and sang for hours more.

By the time I finally crashed into bed that morning, I could only think how lucky we had been to stumble on this family. They seemed to be as happy and content as anyone in the world.

The next morning, after a stately breakfast, we took our leave. The bitumen ended a few kilometres from the village leaving us to face a long, rough and unfriendly stretch of dirt road. We said a final goodbye to our small escort of a dozen cyclists and hooting cars and set out on what promised to be the biggest adventure of all. We were off to tackle the BAM!

The construction of the BAM railway was the most expensive single project in the history of the USSR. Twenty-five billion dollars US had been poured into the venture and hundreds of thousands of young workers from all over the Soviet Union had journeyed to the mosquito-infested swamps of central Siberia to force the line through wild and unwelcoming terrain. It was the dream of the golden renaissance of the Soviet Union. The youth of the nation would push the line through to the immeasurable mineral riches of the Lena River basin and open the doors to the largest mining and industrial development in the world.

The line took twenty years to complete and blew its budget by 1,000 per cent. By the time it was finished in the late 1980s the situation in the USSR had altered, and there was no money left to develop the new mining industries, anyway. Only a few years after its completion, the icon of the Soviets saw the Union decline and then fragment in a collapse that shook the world. The workers who hadn't grown old and died during the construction either gave up on the dream and travelled back to former lives, or turned their temporary workers' accommodation into isolated villages to eke out a living from the land.

In the years that followed, the gleaming metal superhighway saw not the countless thousands of wagons bearing untold fortunes back towards the rest of the world, but the odd passenger train and the occasional timber freighter. A decade later the traffic had picked up a little as the independent opportunists of the new capitalist regime moved in to log the ancient and unprotected timbers of the taiga. By the time we arrived, apart from the steady flow of old-growth forest heading towards the voracious Chinese market, the railway was relatively unused.

We struggled on a further ten kilometres, puffing and blowing as we climbed sandy hills and sped down to crash spectacularly at the bottom of others. We made camp at a beautiful gurgling creek where we were surprised by news from a passing convoy of logging trucks. 'We saw a bear a few kays up the road,' they told us nonchalantly. 'A big one.'

Jesus, I thought, looking at the men sitting high up inside the steel-walled protection of their cabin. I glanced over my shoulder at our still-smouldering campfire then back at the grinning men.

'But that's okay,' the driver carried on. 'If you see it, just shoot into the air and it should run away.' He paused for a moment. 'You are carrying a gun, aren't you?'

'Um ...' I exchanged a worried look with Tim. 'Actually we don't have a gun.'

'What!' The driver stared down at us incredulously. 'You must have a gun! Nobody stays out here in the forest without a gun, especially at this time of year. There are bears everywhere!'

'Oh, really?' I was starting to feel sick.

'Christ!' The driver snorted and pulled his head back into the window. He explained the situation to the other passengers, and they all burst out laughing. 'I hope it's not hungry!' he yelled down to us, then crunched into gear and drove on.

The next day we encountered an unexpected forty kilometres of new bitumen for the ride into Chunsky, the last outpost of real civilization before Bratsk – 400 kilometres distant. Along the way, an expensive black Landcruiser pulled level to glide alongside us. A black tinted window hummed open to reveal the driver, a fat, dark-skinned man with black slicked-back hair. The high-pitched voice of the latest teenage pop star from Moscow ripped loudly through the open window from an undoubtedly state-of-the-art system. Two ovals of shiny black Ray-Bans turned slowly and a gleaming white smile erupted from above a corpulent, smoothly shaven chin.

We chatted briefly. The driver and his passenger were Azerbaijani businessmen, involved in some way in the forestry industry. They were obviously not the ones who chopped down the trees. The guy in the passenger seat – a thinner version of the driver – owned a restaurant in Chunsky and he offered us a meal when we got there.

They flicked up the window after a while and seemed about to pull away, but at the last minute, as though struck by an afterthought, the window glided down again and the driver's black-sleeved arm extended, proffering a fluttering banknote. Tim started to protest but the driver cut him off. 'Take it,' he said, smiling.

Tim did, then waved goodbye as the polished black status symbol disappeared down the road. Wordlessly we stared at the 100 rouble note – about $30 in Australia – and looked at each other incredulously.

Of all the earnest warnings we'd received before embarking on the journey, the most ominous had been the danger of a run-in with the Mafia. 'You are foreigners,' we had been warned. 'Compared to the locals you are rich. In Russia anyone with money is a target. At the very, very best you will both be robbed and left for dead as soon as you set foot in the country, but that is only if you are lucky!'

In reality, it had taken nine months before the Brotherhood had even noticed us. Then, far from the hideous atrocities that had been forecast, we had actually been given money!

We reached the Azerbaijani section of town later that afternoon. The restaurant to which we'd been invited stood out while the other scattered buildings and caravans – tea houses and shashlik stalls – all looked a little rundown.

We parked our bikes against a wall and sauntered to the restaurant, chuffed at the thought of a free meal. The staff hadn't been told that we were coming, however, and looked dubious when we explained our story. They invited us to sit down and eat anyway, but on our tight budget, we weren't prepared to order anything that we might have to pay for. Eventually, a man who knew about us came along and we gratefully ate an excellent, spicy meal.

We made friends with one of the waiters while we were eating: I asked if he knew about the existence of sustainable or selective harvesting practices, but before he could answer, a man in a suit turned to face us. 'I'm a forestry man.' He greeted us with a limp handshake. 'And I can tell you that we certainly do follow selective logging guidelines.'

I looked naïvely into his eyes and believed him. He held my gaze for a moment then burst into peals of laughter. 'Oh, yes!' he shouted. 'We practise selective logging.' He waved his hand at the wall beside him in a gesture that I assumed was meant to indicate a vast expanse of forest. 'Oh, yes! We ...' He wheezed and laughed some more. 'We select a tract of forest and we log it!'

Later that evening, I was pacing up and down a stretch of railway line, thinking hard. Over the past few days, we'd come almost 200 kilometres from Taishet. So far, the road connecting the towns and villages along the railroad had been surprisingly good. But the sketchiness of our map and the pessimistic warnings of the locals told us that things could change for the worse.

'A lot worse!' The locals insisted. 'You'd be better to turn back now.' And while we had no intention of doing anything of the sort, it felt appropriate to put just a little bit of thought into our plan of attack. I paced some more and scanned the girders of polished metal.

The rails were smooth, flat and empty; everything, at this point, that the road was likely not to be. Riding along the rails would be perfect. Endless miles of easy cruising through pure wilderness. But how to do it was still a problem. For one thing, there were regular, heavy bolts protruding from the outer edge of each rail – trains used only the inside surfaces of the rails. Then there were other problems, including the obvious one that Tim had raised: what would we do if a train came along?

We talked about the idea the next morning and decided that if and when I could come up with a practical way of rigging our bikes together so that they could sit side by side on the rails, we'd give it a go. For the moment, however, the road was still rideable, the weather good, and the unknown lay waiting for us. We packed up and rode on.

Fifty kilometres later I dumped my bike on the ground in a screaming panic, abandoning what had until then been a calm but hurried search through my pack for a suit of mosquito-proof rainwear. Ahead of me, Tim had almost disappeared in a cloud of buzzing mozzies, to the point where it was no longer possible to make out sharp edges. This time it was him who was laughing.

Despite the heat, Tim had sensibly put on all his long clothes half an hour ago, when we realised we were about to ride through a swamp. He would be sweating rivers by now, but at least the bites getting through would number only in the dozens, rather than the thousands.

A commando battalion of darting mini-blood-transfusion units found the unprotected leg hole of my shorts and made a kamikaze run towards the weakest point of my defences. Painful chafing at the beginning of summer had forced me to abandon the wearing of underwear, and now, under siege, my control was about to crumble completely. I killed a dozen attackers in a savage swipe at my left forearm. Then they struck. I felt the sickening sensation of forty hypodermic daggers sinking into parts of me usually treated with only the very best of care.

My eyes boggled in disbelief and I let out a choked cry. I flung my raincoat to the ground and hopped around in erratic circles. I took tentative slaps at my genitals and howled hopelessly for mercy. Tim was doubled over with tears of laughter in his eyes. I spotted a creek where it crossed the road only twenty metres ahead. I lurched, hopped and ran towards it. To add to my other concerns, my hair had become a nest of trapped mosquitoes as well. Unable to get out of the thick mop, hordes of them had burrowed deeper, making a pin-cushion of my scalp. I slapped at my head and mashed a few hundred insects into my hair-do. Fresh forces had breached the holes in my T-shirt, and I was starting to suffer heavy blood loss from my belly and armpits as well.

I reached the creek on what felt like the verge of consciousness and scrambled to get out of my clothes. I got my shirt off and freed one leg from my shorts before a sudden wave of bites on my exposed bum toppled me headlong into the freezing water.

I lay in the ankle-deep trickle, twisting and flattening myself to get everything under the surface, then sensed rather than saw the tide of dead and drowning mozzies drift slowly by. I lay still. The roaring agony of the bites slowly subsided and my consciousness made the slow journey back to reality.

We woke the next morning to persistent rain. We struggled on for a few kilometres, but the swamp we were trying to push through was getting soggier by the minute and the service track was now little more than a submerged cattle pad. We battled fallen trees and huge trench-like puddles with perilously slippery edges that stretched for hundreds of metres. Our progress was ridiculously slow. It was still 700 kilometres to Lake Baikal and we decided, eventually, that this just wouldn't do.

The previous day the road had deteriorated gradually but steadily from a wide sandy road to a rutted, corrugated trail to a muddy bumpy service track that went through rather than around dozens of deep and fast-flowing creeks. Each village we passed marked a further deterioration in the road.

Eventually we reached the small, rundown village of Savelyevsky. Dirty children in bare feet chased chickens down the wide, muddy main road lined by a dozen ramshackle log houses. We caused the usual stir on our arrival. The children stopped chasing the chickens and ran over to ogle us instead. A gangly teenager in oversized, grease-smeared overalls had slithered out from beneath a broken tractor to have a stare, and a gaggle of stout old babushkas squawked questions in a loud, unintelligible dialect. A middle-aged woman with hair tied back in a brightly coloured headscarf, and carrying two buckets of water, approached and gave us a level stare. 'And where do you two think that you might be going?' she asked firmly, placing her buckets on the ground and hands on her hips.

We looked at each other uncertainly.

'Um, we're following the train line to Baikal.'

The stare continued. 'Um, could you point us towards the road?'

'There is no road,' she declared.

'But our map ...'

She cut us off with a shake of her head. Her firm features softened slightly to an expression of faint tenderness. Maybe she'd noticed the rows of inflamed red mosquito bites on our legs and arms, or maybe she'd just noticed that we were dirtier and more bedraggled than most of the kids in the village. 'We *do* have a road,' she admitted, hesitantly. Our faces brightened. 'But it's only a winter road.'

'Huh?'

'It's a winter road – you can only get through in winter when it's under two metres of snow. And then only in a tractor.'

'Oh.' We paused. 'Do you think that we could get through on our bikes?'

She looked at us uncertainly, shaking her head. We chose to interpret this as a confirmation. What with the language barrier and all ... 'Great! Could you point us towards the road then please?'

She raised her eyebrows and opened her mouth to protest, but then obviously decided that she was dealing with foreign idiots better left to their fate. 'Cross the railway here in the village then follow the track to the east,' she said abruptly. The tender expression had disappeared. 'It takes you into the swamp.'

We held a conference on the edge of the slimy, swamp-ridden stretch of road and decided that it was time to try the railway.

We heaved our bikes one at a time to the top of the steep, rocky embankment and leaned them against a towering pillar that rose up and over the double tracks of the BAM. It supported one of tens of thousands of spans of electric cables. A thunderclap galloped towards us from somewhere in the distance then reverberated loudly in the humid air. The mosquitoes still roared, but up on the embankment, some ten metres clear of the road and the swamp, they were slightly less infuriating.

A wet and morose-looking forest stretched away on either side. The fresh bright greens of spring had well and truly matured, leaving a much less inviting canopy of dense dark green rising above the white, brown and grey of birch, pine, spruce and aspen. Grey clouds filtered all brightness and joy from the day, leaving a stifling and energy-sapping heat. The occasional crow flapped slowly and grimly through the dampness. Resolutely, I hauled my tool kit from my bike and sat down to try and work out a way of turning our bikes into pedal-powered rail-riding machines.

We armed ourselves with an axe, a saw and a handful of cheap Russian hose-clamps and tottered off into the wet forest. Half an hour later, we added a small stack of fresh three-metre birch poles to our equipment. As we paused for a quick lunch of bread chunks with slices of salami and tomato, it started to rain again.

We were trying to set up our bikes so that they could sit side by side on the rails. Our plan was to join them together using several horizontal poles and diagonal bracing poles to add stiffness. It took us several hours, but eventually we had connected three poles to the seat supports of each of our bikes. We were running out of hose-clamps. There were only enough left to add some crude wooden runners to our front wheels.

We heard another distant peal of thunder. It continued rumbling, growing strangely louder, until we realised that it was a train. We waited some tense moments until the train came around the corner 500 metres away. It was on our side of the tracks! We did some quick scrambling and exchanged a few unsavoury words as the whistling train approached. We struggled to co-ordinate our movements and lift the suddenly awkward and bulky four-wheel contraption over the rails. With less than ten seconds to spare, we sent it hurtling down the steep embankment. We looked up as the train thundered past and saw the amazed face of the driver poking out of the window, gaping at us. The roar of the engine receded into the distance to be replaced by a seemingly endless progression of racing, rumbling wagons loaded high with pine logs. As it rounded the far corner, a tiny hand extend from the driver's window in what was unmistakably a friendly wave.

A few more hours, one more train, a lot of rain and the reserves of our patience later, we were finally ready to test our design. A couple of hasty exits from the tracks had weakened the structure and bent our flimsy hose-clamps slightly, but short of trying to lash on extra poles with the guy ropes from our tent, there was nothing much we could do about it. We made some final adjustments, perched our bikes on the rails, then took some photos and did a little filming as testimony to our efforts.

We pushed the bikes tentatively. They rolled forward a few centimetres. They didn't tumble over. Things looked hopeful.

We pushed a bit further and the wheels started to diverge. We straightened up and pushed on. We made another fifty metres or so before one back wheel thumped off the rail and onto the sleepers. Things no longer looked so good.

We conferred briefly and decided that it might be possible to ride. We climbed aboard and gently eased the combined mass of our bikes, gear and selves onto a dozen creaking hose-clamps. The bikes wobbled dangerously but stayed upright. We pedalled cautiously, trying to stay synchronised – and the thing went to pieces.

I ranted for a while, shook my fist at the sky, the forest and at the endless rails. And also, once or twice, at Tim. After a bit, I settled down enough to take some pleasure in sawing through the three connecting beams – destroying eight hours work in two minutes – while Tim caught the moment on camera.

Late that evening I sprawled on top of my damp sleeping bag in our damp tent writing a letter to Nat, while Tim sat outside trying to make a fire out of saturated twigs and soggy branches. The stifling air was equally thick with mosquitoes and raindrops. I listened to Tim's hopeless anguish through a constant rumble of thunder interspersed with bangs and flashes: 'Come on, come on, light damn you, come on – piss-off-you-bloody-little-buggers! – come on, light, please, come on, light, dammit!'

He gave up at around midnight and we went to bed, exhausted, wet and starving.

The next day we continued a long slog. The sawn-off poles still attached to the bikes made good grips for pushing, and push we did. We tried pushing along the rocks on the outside of the rails, along the sleepers in the middle of the track, and along the service track below, now ankle deep in oozing, sticky mud. In the end, Tim worked out a method of balancing his bike on one of the rails and wheeling it carefully along. While it was possible to walk fairly quickly this way, a momentary lapse in concentration would see the front wheel slide from the rail, bringing progress to an abrupt and often painful halt.

About mid-morning, we ran across a maintenance crew repairing a stretch of the line. About half of the fifteen or twenty men were hard at work sleeping off the effects of a crate of empty vodka bottles. The other half sat smoking on a fallen log. One man walked out to greet us with a handshake and a friendly smile.

They were from Taishet, halfway through a three-week spell working on the line. We joined them for a lunch of stew and before we left, the crew foreman fiddled a bit with an ancient-looking radio and let all the crews working down the line know that we were on the way.

We hit the tracks again and pushed on through the evening. It was exhausting, but eventually a station came into view. Half an hour later, we were being ushered along the road by an excited young man and his little brother.

Our new friend was called Vadim. He had got wind of us from a train driver the day before and had been waiting impatiently all afternoon for our arrival. He hauled us aside and quickly invited us home. Exhausted, we were more than happy to take him up on the offer, but I began to have second thoughts when we were shown into the house.

It was a filthy one-room shack full of buzzing, black blowflies. His mother sat by the window, wrinkled and dirty; she swore at him violently as he came in. We sat down on one of the grimy beds and listened as Vadim boasted of his gypsy heritage, but after a little while, we found that we had run out of things to say. There was a bowl of sour berries and some fermented milk in the kitchen, but there seemed to be no other food at all. I went back to my bike and returned with a loaf of bread. Tim and I tore off some chunks for our dinner and Vadim and his little brother dug in hungrily as well.

There were plenty of beds around the walls of the single room, so Tim and I each chose one. I sunk into mine – almost to the floor – and tried to lose myself in sleep and dreams of being elsewhere, away from these horrible surroundings and back at home with Nat. It wasn't to be, however. Vadim snored like an earthquake and his mother spent the night hacking, coughing and swearing as though she was about to die.

We rose at first light, and left quickly. The only good thing about the village, from our point of view, was that it was where the road started again.

Gratefully, we pushed our bikes through puddles of mud and back onto the wet gravelly surface. We could ride again, and although it was still raining, things felt like they were due to improve. We pedalled through the morning until we reached the village of Turma. Here, we were invited in for a delightful lunch by a lovely old lady and her husband, a stark contrast to the night before, and we stayed with them for a couple of wonderful hours before pedalling on.

It had taken us almost two weeks to cover the 400 kilometres from Taishet, but we had come through and triumphed over all the challenges. It was only thirty kilometres to the city of Bratsk; after that, who was to know? That night, for the first time in a week, we camped to the side of a bitumen road.

Riding the Taiga
Bratsk – Ulan Ude
Mid-Summer 2000

Tim

We drifted into the city of Bratsk amid haphazard traffic of Landcruisers, Ladas and trucks; they swerved about trying to overtake on a road without marked lanes. Every sign of civilization, from bold advertising billboards to impatient drivers and towering apartment buildings, came as a welcome change to life on the BAM. The bitumen roads, mosquito-free air and abundant food were all we had dreamt of in recent days.

As usual at mid morning, my stomach felt close to total implosion. 'Chris, let's find a *stolovaya*!' I yelled, as we rolled down the main street.

I don't have very many bad memories of Russia, but finding a place to eat would have to be one of them. On many occasions we'd traipse up and down streets for hours, searching for a reasonable feed. Since the collapse of the Soviet Union many of the cheap *stolovayas* had closed. During the devastating economic downturn most people discovered that it was hard enough to survive, let alone eat out. With the rise of a wealthy class, cheap venues were replaced with exclusive restaurants, beyond the reach of the average citizen.

The cheaper places were usually hidden behind faceless doors, tucked away in student dorms, or down sidestreets in the basement of apartment blocks. They were relics of an era when advertising and customer service were almost nonexistent.

'Hey, Chris, what about that place over there?' I called out, excitedly. A painted sign had long since cracked and peeled, but the faded letters were an unmistakable clue: *stolovaya*.

We left the bikes opposite the *stolovaya* so that we could keep an eye on them while we ate. Inside we ordered borsch soup, macaroni with rissoles, pancakes, potato salad and tea. Beyond the counter each tea glass had a centimetre of sugar already sitting in the bottom. Sugar is obligatory with tea in Russia; it would just be *nyepravilna*, wrong, without it. It is just as *nyepravilna* as eating a meal without chunks of bread, or potatoes with the peel on.

Not long after we sauntered into the *stolovaya*, a shiny Toyota Landcruiser with tinted windows screeched to a halt and two men with short, waxed hair and black sunglasses stepped out, mobiles dangling from their belts. They wore crisp white T-shirts and dark jeans that had been ironed meticulously. Their shoes were pointy with slightly lifted heels. I thought they looked like city cowboys.

They approached our bikes with an air of confidence, touching the tyres and gesticulating excitedly. The larger man appeared to be scanning the surrounds for the owners. He paced up and down the street asking people, and for a while even stood checking his watch. Eventually, he strutted into the *stolovaya*.

'*Privet*, I am Vladimir,' he said, approaching our table. He then leaned over and squeezed my hand so hard that I could feel the pulse throbbing up my arm. The two men drew up some seats, took off their sunglasses and rested their shiny elbows on the table. Vladimir's hulking v-shaped torso was formidable in the skin-tight shirt. The other man might have thought he was formidable, but his physique was less than impressive. I grinned, hoping that the mud on my face and crusty porridge in my beard didn't put them off.

'So, boys, where are you from?' boomed Vladimir. It turned out that Vladimir had a personal interest in mountain biking and a passion for living life to the utmost. I had the feeling that he was scooping us under his wing with his brutally wide shoulders and toned arms.

'What can we do to help? We will do anything,' he offered.

All I had to do was mention that I dreamed of a replacement gear changer for the bike and we were off.

After dumping our bikes at the local judo club we were rushed off to an outdoor shop. It was typically Russian. There were genuine Gore-Tex jackets going at ludicrously cheap prices, and Chinese junk selling for twice as much. There seemed to be no logic as to how each item was priced or, for that matter, how it all arrived here. In Novosibirsk and Krasnojarsk I had scoured every outdoor and bike shop and failed to come up with a gear-changer, or a tube repair kit. In a city as small as Bratsk, I wasn't overly optimistic. Naturally, I was shocked when a shiny component caught my eye in the only display cabinet. Sure, they didn't sell bikes, had no tube repair kits, but right there sat the exact model of Shimano gear-changer that I had broken. Chris was dumbfounded but Vladimir was unfazed. '*Sudba*,' he said. Destiny.

Vladimir decided on the next course of action: we weren't going anywhere until we cleaned up. We returned to the judo club for the royal tour before being whipped off to the sauna.

Not only was there a sauna imported from Finland, but an indoor pool-spa all set into immaculate white marble. It was simply too good to be true.

In the change rooms, Vladimir dialled a number. Ten minutes later a crate of Bratsk beer arrived.

'Well, I am off; I have got a bit of business to do. I will see you boys in an hour or so. Enjoy the sauna!' Vladimir boomed, before leaving us to it.

I followed Chris, close to skipping with joy, into the sauna. Once settled, we watched the condensed water on our skin trickle down our tortured bodies, carrying the grime from two weeks of riding.

We went in and out about five times, sipping beer and leaping wildly into the pool at intervals. The change of temperature sent my heart racing and I fell into a dizzied euphoria, viewing the world as if it were a dream. Only two days earlier we had been struggling along the railway, drenched in sweat.

If the sauna was heaven, then Vladimir was our unlikely angel. I remembered his use of the word *sudba*, and recalled how often Russian people used it. Lying against the moist timber it occurred to me that our journey had indeed fallen securely into the hands of Russia's firm belief in destiny.

But before we could give ourselves over to Vladimir's itinerary there were more sedate tasks demanding attention. Chris headed off to find the Internet and I did a little food shopping. We agreed on a time to meet, but when that time came Chris was nowhere to be seen. I knew it probably meant he had caught Natalie on-line.

I bought two Bratsk ice-creams and sat on the steps of a department store, soaking in the scenery. At first glance, everything about Bratsk looked a little dilapidated. There were the odd patches of long seeding grass, crumbling walls, flaking paint, rusty factories and streets filled with potholes. Stairwells were littered with rubbish and broken glass; I knew from experience that they almost always smelt of urine. Diverging from footpaths, pedestrians took the shortest routes. I watched three babushkas follow a dirt track off the road, waddling along with shopping bags, then ducking through a hole in a concrete wall and out of sight. In other cities it was common practise to clamber over the railway lines.

A trolley bus jammed with passengers stopped in the middle of the street to collect a woman who waved it down, even though it wasn't an official stop. Every corner was crawling with life. It was as if you could see the very human grease that oiled society. With ageing Soviet machinery and a total lack of funds, the human spirit was surely the only thing keeping the country functioning.

The Russian psyche seemed so open and flexible. Although they are renowned for being overly bureaucratic it seemed that when rules got in the way of commonsense, sanity often prevailed. It gave me such a sense of freedom: anything was possible in this place.

At the same time, everything baffled me. Weaving between traffic, clambering over concrete slabs and down dusty paths, were women in high heels. These *devushki* – girls – and *szhenshini* – women – were supreme masters of grace. They held the same elegance whether they were making their way across ice in winter or crossing a potholed street in summer. Most flaunted stylish dresses and were caked in make-up. They contrasted so starkly with their surroundings that they could have been tourists from a world of wealth, as my mother and sister pointed out during their short visit to Russia.

All day they had been raving about how well dressed the Russians were, but when they came out from the toilets they were horrified. 'My God!' my sister Natalie shrieked. 'Tim, there were no doors or walls, and the toilets were just holes in the floor, and there was poo everywhere!' Meanwhile the steady flow of women exited the toilets as if they were stepping out of a condominium.

On the one hand appearance and cleanliness meant everything, yet on another it seemed that function was more important. Russians respect beauty, but they also accept that living in a shiny world means masking the truth of human imperfection. At least that was what I liked to think.

When Chris, Vladimir and his friend arrived, we rocketed through the streets, weaving in and out of traffic and running red lights. In stark contrast to the looks we usually got on the bikes, pretty girls nodded in acknowledgment as we passed. We drove to the edge of the city and out of the shadow of apartment blocks. After roaring along a dirt track through a patch of forest, we arrived on the shores of the Bratsk Sea. It was a feature of the city that Vladimir was obviously proud of – an enormous dam built into the Angara River valley. This river flows into the Yenisey and on to the Arctic Ocean. At its widest point the dam measures almost 100 kilometres.

In the dying heat of evening, the blue sheen of the water merged with the clear sky and the distant hills in a blurry line on the horizon. We left the car and strode down to the bay where a collection of large fishing vessels, yachts and tin boats were moored. The larger boats were made of steel and looked like ocean-going craft.

Half an hour later we were lying on the deck of a big diesel-engine boat, chugging out into the open water. The city shrank to a grey blemish in the distance. From out here it looked like it was under siege from the endless forest.

Vladimir tapped my shoulder and passed a generous shot of vodka. Altogether we raised our glasses and downed the firewater in an instant. Gazing again at the city, I thought it looked like an artificial outpost of civilization. Bratsk is a city supported by the biggest aluminium smelter plant in the world and by the logging industry, but how did that translate into Mercedes, Coca-Cola, pop music and immaculate clothing?

'Whoohooooo!' bellowed Vladimir. He took off his shirt and stood atop the bow, embracing the breeze.

As the sun edged towards the horizon the engine slowed, and I watched the bow slice through the glassy water. We spent a couple of hours just cruising, and I got to know Captain Pasha. He had the nature of a gentle lion. He was over six feet tall with legs and arms that made Vladimir's look like twigs. Unlike Vladimir, however, he chose not to show off. His hair was a golden mop that matched his moustache and the glint of a gold false tooth. Deep crevices forged into his leathery skin and, as he chewed on sunflower seeds, you could see the muscles ripple about his jaw. The boat was his love and he had spent fifteen years building it himself. He had a wife whom he labelled his 'Winter Love', during summer he lived on the boat. Downstairs he showed me the intricate wood carvings and paintings that were his handiwork. Although he was probably about fifty there was a sense of childlike wonder in him. It was as if his fascination with the world had never been repressed. I could tell that Vladimir admired Pasha for the integrity and earthiness that he himself lacked.

When we arrived back at the docks, Pasha stood silently at the helm, facing the shore. There was something about his contemplative gaze that made me think that he had many stories to tell, and longed to return to the freedom of the sea. His gentle and caring qualities reminded me strongly of someone else, but I just couldn't put a finger on it.

On shore we were whisked away to another world. In an exclusive restaurant we found ourselves looking at a menu of South American dishes. 'What would you like to drink, boys? Order whatever you want!' Vladimir insisted. A glass of beer arrived before the meal and stories began to flow.

'You know, nowadays it's just terrible what's happening in Russia. How can people live on such small wages? You know that I used to have five hundred workers under me. Unfortunately during Glasnost I was put in jail for several years. The Red Cross were even offering me refugee status in Switzerland! Jail, now there's a place you don't want to go.'

His face took on a sour, hard look. Suddenly, I had a different impression of his indulgent lifestyle: he was trying to make up for lost time, but he could never be an innocent again. By the way he skirted around his profession, I presumed that he was involved in some kind of illegitimate business activity. To a westerner, he looked like the kind of person that would be part of the Mafia. Russians refer to organised illegal business as the *Bratva,* Brotherhood, or cooperative; the term Mafia is not used. Anyone with a profitable business, whether it be producing ice-cream or computers, seemed to be operating at least partly above the law. Many Russians believed that every shop, down to the smallest kiosk, had to pay some kind of protection money. In any case, we didn't pretend to understand the system and knew that we were no targets of crime.

In the early hours of the morning, we stumbled back onto Pasha's boat. He was up, waiting to usher us to the beds below. As he tucked us in I realised who he reminded me of – 6,000 kilometres away, Baba Galya was probably settling in for a good night's sleep.

The following afternoon we packed our bikes and waved until Vladimir was out of sight. The bitumen road seemed full of promise as we crossed the 100-metre-high dam wall and rolled out of the city. Five kilometres later, I was watching Chris kick furiously at his toppled bike. He had fallen over on the sandy surface for the third time.

'Bloody hell, mate, at this rate the six hundred kilometres to Lake Baikal is going to be hell,' he cursed.

The bitumen had petered out into a dirt track that was like a giant sandpit, with a few pebbles thrown in for good measure. The council must have had a serious budget shortfall and scattered one trailer-load of gravel per ten kilometres or so! Perhaps the 'expedition god' was letting us know that Bratsk had been a break from reality; life hadn't really become easier.

In the cool of evening we pulled off the road into the shadow of wiry pine and spruce. Although I had enjoyed Bratsk, it was great to get back into our own little world. After dumping the bikes, I plodded off into the forest in search of firewood. There was just the rustle of my feet in the undergrowth and the odd squawk of a surprised bird as it fluttered up through the canopy.

As perverse as it seemed, I loved the sensation of fighting for every inch on the road and eking out a living in the forest. I knew that too much time spent in the city would spoil the taste of porridge and dull the colour of sunset. Out here in the elements one truth was clear and unavoidable: life was supposed to be difficult. I preferred to accept and struggle through that, rather than distance myself through modern conveniences. Although Chris and I disagreed on many things, the passion to live a simple, challenging life was deeply woven into both of us.

I returned to camp with a bundle of freshly chopped wood. Chris had already set up the tent and was sitting by the creek gnawing on the end of his pen. I took pleasure in building the fire and slicing potatoes for another meal. By the time the water was on the boil, the sun was flaring through the forest on its journey towards the horizon.

I stirred the pot with a long twig and peered at the sky. I realised it wasn't just the vivid sense of being alive that bound Chris and I. It was when the roads, bikes, weather and landscape failed, and all that remained was our tortured bodies, that we connected the most. This intimate sharing of subtle agony and reward created a special bond. No one could have fully understood the special intricacies of our humour and routine. By this stage of the journey we had become attached to every little item on our bikes and considered them highly valuable. This even applied to the dirty soft drink bottles that we picked up on the roadside and carried for months on end! We knew each other's habits so well that they could be predicted well in advance. This intimacy was torn apart in cities. The things that we did have in common no longer had relevance and our differences boiled over more easily.

Chris closed his notebook and pulled out the camera. Just a few more minutes and the potatoes would be ready, then I could fry up the sardines. We hadn't spoken in hours, and yet it didn't matter.

It struck me that something had dramatically changed since the beginning of the journey. There was less tension in the camp, and disagreements were often obscure. Now the journey to Beijing *was* life. It wasn't a simple matter of compromising our identities to get on. The journey itself had become inseparable from our identity. In effect, we had found a common passion that would endure as long as we kept cycling.

The reflection of the moon on the stream had replaced the sun by the time I crawled into the tent. As usual I slid into the sleeping bag and rolled over so that I had my back to Chris.

'Good night, mate,' he murmured.

'Good night.'

The following morning we awoke to the sound of heavy rain beating down on the tent. 'Oh, shit,' Chris mumbled, before nodding back to sleep.

Two hours later we lay awake, hungry; the rain was relentless. Resigned to the fact that it was going to be dismal riding, we packed up and headed for the road. To our surprise the wet sand made for easier going. So, like the rain, we settled in for a full day.

The view of the road ahead was alluring. It cut a mud-red swathe through the motley green, rising and dipping as it trailed into the distance. The rain fell from clouds so low that the taller trees appeared to be decapitated. Although we still followed the BAM, the tracks were out of view. Now and then the rumble of a train could be heard from deep within the forest.

We were going fast enough to keep things interesting, but slow enough to observe the landscape. In the swampy river valleys I took note of the craggy firs and spruce, draped in rich mosses and lichen. On higher ground, I kept an eye out for the so-called 'Siberian cedars' that were actually a variety of pine. If I looked hard enough I could just make out the bulging cones that were ripe with nuts. These nuts were a Siberian delicacy that, in the late summer and autumn, took over from sunflower seeds as a snack.

For a while the world shrank to the rattle of my bike, the movement of my legs, and the limited view from my tightly drawn jacket hood.

We huddled under a rickety old bridge for lunch as the rain bucketed down. Chris looked like a drowned rat as he chomped away on a cheese and tomato sandwich. His toes stuck out from the gaping holes at the end of his shoes; my runners were no better. There were so many holes that from above I could see more foot than shoe.

The road turned into a roughly sealed surface. We passed through a village that was built into the hillside of a steep, bowl-shaped river valley. Just beyond, three wet bedraggled babushkas were returning from a day of picking redcurrants and mushrooms. They chuckled and shook their heads when they saw us.

With the heavy cloud, darkness began to set in earlier than usual. The rain increased in intensity, flooding the low-lying land. Muddy torrents gushed down the eroded gullies between the forest and roadside. Despite the conditions, I felt good and rode on far ahead of Chris, taking pleasure in the driving rain that thudded against my jacket and slapped my bare skin.

The downpour cleansed the air and with morning came the heat. By midday we were sweating profusely, taking every chance to dip in streams. It was over thirty degrees Celsius. The road cut a windy path into hilly terrain; flat plains were a thing of the past. Trees grew up slopes like tiered seats in a giant auditorium. If we weren't grinding uphill we were joyfully rolling down, leaning into sharp s-bends. We crossed an endless series of steep-sided ridges, and in between plunged into cool, lush river valleys.

Two days of rigorous riding brought us to the Kuta River which, at fifty metres wide, zigzagged along a deep v-shaped valley. The forest grew right to the edge of small cliffs, some of them arching over the swift current. In the orange glow of evening, fish jumped about in a frenzy.

The road verged away from the river to bypass steep sections then returned to the grassy banks. As we rode alongside the current, I took note of the flowering aquatic plants and purple fireweed flowers that added a splash of colour to the landscape. At a closer look, the forest floor was laden with blueberries and a small red variety called lingonberries. As the mosquitoes took cover in the hot sun, it was easy to believe we had travelled into the romantic version of Siberia I had long imagined.

As we neared the large town of Ust Kut, blistering heat fuelled my irritability. My bike had been plagued by niggling problems. It defied logic that in more than 6,000 kilometres I had been the recipient of less than ten punctures, and yet in 200 kilometres I had patched up twenty-seven! We had run out of spare tubes, patches and glue. Chris reverted to cutting up an old inner tube and gluing bits onto punctures with Russian-made adhesive, which didn't seem to work.

The smooth, unbroken run didn't last long.

'Excuse me, boys. Just stop there will you,' said a uniformed policeman with a machine gun casually slung over his shoulder. He was standing outside a checkpoint on the roadside.

'Oh piss off, just let us keep going!' I muttered. The sight of watchtowers painted with the letters DPS had become routine. They marked the posts of the special road police stationed at just about every intersection, and every entrance and exit to towns and cities across the country. The primary reason was to check whether vehicles were roadworthy and licences were valid. However, since it is compulsory for Russians to a carry an 'internal passport', and the authorities were on alert for Chechen terrorists, it was standard to check personal identification.

'Where are you from?' asked the man. He looked confused, as if not sure whether we were riding motorbikes or, as many people first believed, some kind of bicycle for the disabled.

'We have just come from Bratsk,' I answered, hoping to avoid retrieving our documents. It didn't work.

'Can I see your passports and visas?' he asked. Begrudgingly, we followed him into a little shack on the roadside. He flicked through the passports, amused by the array of colourful stamps. Our visas were separate documents stamped with the title 'Cultural Connections Visa'. He had no more idea of what that meant than we did.

Eventually, he made a phone call. 'Hello, we have here two Australians. They have passports and visas, and everything seems all right. What do we do with them?' There was a long pause, then he handed us two cold beers and strode out to inspect the bikes.

Having dropped his official manner, he sipped his beer and grinned at the unearthly contraptions. His bushy moustache and rounded belly were suddenly far from intimidating. Then, abruptly, his grin vanished. 'I'm sorry, boys, but if you intend to follow the road towards Baikal, I have to strongly advise you to go by truck or car. At the very least, you should only ride by day and spend the nights in villages. There are seven escapees from a nearby jail and they have been ambushing traffic. They are living in the forest and are armed with guns. It would be very dangerous for you.'

We had been warned of dangers on many occasions and were used to ignoring such advice, but I sensed that the man's concern was very real. However, sapped into a state of lethargy by the sun and beer, I wasn't all that bothered. And besides, I was looking forward to a rest in Ust Kut. Under vague direction we trundled into town.

Ust Kut was a collection of tiered apartment blocks sprawling along a narrow, deep valley shouldered by mountain slopes. At the southern extremity was the confluence of the rivers Kuta and Lena. The Lena is the second-longest river in Russia, and the sixth-longest in the world. From the road high along the valley side, a busy shipping port could be seen at one end of the town. I imagined getting on board one of the barges and following the river north to Yakutsk and further on to the Arctic Ocean. It was clear that the local industry relied on trade from up-river and the service of the BAM railway.

The following afternoon I sat on a park bench waiting for Chris. He had wandered off to the telegraph station in a last attempt to get in touch with Nat. We had spent a day getting his bike rack re-welded and searching in vain for tube-repair supplies. I found it remarkable that even in such a small place there seemed to be all the trappings of a big city. To my left was a box-shaped kiosk selling *pelmeni* and beer. *Pelmeni* is a traditional Siberian dish, consisting of boiled meatballs wrapped in pastry and served with sour cream. It is similar to tortellini. Next to the kiosk was a stereo blaring Madonna songs and a dusty Coca-Cola umbrella, complete with a set of red plastic chairs and table. People sat smoking and drinking, rocking back and forth on the flimsy chairs that threatened to give way. To my right was a sweaty-faced man selling *shashlik* kebabs. He prodded at the meat in time with the music, screwing up his face as smoke poured from the grill.

On another bench sat three young boys, probably no older than twelve. One of them had wide, dilated eyes and shivered violently. None had shoes and their tattered clothes were ingrained with dirt. The moment they jumped off the seat it was clear something was wrong. One of them picked up a pole and began smashing it into everything in sight. First it was bins, then a seat, trees and even the footpath. Another boy held a piece of cardboard in front of himself and with aggressive lunging movements stabbed it repeatedly with a knife. The third boy stumbled about in a daze, a cigarette dangling from his mouth.

My attention was abruptly taken by a couple of large men swaggering towards me. They wore Nike T-shirts and sunglasses that were clearly not the two-dollar bargains found in most Russian markets. Even in neat jeans you could see their heavy thigh muscles clenching with brutal strength around their kneecaps. Their heads resembled sledgehammers. Both were chewing gum with sinewy jaws. Behind them two girls, featherweights in comparison, hobbled along on high heels, giggling.

One of the men sent an enormous dollop of saliva to the ground just as Chris returned from the telegraph station. 'Where are you from, huh? All on this bike, well, bugger me. By the way, do you need girls? I have many girls, whatever you need. Or perhaps marijuana? I tell you we have marijuana here like you've never seen.' The girls giggled and we looked up with strained smiles. Then they offered us some *shashlik* instead.

'Oh, I don't know. They're pretty expensive,' I replied.

'For you, they are free. C'mon, let's eat!' the man growled. 'Give us four *shashlik* now!' the brute barked. There was nothing to suggest that the poor vendor would be paid.

More men arrived as we were handed the greasy pork meat. They all showed off bulging arms, shiny sunglasses, short haircuts and western clothes, and greeted each other with bone-crushing handshakes and deep grunting noises.

Chris and I faded into the background as fat wads of money started circulating. I was more interested in gobbling down the hot *shashlik* than anything else. Returning to our bench, I discovered that the three wild boys had taken an interest in our bikes. 'Don't touch!' I yelled between mouthfuls, and watched them scurry away like frightened mice. I hadn't meant to be so aggressive and felt bad.

After licking the skewer free of luxurious grease, I left Chris to buy some food supplies. Not far away several glum old men sat in front of buckets of shrivelled potatoes that were obviously leftovers from the previous year's crop. I approached them but before I could finish asking for the potatoes I was interrupted.

'Hello, take this jacket! Buy this!' I looked over to see a gypsy woman holding up a fake leather jacket.

'No, sorry, I don't need it. Thanks,' I replied.

'Take it! Take it!' she insisted.

'What, you mean for free?' I asked with a grin.

'No. For five hundred roubles.'

'Well, I don't need it!'

Meanwhile, the potato men were squabbling over who would find a plastic bag for my potatoes.

'Come here, boy! Come here,' squealed the gypsy woman. 'Closer! Closer!' She sat squat like a plump walrus. 'Give me your hand!' she demanded. I held out my hand and she examined it with a passing glance. 'Now, if you put twenty roubles into my hand, I will tell you your future.'

I laughed and walked away. By the time I returned to Chris, the gypsy and her family were huddled around him.

'Give my child sweet biscuits!' she was screeching.

The three boys were still standing behind a tree, hiding their arms inside long-sleeve jumpers. Now and then they looked down their tops and took deep breaths. Then one boy ripped something out of another's jumper. It was a plastic bag, probably full of glue. I watched as the boy began breathing into the bag with the desperation of someone close to drowning. His eyes were wide and lifeless.

Eventually, the gypsies walked off in a sulk. Chris had handed out some biscuits but nothing more. We were left with the glue-sniffers, who were clinging onto a fence, rocking it back and forth in a rage. When they grew tired of the fence they picked up rocks and began hurling them into the air. Meanwhile, the diners in the Coca-Cola café continued to drink and smoke unperturbed.

Suddenly, someone was standing in front of me. 'Hello, I am from Khaborovsk!' said a tall man in a beige suit. His head was remarkably egg-like in shape and an extremely wide part in his hair exposed a shiny scalp.

I shook his extended hand and met his magnified eyes through thick, rectangular, Soviet-made spectacles. For a moment I was lost for words, then I told him our story.

'That kind of route, hey,' he exclaimed, chuckling. 'Marvellous, boys, just marvellous!'

He seemed like a well-spoken, upper-class gentleman. Only the eyepiece and fob watch was missing. As it turned out, he was an engineer who had been called in from Khaborovsk in eastern Siberia to work on a problem at the Ust Kut power station.

As we chatted, I watched the rest of the scene develop out of the corner of my eye. The local thugs were again approaching, the glue-sniffers were digging up the footpath, and the gypsies sat on a nearby bench keeping a close watch on us.

It was a great relief to mount the bikes and ride away.

We didn't hesitate to cross the Lena River and head for the solitude of the forest. I had arrived in town in desperate need of a rest, and yet felt more depleted as Ust Kut slipped from view.

A day out of Ust Kut, I struggled along an inclining sandy road. The hot, almost viscous air was choking. In desperation, I welcomed a crash now and then – they seemed to refresh my muscles and provide legitimate breaks from the torment. I guzzled water by the litre and yet felt my mouth become claggy as soon as the drink bottle was in its holder. Any momentum was pegged back by the gravel and sand, and a need to concentrate on balance. I cursed the odd log truck that came roaring around the corners, showering us with stones and clouds of dust.

We followed the Lena before turning east along the tributary Niya. After climbing for several hours the road made its first descent for the day. I clicked my gears down a fraction and felt the rush of air cool my sweat. We had made a late start and the sun was already low, tinting the forested spurs a soft gold. These spurs dropped off from a plateau into the gorge where the Niya flowed, hidden from sight. The thought of icy, crystal-clear water was reassuring.

As I switched my attention back to the road, I faced a different reality. Travelling at full speed, I had verged off into deep gravel and was fast hurtling out of control. The handlebars rattled violently as I struggled to correct my direction.

The next sensation was that of my bum scraping along fifteen metres of gravel with my elbows digging in like brakes. Somewhere behind lay the corpse of my bike. When I rushed back to examine it, I saw that the gear and brake cables had been ripped clear off, and the handlebars were severely bent. I could fix the handlebars but Chris, who was ahead of me, had the only spare parts for repairing the cables. I would have to go on without gears or brakes.

Half an hour later, the back wheel began to swerve. It was a puncture. When I removed the wheel, I managed to rip the grain off the axle bolt, which meant I couldn't replace it securely. Three tubes deflated as quickly as I pumped them up; and I tried desperately to improvise for the damaged bolt. A shadow crept over the road and with it came a cloud of mosquitoes.

An hour later one of the tubes, fixed with Russian adhesive, finally remained firm. Relieved, I sat down only to feel the seat give way and my bum come to rest on the narrow steel frame. The nylon meshing of the seat had ripped. I looked down to see blood from my grazed buttocks dripping onto the chain. There was no time to stop though – the mosquitoes were still upon me.

Twenty metres later my drink bottle rattled free and fractured, leaving a wet patch on the road. Not long after that I had to stop to fix the broken mudguard that was rubbing against the back wheel.

Was my bike ending its life?

Thankfully, Chris came back to see what the hold-up was. No sooner had I stopped to tell him the story than a car came to a halt beside us.

'Hello! We are great Russian people. We live in the village of Zvyozdni, and we would like to invite you to our home for the night. We really are good people, so don't worry.' I turned to see a middle-aged couple grinning from the window of their Lada. Chris took their address.

As the car disappeared around a bend, he turned to me. 'Tim, it would really be a good idea to stay with them. Several drivers have warned me about the armed jail escapees. Apparently the group are living between the village of Zvyozdni and Niya.' They were the next two villages on our route.

With the bike repaired, we set off again. We had just rounded the first corner, however, when two road workers leapt out in front of us, wielding shovels. We shot past, pretending not to see them, but two minutes later their giant truck roared down the hill in front of us and came to a halt. We had only covered thirty-five kilometres, but it seemed we were destined for a day of drama. Soon we were squatting in the roadside trench downing three compulsory shots of vodka. Each was preceded by the chinking of glasses and a triumphantly aired, '*na zdorovi!*' To your health.

Afterwards, the men opened a tin of fatty chicken pieces. We dipped our fingers in and brought the slimy delights to our mouths. As my mind sank into a warm fuzzy state, I gazed at my dirt-brown shirt that used to be white, and at the glass in my hand that was actually an old chipped jar. My bloodied elbows and bum stung with the profuse sweat. Meanwhile Chris was grinning and licking his grease-stained fingers clean of chicken remnants. His tattered shorts had the trademark rip in the arse, but in recent days it had extended to a gaping hole through which his entire right buttock was blatantly obvious. Several attempts to sew them up had failed.

As filthy and unhygienic as our party was, it occurred to me that it didn't matter. It was one of those moments when you become so deeply involved with the experience that you begin to blend in with the dirt. I thought of my initial aim of the journey and realised with satisfaction that a large part of it was coming to fruition. The men lit cigarettes and laughed. It would never have occurred to them that, for me, this was the most profound moment in the journey to date.

Eventually we wobbled down the road towards Zvyozdni. With our high metabolism the tipsy sensation passed quickly, but not in time for me to realise that there was something wrong with my bike – again.

'Chris, my back wheel feels really strange, can you have a look for me?' I asked.

'That's because it's dead flat and it's probably been dead flat for the past five kilometres!' he announced, breaking into side-splitting laughter. I was past the point of caring and just got off to push.

It was almost dark by the time we pushed into Zvyozdni. The streets were playing host to summer evening life. Babushkas were out in force on their balconies and on the street outside their wooden homes. The collective sound of their constant babbling resonated through the still, sultry air. Dogs sniffed about in piles of half-burnt rubbish, barking now and then at nothing in particular. Villages like Zvyozdni were purpose-built to house the labourers who had worked on the BAM. The mish-mash of apartment blocks and wooden houses differed from most villages we had passed through.

Midway along the main street, I noticed a middle-aged couple in the process of a fitful domestic argument. The woman's face was etched with so many lines that not a smooth patch of skin remained. There were only two relatively flat surfaces, and they were covered in thick, red lipstick.

As we passed, she screeched and insulted her partner as he fossicked away in the boot of a Lada. In her rage the woman began slamming the car boot down on the man's back. I was astonished to see that apart from the odd flinch, he carried on with his business as if it was a regular occurrence. We kept moving, glad not to be acquainted with such crazies.

We continued on, trying to find the home of our hosts for the night. Suddenly a car pulled up alongside us. 'Where have you been? Come on, our house is down this way!' someone screeched from the passenger seat. I looked closer. It was the wrinkly faced woman. It was her after all who had invited us to stay in Zvyozdni. And so begins our time with the woman who beat her husband with the car boot, I thought. It would surely be a perfectly fitting end to the day.

After rolling the bikes into a garage we followed the couple up a dingy stairwell to their apartment. The husband was a short man with thick glasses and a clean blue shirt. His name was Alexsei. Like his wife he had very few patches of wrinkle-free skin. Under his eyes were deeply set semi-circles that looked as if they had been painted grey.

Although Alexsei was quieter than his wife, he had a drab, unchanging tone of voice that was only broken by a sniggering laugh.

Unfortunately, dinner was served with two bottles of homemade *samagonka*. Alexsei's eyes lit up and he sniggered before coughing and spluttering on his own cigarette smoke. We were bullied into having two shots. It was considered bad karma to open a bottle and not finish off its contents.

More than anything, I wanted sleep. The vodka, however, had brought Alexsei to life, which was most noticeable by the sudden rise in the number of obscenities per sentence. They weren't just soft, playful expressions, but a barrage of filth. The more he drank, the more his wife scolded him, and on more than one occasion she slapped him hard across the face. He just sniggered and spat into his smoking ashtray.

Eventually, I weeded out some interesting information.

It turned out that Alexsei was the retired chief of police for the Zvyozdni district. He was able to confirm that seven prisoners had escaped and that three of them were brothers. But they posed no threat to us – they had all been shot dead in the forest earlier in the day.

We also gleaned that he and his wife had three sons. One of them had recently died fighting in Chechnya; the other two were unemployed and still living in Zvyozdni.

At some point the term *bomzsh* came up in conversation. It was the Russian equivalent of 'bum' or 'tramp'. I had heard it before but was still unsure of its meaning. Alexsei was eloquent in his definition. '*Bomzsh*! Well, basically, that is you without bicycles!' he said, sniggering. Even his wife giggled at that.

Later, when a blind-drunk man fell through the doorway, we had the pleasure of meeting the eldest son. Fuck was the only word I could make out as he delivered an epic tirade aimed at his father. Alexsei argued back in a similar fashion until the wife, to whom we were not introduced by name, stomped over to her son and struck him deftly on the skull with a clenched fist. 'Idiot! Fool,' she screamed.

The festivities dragged on until 4 a.m. I went to bed feeling as if our healthy cycling routine had been badly broken. The vodka over dinner had felt like little glasses of bad health. It seemed ludicrous that we had opted for such hospitality when there was perfectly nice forest stretching thousands of kilometres in all directions from the village.

In the morning I headed into the vegetable garden behind the apartment block to repair my torn bike seat. Next-door the charcoal remains of a garage were still smouldering. Apparently, it had burnt down the day before our arrival.

For hours I sat prodding at the torn mesh with needle and thread. Meanwhile, Chris and Alexsei went about fixing my punctured tubes. Each attempt was shortly followed by a loud hissing sound as another patch broke free.

Alexsei's wife, looking even more wrinkled without make-up, lay on a deck chair next to the carrot patch, taking deep drags of a cigarette and exhaling heavily. Her plan to go berry-picking for the day disintegrated when her son arrived with a two-litre soft drink bottle of *samagonka*.

With each successive repair failure our hopes of getting back on the road also disintegrated. By 4.30 p.m. I was reaching the point of intolerance. By 5 p.m. I was desperate. Alexsei and his son were wildly drunk, and his wife turned on me after I broke her one and only threading needle.

Finally, the bike seat was ready. I worked feverishly with Chris to sort out the tube situation. The Russian glue and cut-up rubber just wasn't working, and neither was Alexsei's vulcanising repair system. After some desperate searching, I found deep in my coat pocket a stray patch. It was our last chance. I applied it to the puncture with glue, put the tube in the tyre and pumped it up. Suddenly the air came gushing out – I had ripped the valve from the tubing.

Chris pumped up a tube for the twenty-third time and something unprecedented happened – it stayed inflated for more than three minutes. We put on a smile and announced our departure. The family strode out of the vegetable garden to shake our hands and have a group photo taken. Twenty metres from the vegetable garden my tyre was already dead flat, but I was determined to keep going. I continued to wave and pedal until I passed out of sight behind a fence. At least we had officially left Zvyozdni.

Two hundred metres on we stopped to eat lunch and discuss our problem. 'I had a cycle touring manual once and it was useless,' said Chris, 'but I do remember one thing. An emergency technique in the event of a ruined tube is to stuff your tyre with grass.'

The thought of riding on a grass-stuffed tyre for 500 kilometres to Lake Baikal was enough to inspire a final puncture-repair attempt.

I took a small piece of copper wire from my tool kit and retrieved the tube with the severed valve. I was then able to wind the wire around the rubber and valve, working it like a mini tourniquet. It was a long shot, and Chris had little hope the idea would actually work. But, miraculously, it did. And so we rode off with the certainty of our journey as fragile as ever.

For the first time in weeks we had a smooth, unbroken few days. The view along the Niya valley was supremely pristine. The nearby trees, with twisted, gnarly fat trunks, were dressed in thick shoals of moss, and the forest floor was like a spongy mattress of multi-coloured mushrooms. The road had fallen away in many places and there was negligible traffic. The terrain became increasingly hilly, and I began to anticipate the Baikal Range, the mountains that surround Lake Baikal like enormous castle walls.

We passed through the villages of Niya and Magistralni, where most of the vehicles were off-road trucks, four-wheel drives and motorbikes.

Locals repeatedly informed us that crossing the Baikal Range would be impossible. 'There is no road going over the Baikal mountains! You realise you will have to walk, and you won't make it. The gravel stones up there are the size of footballs. I can't even drive over there in my four-wheel drive,' said one man who was angered by our indifference.

Further on we descended into marshy land where the forest was clearly being harvested. In the village of Ulgan, children described how Japanese businessmen often visited by helicopter. 'They are taking our forest! A few years ago there was good forest right up to the edge of the village. Now you have to go a long, long way to find berries, and hunters also have to travel far,' complained one boy.

Not far from Ulgan I caught my first glimpse of the mountains. The high series of craggy peaks ran right across the horizon and cut a jagged silhouette into the pale blue. They launched far above the forest, draped in small white glaciers. A shiver of excitement ran through me. The treeless terrain with a network of crevices and snow-choked gullies was the first true mountains we had come to in almost 7,000 kilometres.

We camped at the base of the steep slopes and awoke in anticipation of a rigorous challenge. The day began under a burly, overcast sky that precipitated light rain. The road soon deteriorated so badly that we were dodging cavernous gullies and potholes large enough to swallow a Lada. Sharp shards of slate and rocks fallen from above replaced the gravel.

The high peaks were shrouded in misty cloud that swept across barren slopes, curling and wafting like smoke blown from a fire. Now and then, through the thinner mist, I could make out the white patches of snowdrifts clinging onto perilously steep terrain. Further on we passed over bridges that consisted of a few planks and logs laid across the rapids and bound with fencing wire. Each plank was just wide enough for a car tyre.

Then the road began to rise and, suddenly, the forested plains slipped from view. We were surrounded by the mountains. Glancing up I saw thin white strips of water gushing their way down from unseen heights like unravelling toilet rolls from the heavens. I felt dwarfed by the rocky slope that rose to the right. It was exciting to be back in the grandeur of the mountainous terrain that, although enveloped in clouds, began to reveal the detail that had been a mystery from a distance.

Mosquitoes biting at the ankles, legs burning, fighting to keep balance, dodging boulders, we cycled on. The hills were interspersed with rivers that gushed right over the road, forcing us to push through with icy cold water up to our shins. The landscape was just like an enormous mound of gravel and our route was a fragile ledge that could crumble at any moment. Then the road made a sharp turn. This was where the BAM railway on the valley floor below passed into the tunnel and under the wall of towering rock. We would have to go up and over the saddle.

I looked at Chris and he smiled. This was it. There would be no downhill or even flat until we were over the other side.

At times it was so steep that my front wheel lifted off the ground. Large rocks made balancing on the bike acutely difficult. As we rose, so did the clouds, revealing razor-backed ridges that looked black and menacing. From below, the constant roar of a river could be heard from where it tumbled down a series of steep gullies.

Then, quite abruptly, the road flattened out and I caught up to Chris. 'Well, mate, I guess this is the saddle then.'

It was an unremarkable, swampy patch of land crisscrossed by a decaying rail line network. Scrubby birch lined the roadside and a shallow stream sluggishly flowed over thick brown silt. It was a little disappointing after all the graphic descriptions we had heard from the villagers. Sure it had been hard, but only for a couple of hours.

The anti-climax didn't diminish the achievement for us, though. Crossing the ridge signalled the last day of one of the most vivid experiences of the journey up to this point. Until now, Lake Baikal had been a mythical place. That little swampy saddle was proof that we had really made it somewhere.

All that was left to do was start rolling down. Halfway down, near the village of Godshigit, we stopped for a rare treat – a dip in the famous Baikal hot springs.

We spent several hours lazing in the hot pools that smelt strongly of sulphur. The weightlessness was soothing and contrasted dramatically with the force that was applied to push all eighty kilograms of bike and gear up the mountains. There were two pools: one bearably hot, and another that felt close to boiling.

In the less daring pool I lay back and peered up at the peaks through which we had passed. No matter how relaxed I was, I still wanted to be up there in the wind. There was a certain feeling of freedom that came just from running my eyes across the treeless space. Later, as a rainbow made its way out of the clouds, I wondered if Bruce was somewhere up there.

To our surprise we were denied a view of Baikal until the following afternoon. A series of lower hills separated the mountains from the lakeshore. Blessed with clear weather we stopped frequently to film and take photos. The clouds had parted to reveal an incandescent blue. With the sunrise the grey sloping giants were awoken from their modesty. Lower mountains, olive green in colour, bore slopes where even the scraggiest bushes struggled to cling on. In many places the green was broken by scree slopes where rocks tumbled and seemed to flow like rivers. In the shadowy crevices the trickling waterfalls and snow shone a brilliant white. Unlike the mist of yesterday everything was crystal clear. In the intense heat, the idea of snow seemed far fetched.

The lake appeared just as the road turned to bitumen and my legs felt as if they would splinter under the strain of more uphill work. Through the trees the unmistakable blue glittered in the sun and mountains launched straight up from the far side, snow drifts glistening like jewels embedded into the cliffs.

Cevero Baikalsk was a bustling town crisscrossed by apartment blocks and surrounded by a sprawling mess of wooden shacks and train carriages. It had been built in the '70s purely for the BAM railway workers. Nowadays harvesting the famous Baikal omul fish, a member of the salmon family, is a core industry. I found it strange that so many cars filled the streets when they were confined to such a small area. The only roads that were navigable led to the neighbouring fishing village of Nizshneangarsk and the hot springs. In winter there was an ice road – a route marked on the frozen lake when the ice is thick enough – along the lake that led about 500 kilometres south to the city of Irkutsk.

The population of Cevero Baikalsk was an intriguing mix of nationalities. Many of the workers on the BAM had been recruited from central Asia. When the railway was completed and basically abandoned, many people, reluctant to leave, had found other means of making a living. Interestingly, by crossing the Baikal Range we had officially crossed into the Republic of Buryatia, which is home to the Buryatians, close relatives of the Mongolians. In the market of this far-flung settlement one could find Azerbaijani food, Buryatians with Mongol faces, gypsy families and Russians from all corners of the country.

For us, Cevero Baikalsk was where the road ran out. From here, our task was to seek passage on a ship that would take us about 250 kilometres south-east to the far shore, where we could rejoin a road.

We were skirting around the central square, when suddenly a fierce shouting began. 'Hey! Tim! Tim! Australians!'

It was Slava. I had talked to him on the outskirts of Bratsk, where he had handed us a bottle of 'Baikal Mineral Water'. Now he was leaning against a car with his arms crossed above his pot belly. His face seemed to run in parallel lines, his chin just as wide as his forehead. His eyes were clenched tightly between tensed brows as he squinted into the sun.

'What took you so long?' he boomed, as we approached and shook hands vigorously. Within minutes we were following him home. Unfortunately, he had forgotten his house keys and tried to break in through his own window.

'Don't you know, it's normal for us Russians to get into our homes like this,' he said.

Once inside, it didn't take long before a steady flow of friends arrived to meet the famed Australians. One visitor was Sasha, a man with the erect posture of a policeman. In his train conductor's uniform, I mistook him for an officer come to check our visas. His hair was short and thick, combed back in a stiff series of waves. He wore sunglasses perched above his forehead and when he smiled they moved ever so slightly, making the grooves around his eyes apparent. He was full of energy and never without another question or suggestion.

'Have you swum in Baikal yet? Have you talked to a captain about getting across to the other side? Do you have a wish to do such?'

Dinner was almost ready but Sasha convinced Slava's wife that a turn on the lake was obligatory. After a trip on the open water, we returned to port for an impromptu swim in the icy water. Dripping wet and shivering violently, we returned to Slava's home and a celebratory chorus.

'Don't be shy, eat as much as you can, be at home, eat! Eat!' demanded Slava's wife. I looked down at the table and my pulse rose. There was an array of salted and cooked fish, an endless supply of *pelmeni,* potato salad, cucumbers and tomato. And, of course, vodka.

Next came the *banya*. Inside, Sasha grasped the *veneg*, a bundle of birch twigs and leaves, and dipped it in a pot of boiling water. I lay down on the timber slats before he began whipping my back and legs in a mad frenzy. '*Mechta? Mechta!* Isn't this just a dream? It's a dream!' he kept saying. It felt as if my skin was being singed and boiled; at any minute it would be ready to peel off.

The session lasted three hours. I watched in amusement as Chris stumbled out naked with glowing red skin, unable to focus his eyes. The grin on his face suggested extreme pleasure. Before returning home to party, we agreed that it was the most luxuriant *banya* we had ever had.

I rose at 10.30 a.m. feeling guilty for the sleep-in and as I tiptoed to the kitchen for a glass of water, I was greeted by a cacophony of snores rising from the bodies lying in the lounge and bedroom. More than happy, I returned to bed. Perhaps, after all, it was a well-deserved rest.

When I awoke again, the activities were already in full swing. There was a platter of food and talk about an excursion to a nearby spring. As for passage to the opposite shore ...

'Five thirty this afternoon, it's all organised,' Slava said, proudly. 'The captain is a bit eccentric and he is transporting frozen fish, but he will let you on board.'

Come 4.30, we downed a salutatory shot of vodka and cycled off towards the port. Slava drove behind with all our gear – it had taken extensive persuasion to convince him that we wanted to ride.

The whirlwind of laughter, celebration and good food continued right up until we were sitting on the ship waving goodbye to our friends. Little more than twenty-four hours after Slava waved us down, we watched him shrink into the distance. We were stunned. So much had been packed into such a short time and the generosity had been so spontaneous. I thought about what we had given them in return – it amounted to little.

Eventually, I turned my back on Cevero Baikalsk and realised that we were already forging to new horizons. The ship was a large steel vessel with cranes for moving the containers of frozen fish. As my jacket sleeves flapped wildly in the blustery breeze, I watched the hull crash through large swells. To the west the last rays of light glinted off wave crests. It was more like a sea than a lake.

Rising from the distant shore, the mountains lurched from the water, blotting out the sun. It was possible from our position to get some idea of the grandeur of the lake, but the statistics were still mind boggling. Baikal is a word derived from the Buryatian word *bai-kul*. It means rich lake and is the world's largest lake, containing about one fifth of the earth's fresh water. It stretches 636 kilometres long and reaches 1,624 metres at its deepest point. They say that some people get vertigo when swimming in its waters – it is possible to see forty metres down on a still day.

Nightfall brought a bitter cold. We crawled into our sleeping bags with the sound of water lapping at the bow and wind whistling over the freezing steel. I peered at the stars and settled in for a sixteen-hour journey.

At 4.30 a.m. I braved a frosty dawn to film the sunrise. The pale clouds that hovered over silhouetted peaks were gradually transformed into a molten swirl. The lake's surface turned to liquid glass and reflected with flawless symmetry. I watched as the glow brightened like steel in a fire, until the sun burst over a saddle and shed the first rays of warmth. For a long time I had wondered what could be so special about a big lake. Now I understood that there was something unspeakably beautiful and complete about the moody waters and haunting terrain. The calmness induced a feeling of purity and permanence. It was not hard to understand why many of the lake's features are of significance in the traditional shamanic religion of the Buryatians.

Later I shared a bite of omul fish with the captain and a colleague. They had been up all night chatting over a bottle of vodka. When it was light enough, the captain blew out the hurricane lamp and crawled into bed. It was as if the magic of night had vanished, chased away by the sun. I had the feeling that years on the sea had turned the captain nocturnal.

The east shore was a surprise. Twisted pine trees, craggy with age, leaned from the forest edge casting elegant shadows over a sandy cove. The water appeared silky and inviting. After stepping off the boat we had lunch on a beach of fine yellow sand. Removing my tattered running shoes, the sand tickled and massaged my feet. This was the kind of paradise I had dreamt of all through winter, when cold toes had plagued my every moment.

We took a swim and washed away the mental anguish of the last weeks. Under the crystal clear water, fragmented light needled its way to the sandy bottom in slender, wobbly shafts. Later, I lay on the beach and felt the sun flatten my goosebumps and render my skin bone-dry. The little wooden village in the distance and a sandy peninsula jutting out into the silvery-blue water reminded me of the tropical coast in Queensland. It was hard to believe that in winter temperatures of minus forty degrees Celsius were common in Siberia.

I was reluctant to say goodbye to Baikal, but once it was out of sight I just wanted to ride. Our aim was the Buryatian capital of Ulan Ude, 350 kilometres to the south-east. There we planned to dump the bikes for a month and travel by train to the Altai Mountains for a hiking trip.

During the four days it took to cycle to Ulan Ude, the exhaustion that had been masked by adrenaline came to the surface with a vengeance. I rode slowly, without the spark to fly down hills and motor across flats. Time felt drawn out and my stomach throbbed endlessly, even though I ate as much as humanly possible. Between Baikal and Ulan Ude lay another mountain range, yet I felt too tired to be excited by it. I wanted to get the kilometres over and done with! I lost Chris on one occasion – rode past his flag without seeing it – and became enraged. Maybe it was just coming down after such an enthralling time, or a sign that I really did need a break.

When we finally rolled out of the shadow of the mountains and into a valley choked with apartment blocks and smoke stacks, I was overcome with relief. I pulled up next to Chris and sat silently. We could just make out a sign in the distance: 'Welcome to Ulan Ude'.

Ulan Ude was different to any other Russian city we had visited. The roads were narrow and bustled with chaotic traffic. A large percentage of the people were Buryatians with distinctly Mongol faces. The bus stops had oriental spires rising from the roofs and the city centre was particularly untidy.

In the central square the giant head of Lenin towered ten metres above all else, in danger of toppling and rolling. We spent hours in an unsuccessful bid to find a Visa cash advance facility. As time passed we became desperate for a safe place to leave our bicycles.

Our plan was to take the train to Novosibirsk and then bus and train it to the Altai. Chris went to enquire about tickets while I rested outside the train station. As if from nowhere a small Buryatian man appeared beside me. He wore an American baseball cap that threatened to swallow his small head whole. In fact, the rigid glasses on his nose were the only things that kept the cap from falling over his eyes. He wore sports pants and a grotty coat, and in one hand carried a shopping bag with a loaf of bread and a folder.

He introduced himself as Misha and was soon asking the inevitable questions. I was going through the tired rigmarole of explaining the journey when he said, 'Well, it would be better to leave your bicycles with someone rather than in a carpark. You are welcome to come to my place.'

It was later, in his *banya*, that I realised my mistake. The three of us had been sitting on the wooden seat when Chris walked out to cool off. Our new friend suddenly shuffled close to me and whispered something incomprehensible.

'Sorry, I don't understand,' I replied.

He said it again, but I was equally baffled. Suddenly he moved his hand to my leg and insinuated sexual relations. Now I understood.

'No, I like women. I like women, not men. Women I like!' I stated, emphatically.

'Oh! Oh! But you are so beautiful! I liked you the first time I saw you! C'mon, why don't you try?' he pressed.

There didn't seem to be any point in arguing with the man, so I strode out.

'Oh why? Ask Chris. Maybe Chris wants it!' were his last words before I slammed the door shut.

Outside I stood naked, speechless. I stood there gazing into nothingness, water dripping off my body. Chris was placidly preparing to go back in. Silence prevailed and the steam wafted off my cooling back. I didn't utter a word until I was clothed and ready to leave for the train station. My first reaction was to take the bikes and get out of there – only our train was leaving in less than an hour. We had no choice but to trust that our bikes would be safe until we returned.

What got me wasn't the fact that he was homosexual. It was his unrelenting begging, his refusal to take no for an answer, and the way he had lured us to his home.

As the carriage swayed and creaked over the ruts toward Novosibirsk, it occurred to me that in the past month much of the challenges had involved running the gauntlet of Russian hospitality.

Siberian Paradise
The Altai Mountains
Late Summer 2000

Chris

The sun was down and the lights of Ulan Ude had long since faded behind us. The fire in Tim's eyes, however, was still burning bright.

'That bastard!' he exclaimed. 'That absolute little bastard. I can't believe the way he wouldn't take no for a fucking answer!' He simmered for a moment, and the polite, well-dressed Russian lady sitting on the seat beside him discretely inched a little further away. 'The way that he bloody well told me that I should think about it. Fuck!' He thumped his fist into the upholstery. 'I've got nothing against gays or anything, but I came closer to punching that little bastard than I've ever been to hitting anyone in my life!' Tim closed his eyes. 'You'd better do the talking when we go back there again, mate. If he tries to come onto me again ...'

I had no real idea of what was going on until we boarded the train and Tim told me about the incident.

'It's all right. Just forget about the guy for a month and lose yourself up there in the mountains. We'll go back, I'll do the talking, we'll grab our bikes and leave ... Unless, that is ...'

Tim looked at me incredulously. 'What?'

'Unless, of course, you feel like taking him up on his offer of getting all his friends around and having a big *banya* party?'

Tim was in no mood to appreciate my joke.

'Get stuffed mate! When we get back we're going to grab our bikes and leave straightaway.'

The clicking wheels of the train marked the time. Three days in transit merged steadily into one as we rode ever westwards. I sat huddled against the window in a sullen, watchful mood, as roads and tracks flashed past outside. Tim and I had rebuilt our friendship over the summer, and although we still had the occasional yelling match, we'd been getting along really well. Living with him at close quarters indoors, however, brought out my intolerance for his 'Timisms'. I gazed at the road and recognised a stretch along which we'd cycled more than two months ago. The memory tugged at my heart and I wrote morosely in my diary:

Wishing that I could just get out there for an hour to ride, clear the mind and feel the thoughts start to flow again. The fresh air, the clear blue sky. Just an hour, I know, would be enough to lift me right back out of this gloom.

When we finally reached Novosibirsk, we checked into a hotel and spent a day scouring the markets, buying food and supplies for the walking trip. We were also waiting for our British mates, Brendan and Ray. Tim had met them during the Wilderness Guide course in Finland. Initially, we'd been planning a two-week walk in the Arctic section of the Ural

Mountains but decided instead to trek through the Altai Mountains. The Altai range is situated on the borders of Russia, China, Mongolia and Kazakhstan, about 800 kilometres south of Novosibirsk. Ray had quickly agreed to the idea over e-mail, and then Brendan thought he might to come along, too. At any rate, Tim and I were set for a big one.

Brendan and Ray turned up the next day. It was good to see them again and it was a relief for both of us to have other people to talk to in English. We munched greasy pies on the station steps and talked for hours. We all had a lot to catch up on, but when we started talking about our plans for the walking trip, it became clear that we had radically different expectations about what the journey would entail.

Tim and I spread out our maps to show Ray and Brendan what we thought would be a promising sixteen-day route. They looked at each other in disbelief, then Ray exploded. 'Sod that, you crazy Aussie buggers. You'll have us walking every bleeding day!'

'Well ... yeah.' It seemed obvious. 'And?'

'*And*,' Brendan said, cradling his didgeridoo protectively, 'you simply won't get me taking me didge up that high. It's cold up there, see, and me didge don't like the cold.'

My mind was whirling. 'Are you really thinking of taking a didgeridoo on a mountaineering trip?'

'Jeez!' He guffawed. 'Ya don't think I brought it with me all the way to the middle of bleeding Siberia just to leave it behind now, do ya?'

A day later, the four of us were standing in the evening sun on the banks of the river Chuya, waving goodbye as a convoy of coal trucks – our lift – rumbled off down the road. They disappeared and we were left with bulging, heavy packs and the prospect of two weeks in the Altai. It would undoubtedly be a spectacular time, but somehow, like most of our journey, it was largely unplanned. All we'd managed to agree on was that we would walk for a day and a half up to a little lake in what looked to be a nice alpine valley. We'd see how that went, and take it from there.

Our first afternoon went well. We walked a few kilometres up a dry creek bed found a place where we could stretch a large groundsheet over the top of two adjacent boulders to form a sort of long, narrow sleeping cave. The following morning Tim and I got up bright and fresh and ready to go. Brendan and Ray were still fast asleep. As we waited, we started to realise what we might be in for. I became impatient and some of my frustration started to spill over onto Tim. By the time they woke – 11 a.m. – we were bickering, and by the time everyone was finally ready to go – 1 p.m. – I'd just about gone round the bend.

We climbed upwards along the steep banks of the creek and later found an overgrown vehicle track, which made progress easier.

Towards the top of the climb, we began to get a view. Behind us, as we climbed up and out of the river valley, a panorama of craggy ridges and slowly diminishing foothills stretched away into the distance. We climbed further and the vegetation thinned out, becoming twisted and alpine. When we neared the top, the views were spectacular, but nothing had prepared us for what came next.

Due to our carry-over cycling fitness, Tim and I were a fair way ahead of the other two. We climbed enthusiastically up the last pinch, looking back down on the river where we'd started – 1,200 metres below – then raced each other, laughing, to the crest. Tim got there first and I crashed head-first into the bum of his backpack as he came to an abrupt halt. I climbed to my feet, chiding him, but stopped in mid-expletive as the panorama caught my eye and I turned to gawk open-mouthed at the view.

A broad grassy valley, ringed by trees and with a few silvery creeks trickling down the sides, stretched out just a little way below. Halfway down, I could make out a tiny hut with a thin tendril of smoke climbing steadily from the chimney, and spread out across the slopes, a herd of wild horses raced each other through the rich green grass. At the bottom of the valley, several kilometres off to our right, an oval-shaped lake glistened serenely, the dead-calm surface presenting an upside-down image of the wondrous prospect that lay beyond.

Slowly I lifted my gaze from the magnetic beauty of the lake to take in a view that literally dominated the horizon. From left to right a towering, savage, rocky ridgeline bit into the sky. Sheer cliffs soared hundreds of metres above rough scree slopes and impossible pinnacles towered majestically upwards as though reaching out to touch the sky. The sun was slowly setting behind us, painting the entire ridgeline a fiery orange. I stood transfixed, oblivious to the sound of Ray and Brendan struggling to join us. My gaze slowly focused on one of the rocky peaks. We hadn't planned our route from here on. The Poms wanted to stay a while and that suited me just fine. My mind registered an appointment and I broke out in a manic grin. That peak was mine!

We camped by the lake and spent a day relaxing and exploring the valley. The owners of the hut were an elderly couple of semi-nomadic Altai sheep and horse herders who had their two little granddaughters up from the city for the school holidays. They spoke a little Russian as well as their native Altaic and we soon made friends. They spent every summer in the mountains, rearing their flock of sheep and their herd of horses, coming up on horseback and living self-sufficiently for months.

We trekked to the top of the valley, climbed small pinnacles and shot reams of photos and video film. Brendan played beautiful, haunting tendrils of rhythm on his didgeridoo that echoed from the crags all around. We watched the horses frolicking in the valley beyond and had tea with the locals in their hut. No matter what I did, it seemed, my eyes were always drawn to the monstrous range towering above.

We made a brilliant tent sauna that night by heating rocks in the guts of a huge, raging bonfire. After a few hours, when the fire died down a bit, we shifted the red, glowing rocks into a shallow hole nearby and erected a dome-tent over the furnace. We climbed in and poured bottles of water to unleash steam before running outside and jumping into the freezing lake to swim naked under the stars.

The next day we set out with small packs and climbed 1,000 metres to one of the nearer peaks on the mighty range. It was rocky and wild, and we had to do a lot of exposed scrambling to reach the summit, but the view from the top was worth the effort. Before us – twenty kilometres or so further to the south – we could clearly see the next big range. It was the main one: the Altai Range. In places, it rose nearly 2,000 metres above us. The peaks were white and icy and the saddles filled with snow. This was part of what Tim and I had come for: mountaineering. We'd brought crampons and ice-axes. Ray and Brendan had not.

We returned to our camp late in the afternoon, and after a short investigation, Ray and Brendan discovered that they had not brought enough food to last the trip. With all our camera and video gear, our tripod and climbing equipment, Tim and I were on lean rations already. Our packs weighed close to forty kilograms each, and we had no food to spare. The Poms sortied off towards the hut to see if they could buy food from our friends and returned a couple of hours later, lugging a large plastic bag. They made sure they had our attention, then opened it to reveal half a carcass of a freshly slaughtered sheep.

It is quite difficult to do, but I nearly choked on the last mouthful of my dehydrated mash potato. 'What the bloody hell are you two going to do with that?' I asked, utterly amazed.

'Wha'd'ya think, mate?' Ray asked me, chuckling. 'I thought you colonials were meant to be good at this bush-tucker thing or something, like?' They sniggered to each other. 'Seriously though, we're going to have to spend most of tomorrow here smoking and drying this meat, so we're not going to be able to go on in the morning.'

We sat up into the evening, talking. Brendan and Ray sliced up their meat and hung it to dry on a hastily lashed-together wooden frame over the fire.

Ray and Brendan had a dream of travelling together on horseback across the steppe, from Mongolia to Europe. It was much the same idea, incidentally, as the one I'd had when first deciding to leave university and head to Russia. Tim and I laughed and told them that if we were anything to go by, then they could probably expect a fair amount of 'interpersonal conflict' along the way. We gave them some stories as evidence and they seemed amazed that we had made it this far.

'So what you're saying, Chris,' Ray joked, 'is that after living with Tim, married life is going to be a breeze!' Everyone burst into uproarious laughter, but try as I might, I couldn't for the life of me see the joke. To me, Ray had just pronounced the most blaringly obvious fact in the universe. How on earth could anyone compare the trials and tribulations of living with Tim to the joy I was expecting from being married to Nat? I shook my head, confused, and they laughed all the more.

I got up early the next morning and made a quick breakfast of instant porridge with Tim. He had decided that he would carry on ahead for a day, walking fifteen kilometres down into the next big river valley, where he'd wait for us. I was going to take the opportunity to climb the towering mountain I'd first seen on arrival in the valley. And the others, still sleeping soundly, were probably going to deal with the rest of their hunk of sheep.

I'd already spied out my route. First I would ascend around 1,000 metres to a peak similar to the one we'd climbed the previous day, only about five or six kilometres further away. From there, I'd try to traverse a kilometre across an extremely exposed and jagged-looking saddle to reach the soaring peak in the distance. My peak.

'If I'm not back by tomorrow,' I told the half-awake Englishmen, 'come look for me, all right?'

I scrambled steadily up through the treeline, and climbed further on steeper and steeper rocks until I finally reached the first summit around lunchtime. I stopped and had a bite to eat, admired the view and steeled my nerves to press on.

I worked my way tentatively out onto the top of the saddle, scrambling and scaling big boulders and rock formations as the crest narrowed to a knife-edge. I crawled cautiously out along a narrow ledge of rock and saw with dismay that it ended in a vertical drop of about ten metres. I took a breather and weighed up my options.

I was born with neither the skill nor the inclination to be a rock climber, and although the rock face was generously creviced with hand and foot holds, I decided against taking the risk. The rock was flaky, and I didn't have any ropes. A slip would more than likely transform me into a bloody pulp among the rock heaps half a kilometre below.

I crawled backwards and gingerly climbed down a crack off the side of the ledge. I eased my way around a little way, onto another tiny ledge that protruded out a centimetre, but it didn't continue and I had to go further down.

I reached the bottom of the high rock pillar and found myself standing at the very top of a long rocky chute that cascaded down into a gigantic scree slope below. The gradient was about eighty degrees and it stayed that way for hundreds of metres.

The vast slope was littered with loose rocks and stones and I could hear a constant background clatter as boulders slipped downwards in mini-avalanches.

I inched my way along the top of this slope, willing myself to stay calm and to not look down past my shaking legs. I kept all of my weight on my toes and pressed my arms, chest and face up against the rock face in front of me, straining with all my will to adhere to it. Every time I lifted a foot to move, rocks clattered downwards and I had to test carefully before trusting my weight on anything.

After travelling thirty metres in half an hour, the end of the ordeal was in sight. Just two steps away was another flat ledge and after that, the obstacles looked more manageable. My self-control and my strength had almost left me and I was desperate to get away from the brink of that terrifying fall. I took one careful step forward then tried to make a quick lunge to safety.

As I pushed off with the toe of my right boot, the rock I was standing on dislodged and went plummeting down. I crashed downwards. Gravity seemed hell-bent on sending me to my doom, but in a reflex action I managed a desperate grab at a small rocky protrusion on the solid face above me and checked my fall. I wasn't able to hang on and the shock removed the skin from my fingertips and nearly wrenched my arm from its socket, but at least I wasn't falling. I slid very slowly downwards with the rocks, pressing myself flat and digging my hands and feet desperately into the moving mass.

The slope was so steep that I was standing virtually upright. I felt like a very small bug clinging desperately onto the top of an extremely high wall – only this wall was sliding. Within a second, I was beginning to pick up speed, but at the end of that second, just moments away from careening down to death or serious injury, my foot found a stable rock and I stood still.

The world held its breath while my heart pounded furiously. A cold sweat was pouring off my skin and I dared not move until I was sure I wasn't going to take off downwards again. Carefully, I climbed back up to the safety of the ledge and there I sat, regaining my composure, thinking of how much I loved Nat and mentally thanking each and every god I could ever remember hearing of.

The going became easier from there and, within half an hour, my panic had given way to a towering optimism. It was by far the most technically difficult and dangerous scrambling and climbing that I'd ever done, but I was being very careful now and was loving it.

I reached the saddle and began to climb up the ridge to the mountain on the other side. The climb was steep and exposed but much safer than the descent now behind me. I reached the top and stood like a king claiming virgin territory. I spun around and exulted in the view of mountains and mountains and mountains. As far as I could see, in every direction, towering peaks and valleys that stretched away to every horizon. The peace and tranquillity of this wild world was seeping into my consciousness, and every day I was feeling a stronger sense of calm.

If only Nat could be here with me, I thought. This is heaven!

I reached camp at one in the morning and found Ray and Brendan eating their fifth meal of mutton stew for the day. I was exhausted but also deliriously happy. I told them of my day's adventure and they seemed relieved that I'd made it back. I was glad too.

We broke camp the next morning and walked down the valley to find Tim. The trail became indistinct, and we split up to try and find a way through. Brendan, a little short-sighted, thought he saw Ray in front of him with his back turned and sneaked up to give him a surprise. He stopped only a few metres short, though, looked again, and slunk back, terrified. He'd been about to land a walloping whack on the shoulder of a big brown bear!

We found Tim collecting firewood and he led us back to an empty cabin near where he'd been camping. Compared to the scant shelter of our tent, this was a veritable mansion! There was a two-room hut – slightly musty and rat infested, but fantastic nonetheless – that became our home, a traditional log and bark *yurt* of the semi-nomadic Altai people, a smelly pit toilet and best of all, a log *banya*.

Tim had the furnace heated and the water barrel filled. We dumped our packs and gladly jumped in to steam the dirt from our bodies. It was fifty metres to the river on a rocky, slippery path strewn with tree roots, and we raced there and back a couple of times, in between bursts of almost unbearably hot steam, to dive into the freezing alpine torrent. On the way back after our second exhilarating dip, however, Brendan slipped and stepped heavily on a sharp rock. He gashed the sole of his left foot badly, and after we'd bandaged it up, he decided that he'd best not try to walk on it for a while. We moved into the hut and waited another two days while it healed.

After Brendan recovered, we walked south-east for a few rainy days, up the banks of the gushing River Shavla until we reached Lake Shavlinskoye. It was a pristine, jade-coloured alpine lake set like glass in the bottom of what was almost a deep crater surrounded by snowy peaks and alpine mountains. On the far side, vertical cliffs rose straight from the water, towering hundreds of metres into the air.

Scattered about we found clusters of age-old shamanic totem poles. Woodcarvings of long, hideous faces stared menacingly from crooked poles, and the occasional tree trunk was carved with the dancing face of a forest sprite. Some of the carvings were obviously new, others had been vandalised and others again were strewn with the drying underwear of a party of

Russian walkers. But the majority of the figures were clearly hundreds of years old, remnants of an otherwise forgotten culture that had inhabited these mountains for centuries. They lent a sombre aspect to the magnificence all around.

We camped by the lake and enjoyed a sumptuous dinner of instant mash potato and mutton (by this stage Ray and Brendan were willing to swap their meat supplies for just about *anything* we had to offer). We sat up late, talking of our plans to find a way up and over the main range the next day, but when Tim and I got up early in the morning, we were in for a surprise. We hung around, kicking stones and getting increasingly frustrated until mid-morning. Finally, we stormed into their camp and tried to get them moving. I prodded Ray's sleeping bag with the toe of my boot and he rolled over angrily.

'We need our fuckin' beauty sleep, so sod off!'

The previous evening they'd seemed keen on finding a way through the mountains, but now they'd changed their plan and seemed completely unconcerned about how it would affect us. Tim and I spent an hour arguing about what we should do. Tim was annoyed, but still tempted to stick with them, while I was really pissed off and wanted to keep going. Eventually, Tim agreed to come with me. It was the thought of spending most of a week walking back the way we'd come, rather than crossing the range and completing a round trip, that changed his mind more than anything. It would probably be a long time before either of us was able to come back to these mountains again, and six more days was still a lot of time in which to explore.

We woke the Brits again and told them our decision. We agreed that if we didn't see each other beforehand, we'd meet for a beer at Novosibirsk train station a couple of hours before their train was due to depart. From Novosibirsk, Ray and Brendan would take the train west, back to Finland, and Tim and I would travel east again, to our bikes in Ulan Ude.

They were good mates and it was sad to say goodbye, but Ray had changed a lot. As for Brendan, although he was a really nice guy and played an incredible didgeridoo, he often seemed pretty bent on getting his own way. We said goodbye and headed off around the edge of the long, oval-shaped lake and up into the mountains. It was back to the two of us again.

We spent the day climbing to the headwaters of the river and found ourselves in a huge flat rocky bowl. The river started in a series of small tarns fed by the run-off from several gigantic glaciers that stretched upwards to the glistening peaks all around. We climbed further and camped in a cleared patch on top of a rock pile at the bottom of a glacier. The night air was haunted by the sounds of avalanches and the eerie groans and sharp cracks from the melting ice-mass, weeping as it retreated beneath the fierce heat of summer.

The best map we'd been able to buy of the area was a 1:250,000 sheet – one centimetre of the map showed 2.5 kilometres of the ground – and this made navigation sketchy and haphazardous. We wanted to cross the huge ridge before us, but we weren't sure if and where we would be able to do so. By a combination of visual sightings and guesswork, we followed the glacier to its very peak, and then climbed upwards onto a steep rocky scree slope bounded by the solid, near vertical walls of the mountains. We climbed steadily for hours, curving away from the bulk of the glacier and around to the left until a snowy saddle came into view to our right.

'Over there. Tim, mate! Look! Woohoo! That must be it. Yes! We've found it!'

Tim took one look and dug in his heels.

'No way, mate. I don't reckon that's it. And if it is then there's no way I'm going to climb it, anyway. That scree chute leading up to the top is way too steep!'

'Huh?' Tim wasn't usually like this. He'd been fine with the heights on Mount Elbrus the year before, and the stories he'd told me of his risky mountaineering feats in the United Kingdom and Eastern Europe had been enough to make my blood run cold.

'What do you mean it's too steep, mate? That only looks a little steeper than what we're on now.'

'Bullshit, Chris!' Tim *really* didn't like the look of that saddle. 'If those rocks are anywhere near as loose as they are here, then it'd be impossible to climb.'

'Okay then, mate,' I agreed, still uncertain. 'We'll keep on going round here then and see if we can find another pass a little further along. But if we can't, then that one there definitely looks like *one* way across, so maybe we could at least have a look at it on our way back. Right?'

We kept on climbing, still curling round as we hugged the rock wall on our left, the scree slope getting steeper and steeper. Every footstep slid backwards, and although there was no real danger of falling, we had to work hard to make progress. Eventually, a saddle came into view. The climb up to it was extremely steep and the loose rocks were becoming dangerous.

It was a long, long way down when I looked back between my legs to see Tim a little way below me taking off his pack and bracing himself against a boulder.

'What's up, mate?' I called.

'It's too steep, Chris. I just don't feel safe.'

'It's not too bad.' I tried to encourage him. 'Just don't look down. We're not far off the top now, anyway.'

'Nah. Look, I'm sorry mate, it's just ...' Tim was upset. Somehow he'd lost his natural recklessness and along with it his head for heights. 'It's just like ... I didn't make it up Elbrus last year and before that, the last time I did anything really challenging in the mountains it was with Bruce. And now he's gone ... I don't know. I'm sorry. I just can't do this right now.'

'That's okay.' I thought for a moment. 'How about if I leave my pack here and scoot up to the top. If it's good and it looks all right on the other side we can try it then, right?'

He agreed, and I set off, much lighter without my pack; and after five minutes of hair-raising scrambling I reached the crest.

I crouched down on an extremely narrow precipice and took in the glorious view. An overwhelming sense of vertigo swept over me and with hundreds of metres of steep falls on either side I couldn't trust myself to stand. It was a wonderful view, though. Magnificent peaks and ridges stretching away ... But hang on ... I looked again and started to recognise some of the features. I wasn't looking south toward the peaks of the Altai in China and Kazakhstan at all; I was looking back down at the lake where we'd camped two nights before!

We'd climbed the wrong bloody saddle! I looked around carefully and realised that I'd practically ascended to the top of a little island peak that protruded north from the main east-west range. We'd climbed around in a circle!

'Bugger it!' My yell resounded and echoed from a dozen different mountains. I laughed at myself, then scrambled down to tell Tim.

The break had done him good. I told him the bad news and he grinned.

'Good thing it was you that climbed up there then and not me, isn't it?'

'Yeah ... right.'

'I've been thinking, though, mate. That other saddle over there is actually lower than we are at the moment. I reckon that maybe I'd be ready to have a go at it if we could get over there.'

We scrambled back down the scree slope, sending hundreds of kilograms of loose rocks catapulting loudly down before us, then traversed over to the other side of the slope to reach the bottom of the chute leading up to the new saddle.

It was steep, but no worse than anything either of us had done before. Tim went first and he looked a different person to the one I'd seen just a couple of hours before. He slammed his ice-axe into the hard snow that still clung to gaps in the rocks and drove upwards with his legs. I swung my own axe and followed, scrambling in places, and after about fifteen minutes, we reached the top.

The landscape ahead equalled any that I'd seen before in sheer, captivating beauty. A vast, white glacier stretched out below us and a magnificent river valley with ice-capped mountains on either side flowed into the distance.

We cooked our usual lunch of textureless mash potato and considered the glacier below. Neither of us had ever tried to cross such a large glacier before, and we were nervous about the danger of hidden crevasses. Luckily, though, we spotted a party of Russian climbers coming our way. We watched carefully as they weaved their way across the huge ice mass. Later, we were able to safely follow their footprints across the melting surface.

We climbed carefully off the glacier to reach dry ground and entered the amazing world of a warm, green and grassy valley blocked at one end by an ice cliff and scattered here and there with rocks and snow. We walked till dark. Exhausted and unable to find a suitable spot to pitch our tent, we simply set up on the gentlest slope of a scrubby hill, climbed in, and collapsed into instant sleep.

We woke early the next day to a beautiful sunrise of wispy orange clouds and a light dusting of powdery snow. We had four days and about 100 kilometres till we'd reach the road, and we were short on food. We'd added an extra day to our journey when we split from Ray and Brendan, and having eaten too much already we were now having to cut back to two-thirds rations to make our supplies last the distance. My trousers, which had once been a little tight, now slid easily halfway down my hips and Tim, constantly starving at the best of times, had adopted an 'energy conservation strategy'. When he wasn't walking or busy making or breaking camp he would lie perfectly still, willing his body into a sort of hibernation while he waited for the next meal.

I cooked our meagre ration of instant porridge for almost half an hour, adding extra water and watching the oats swell into bloated puffs, until it looked like a decent-sized meal. I spooned a generous half of the slop into Tim's bowl, added a handful of sugar and pushed it towards him. He sprung into instant life, sat bolt upright and wolfed down the meal in what seemed like a few spoonfuls. He carefully licked every last trace of sustenance from his bowl and his beard, then burst out of the tent and quickly started packing all his gear. 'Breakfast energy doesn't last long!' he explained in between shoves. 'Gotta get a move on now before it all runs out again!'

We stormed down the banks of the River Karagem. We'd crossed it where it started, just below the glacier, the previous day, but within a few kilometres it had become a deep, wide torrent of raging white water. We stomped down the valley across slippery rockslides and through rough, wet scrub. We crossed tributary rivers running off glaciers; the water was so cold that my calf muscles cramped up and my feet snap-froze so badly that I reached the far side crying out in pain. We both faded around mid-morning, but after a small and invigorating lunch we were back on foot and charging through a heathy swamp, southwards along the banks of the river.

It started raining later in the afternoon, but things improved when we found an overgrown vehicle track next to a long disused field. We literally raced along for a few kilometres before unexpectedly spotting a large wooden walker's hut in the distance.

We approached it eagerly. People often leave surplus food behind and we gloated about our chances of finding something extra to eat. If we were lucky, there might be an abandoned block of chocolate. Or maybe someone would have left behind a packet of pasta and a tin of meat.

We raced to the door and I swear I actually saw Tim drooling. But, to our dismay, inside was not the cupboard full of ownerless food we'd been hoping for, but half a dozen startled girls wearing the T-shirts of the Moscow University Trekking Club.

I could see the bitter disappointment in Tim's eyes. He turned his face into the drizzle and glared heavenwards. I could almost read his thoughts. *Food*, God! It was a nice warm hut full of *food* that we wanted! Not a nice warm hut full of *beautiful girls*, darn it!

But then, as though in answer to his ad hoc prayer, one of the girls moved away from the table to reveal a huge pile of freshly cooked pancakes. Our knees began to wobble violently and Tim started drooling again.

One or two of the girls still looked frightened, but the others were intrigued. One of them cautiously invited us in to share a pancake and dry out by the fire. We left our packs outside the door, stripped our dripping jackets and headed inside for a comfortable hour of conversation and a mouth-watering pancake or two as our clothes steamed by the fire.

A little later, we were joined by another large party. They had arrived earlier in the day, and now they were returning to the warmth of the fire after setting up their camp in the forest. One couple was carrying a six-month-old baby on a ten-day walk along a similar route to the one we'd taken. Another man said that in the twenty years he'd been walking in the Altai Mountains, we were the first foreigners he'd ever encountered.

The most important thing we learnt, however, was that only two days' walk away – about forty kilometres, and just off the edge of our map – was a little village from which we would be able to hitch a ride back to the main road! We would no longer have to walk at a forced march and more importantly still, we no longer had to ration our food.

We talked for a few hours then went to set up our camp and have dinner on a sandbar by the river. I crawled into the tent, stuffed to the point of exploding, and drifted off to sleep while looking out through the mist at softly shrouded stars.

Half a day later, we were sitting in the grass near the top of a high pass on a huge, rolling plateau. We were almost 3,000 metres above sea level, with the steep and rocky mountains behind us. All around were huge, softly rounded hills flanked by steep glaciers that descended onto the shimmering steppe on the horizon. We'd passed some yaks earlier in the day – Tim had chased them up a hill with his camera – and now we sat with our boots off, finishing off the remains of our lunch, watching as a party of five toiled slowly towards us up the slope.

They looked even more haggard and emaciated than Tim! I looked closely at the guy in front and decided that he'd recently added two new holes on the smaller side of his trouser belt. They dumped their packs and stopped to talk.

'Whereabouts have you been?' I asked.

'Oh, we've been out exploring glaciers and climbing mountains just over the border in China and Kazakhstan.'

'Wow!' These guys were hardcore!

'We've been out for twenty-six days, and now we have to hurry because we're all late getting back to our jobs and our families in Moscow.'

We walked with them and were amazed by their stories. They'd carried only 500 grams of food per person per day during the trip, and each of them had fallen down at least one crevasse.

They were doing it for the record, apparently, and they told us of a whole new world of Russian adventure walking.

Apparently, groups of adventurers went on expeditions every year then submitted a detailed report, complete with photos and descriptions of the climbs, the new routes and the difficulty involved, to a panel of judges. The winning group was awarded a prestigious prize – the leader of this particular group had received it once. But more amazing was the news that there was a whole library of these expedition reports, complete with hand-drawn maps to previously untrodden places sitting virtually unknown in Moscow. This untapped source could be a gem, I thought; and my mind fired up instantly, making grand, but momentary, plans to set up an adventure travel business bringing tourists to the wildest places in the former USSR.

We agreed to ride with them back to the road, and if possible, to the train line. There were five of them, too many to fit into one car, and so with the two of us, we could split the price of two taxis seven ways and save money all round. This sounded fair enough, but we were dismayed later that evening when we found a loaded hay truck from the village, the owner of which was willing to give us a ride.

The Russians agreed instantly, but I felt that it was a bit of a shame. We'd been planning to walk the rest of the way into the village the next day; and both Tim and I were sad to find the opportunity gone and our trip finished so abruptly. But like they'd said, it would be cheaper to catch the taxis as a group; and with native speakers to do the bargaining, it would save us a lot of hassle. We threw our bags on top of the huge pile of hay and climbed after them.

That was it. Fifteen days of walking over in a flash, with only endless hours of transportation to take us back to our bikes.

The truck lurched away, and as it started trundling down the road, I looked at Tim, sitting high up on a pile of hay, smiling sadly. He caught my gaze and shrugged.

'Ah, well. Looks like that's that. I suppose we'd better go check out Mongolia.'

Riding Rough

Ulan Ude – Gobi Desert, Mongolia

Early Autumn 2000

Tim

Rain fell, sometimes hard, sometimes as spittle, but never consistently. Cars crashed through swelling puddles, sending a wall of brown water towards shopfronts and unlucky pedestrians. Disco music blasted from a plastic marquee where a drunk couple danced. Beyond them, a babushka with bowed legs hobbled along, clutching a plastic bag full of food scraps scavenged from overflowing bins.

My head throbbed and I wandered in a daze. Chris and I had arrived in Irkutsk earlier that morning; we were spending a few hours apart before our evening train to Ulan Ude.

As aimless as the rain, I turned into a shopping centre. Racked by tremors of hunger and bewildered by the contradictions of the city I took refuge in a café and bought a beer to settle my nerves. There I opened my diary and toyed with the idea that the shopping centre was a veneer slapped over the reality of the destitute, the unhealthy, and those who struggle to make ends meet. Yet, neither those who wore the designer labels nor the dank rags looked like they had any life in them.

For fifteen days in the Altai we had not known the date or time, or heard so much as a distant car. The rivers had gushed through precipitous gorges with crystal blue water, and mountains soared above lush forest and high alpine plains. I had felt at ease and no matter what the conditions, they never appeared as hostile as the city. The day I'd walked ahead of the others, I climbed a peak and lay a photo of Bruce, together with a flower, under a rock. I couldn't think of a more ideal place to let his spirit rest.

I was convinced, that despite progress, the wilderness and simple ways could still be of benefit. In the wilderness there was no room for the bullshit splattered across television screens and the hyped-up advertising campaigns. It occurred to me that there is no mountain too high or weather too hostile – it is simply the way things are. In the end you are forced to be true to yourself, and the important things really become clear. There is no point lying to nature because it won't listen. Furthermore, once you step outside cities and roads, money is meaningless. On the alpine plains a CEO could shoulder up alongside a factory worker and neither would be advantaged.

Realistically, the experience in Altai reinforced the notion that it's important to look after nature, and keep areas of wilderness even in an advanced world. It didn't mean cities should be obliterated. In some ways, the state of the earth could also reflect the state of human health. Getting out and experiencing nature could be promoted as a way of balancing city life. As a source of solitude and replenishment of the human spirit I know of nothing better.

But what of the guilt I felt sometimes as a 'wealthy' westerner passing through Russia? Was it really escapism? Perhaps, but only if I returned to Australia and forgot what I had learned. I remembered the message I had read in countless mountaineering books: 'We don't go to the summits to escape, but so that when we come down we can live a better life in civilization.' As long as I could apply what I learned from our adventure to life at home, then it would have all been worth it.

Rather than feeling guilty, it was probably better to understand how privileged I was. I had the opportunity to live a healthy life in the city, and the resources to visit the wilderness and foreign places. In short, I had the freedom to appreciate the advantages of many different environments and ways of living.

'Should I get the *banya* fired up?' someone from behind me said. I cringed. We were at a bus stop in Ulan Ude, waiting for transport to the place where we had left the bikes. By some coincidence Misha, our Buryatian friend, had seen us on his way to work. I had had a month to forget about the unfortunate experience in the *banya*, but suddenly it all came back.

After some rushed, much-needed repairs to the bikes in Misha's yard, we wobbled out of Ulan Ude and into the setting sun.

I hadn't been on the bike for a month, and the sudden flurry of air enlivened my senses. The days of stagnation on the train vanished, leaving behind an ability to think more clearly. Even as we slipped out of the city we were setting our sights on the next goal – reaching Ulaan Baatar in Mongolia. There remained 350 kilometres to the border and a further 450 to the Mongolian capital.

The familiar forest of spruce, pine and birch quickly dissipated, to be replaced by thick hardy bushes and stocky trees. Parched green hills rose well above wide flood plains and shallow streams. The ridges looked like the bony spine of a rotting corpse. When the sun was low, the grass appeared not green but a dry yellow. Gradually, the grey earth became red, punctured by islands of tight-fisted grass. The view spanned clear horizons and although pyramid-shaped hills rose here and there it lacked prominent features; distance became harder to gauge. Suddenly, I felt like a tourist in an alien land. Camping on the sandy earth left me pining for the seclusion of the forest, and made me realise that Russia had become a second home.

It wasn't just the landscape that was changing. The Buryatians, although Russified to a point, were distinctly different. The following evening, near the town of Gusinosersk, I was hailed down by a man intent on talking.

'You know that this, Buryatia, is the home of Genghis Khan. You see, up in those mountains the Russians mine the diamonds and gold. We cannot. As Buryatians, disturbing the earth is sacrilege. By the way, you see that smoke stack there? That is the highest in Buryatia,' he said, pointing to an unremarkable chimney rising from a rusty old factory. 'You understand, we have clean, fresh air. And by the way, have you noticed how here in Buryatia all Russians work and we stand around and watch? Our God forbids us to work.'

I wasn't convinced that he spoke for all, but most likely there was an element of truth in his eccentric ravings.

Further along the road we passed blue satin sashes tied to the branches of trees. Cars often stopped and the passengers offered drips of vodka to heaped cairns: one flick of vodka to the sky, one into the air, and one onto the rocks. As far as I could understand, it was for good luck and happiness; and it was bad karma to not stop at each and every sash and cairn.

Some of the Buryatian superstitions bore a resemblance to common Russian beliefs about good luck and the right way of doing things. Russia was a blend of cultures ranging from Europe to central Asia and the Far East. This complexity always made it appear that the culture was plagued with contradictions. For example, Russians were caught up in systems and laws similar to that of the Europeans, yet turned to 'destiny' and 'luck' to show them the way; they could be intensely cold and yet be the most hospitable and open on earth; they were overtly materialistic and yet deep-spirited; they could be incredibly moral, hard working and disciplined and yet be openly lazy and apathetic; they were great ones for following pragmatic plans and yet thrived on spontaneity.

The country escaped definition – it wasn't Europe, it wasn't Asia, and it wasn't even a northern or southern culture.

That evening, as I pedalled fiercely to reach a hilltop, a petrol tanker stopped in front of me. The driver stepped out, motioning for me to stop. 'C'mon, have a couple of shots of vodka with me,' he urged.

'Oh, no, I had better not. I find it pretty difficult to ride after vodka,' I replied.

He peered down at me in sheer anger and puzzlement. 'And you think it's easy to drive a petrol tanker after a couple of shots of vodka?' he yelled.

His pleading trailed off as I breasted the crest and set off down the other side. The bike whizzed with ease, and I felt the sweat cooling. As the sun glided down to the west and the land opened out before me, it occurred to me that the difference between western and Russian culture was perhaps rather simple. A Russian almost always first thinks with his heart, and then with his head. That would explain the lack of rationale at times, and also the spontaneous generosity and flexibility. Russia was starting to make sense ... yet ironically it was fast becoming a memory.

The light of evening soon became fragmented by craggy hilltops that cast long shadows. The translucent grass blades became dull and still. I was brought back to the here and now by the sudden cold and stopped to put on a jumper. As I did, a Volga car – the Statesman of Soviet cars – pulled up. The brake lights glowed like mini suns at dusk. It was a Buryatian couple wanting to invite us to dinner.

As we approached their settlement it was the barking dogs that struck me first. Then the shouts of a woman telling the dog to shut up. The village was situated in the shadow of a hill upon dry floodplains. In the still air not a bush trembled and from a distance you could make out a thousand conversations. It seemed that the dust had settled in streets that were usually enveloped by torrid dust clouds stirred by wind, four-wheel drives and cattle. Like the wooden villages of the north, this too nestled into the landscape with minimal disruption to the view. The houses, however, were built with stone and layered with an earthy paste. Many appeared to grow from the earth itself.

Our hosts for the evening owned a modest home, yet it was probably one of the larger ones in the village. The Volga and an Uaz, a Russian-made jeep, parked out front meant that they had probably held roles of importance in Soviet times. The man wore a tightly buttoned shirt and had a plump neck. His dress pants, although old and well-worn, were spotless, in line with the rest of his attire. I could only look in amazement at his mirror-gleam shoes; they seemed to have an uncanny ability to repel the dust they trod upon. His face was wide, with cheekbones that panned out like two inverted frying pans. His nose barely rose higher than his cheeks, and his eyes resembled slender crescent moons. The curvature of his eyebrows equalled a mouth that constantly cut an arcing line beneath his heavy features. Meaty forearms and legs complemented his thickset torso.

He cast a proud figure, yet seemed humble. What I didn't know was that he was almost sixty and a grandfather. The couple ushered us into the home, tut-tutting, as if to say, 'don't be silly' when we proposed taking off our shoes. Not for the first time, I was left wondering whether I would take someone off the street with such ease.

The man's wife was also thickset and muscular. Her agility and thick black hair were deceptive – she was almost sixty.

It wasn't long before we were seated in the kitchen. Although we had been showered in meals and hospitality all through this journey, I never took them for granted. Even a day on the bicycle, let alone a week, made a home-cooked meal hard to resist. Along with the meal, of course, came the ubiquitous bottle of vodka.

On this occasion Chris and I felt that alcohol could only prove beneficial. If our hosts wanted to celebrate, then damn it, we would too!

It turned out the man was the former director of the collective farm. He had worked in the fields with sheep, and in the office with local government. As he drank, his smile grew. He told us again and again of his Mongolian friend, a cosmonaut. Family albums by the armful arrived and we spent an hour flicking through the black and white photos. They had four children and nurtured high hopes for their futures. It struck me that these concerns were no different to those of parents in Australia.

But then his smile was crossed by a look of anger. 'It's all messed up now; no one knows what tomorrow will bring,' he said, lamenting the changes that had befallen his country. Looking at the photos and listening to his heartache, we were in no doubt that the Russia we were experiencing was a very different Russia to that of ten or fifteen years ago. The glossy photos of cosmonauts and rockets with the USSR symbol gave the impression of a time of glory, optimism and excitement. Compared to those glory days, our friends seemed to be living in a country shattered to pieces. Nowadays, it seemed that Russia was still reliant on systems set up during the Soviet Union, even though those very systems were falling apart. As the public buses ground to a halt, the hot-water pipes rusted beyond repair and the power stations fell into further neglect, what would the future bring to Russia?

Fortunately for us, the man happened to have a tourist map of Mongolia, which had a scale of 1:2,000,000. Little did we know that it would become our sole source of navigation later on.

As we rode out of town the following evening, it felt as if we had been wished good luck and sent on our way from Russia itself. It had been the final spontaneous display of everything that encapsulated the warmth and generosity of almost twelve months in this wonderful country.

Two days later the border of Mongolia was in sight.

With a bowl of porridge in hand, I wandered towards a nearby hilltop and sat beneath a lone tree. Leaning against the trunk, I breathed a sigh of relief. I wanted to be alone with my thoughts; I wanted to think about what this day would bring.

For more than two years I had been living in the northern forest lands of Finland and Russia. This part of the world had become my life, my passion and home. Now that we were leaving, I wanted to hold onto it like a baby to its mother.

I peered into the distance and tried to adjust my eyes to the details of the horizon. I thought that if I looked hard enough I could solicit some kind of certainty about my future.

'Hey, Tim ... ready to go?' came Chris's voice.

From our camp site, we descended towards the border town of Kyakta. 'Mongolia 10 km', read a sign. The bikes sliced through the mist, freewheeling, gathering speed towards the end. I was tempted to pull on the brakes. It all felt too early to be leaving Russia.

The road abruptly flattened out and we rolled into the centre of town. Several cows lazed about the bus shelters, others lay in the middle of the road, in the full knowledge that drivers would avoid them. Box-shaped kiosks lined the main street; and as our momentum slowed, we observed tubby women in blue and white aprons preparing for a day behind the counter.

As we neared the town centre, I was puzzled by a vibrant display of reds, yellows and pinks in the mist. They seemed to melt and swirl into one another like running paint in a watercolour. I squinted into the mist, trying to work out what it could be.

'Children!' I burst out as the present snapped into focus. They were children! There must have been about a hundred of them. The girls wore black dresses and white tights with frilly ribbons in their hair. They walked hand in hand with their mothers and clasped gigantic bunches of flowers. The boys, no older than eleven, wore bow ties and also carried flowers. Their crewcuts had grown out to thick tufts of hair and had been slicked back meticulously. The vision contrasted starkly with the kids we had seen over the last months just lolling casually by rivers and playing games on the street. There was something familiar about this sudden change in tempo, but we remained stumped. It was Chris who clicked first.

'It's the first of September, the first day of school!' he shouted.

But the haircuts and long pants had a greater significance than the first day of school – summer was over and autumn had begun. With the warm weather behind us, it was clear that there was no time to waste.

We had things to do before we left the world of vodka, babushkas, taiga and *pryaniki* behind. The first was to call Baba Galya. The second was far less significant, but equally as satisfying: stuffing ourselves with a final meal of *pelmeni* at the local *stolovaya*.

With the camera rolling on a tripod fixed to the back of Chris's bike, we pedalled off in the direction of the border.

Eight thousand kilometres of cycling down, I focused in on the final stretch.

Our hopes of surging through the border were short lived. I pulled on the brakes in a panic. The road ahead was locked off by giant iron gates. Traffic was banked up and truck drivers sat at the wheel chewing sunflower seeds. Nearby, Mongolians sat around piles of bulging striped bags. A lady wandered about, desperately trying to sell ice-cream from a milk can. Where was the road? Where was Mongolia?

The crooked door of an aluminium shack eventually swung open and slammed backwards into the wall. A soldier in a fading khaki uniform sauntered out. He smiled and spat out sunflower shells on the ground. 'Sorry, you'll have to wait. We are closed for lunch right now. We will open at two,' he said, before returning to his shack.

We waited for two hours before a soldier returned with our documents.

'Sorry, guys, your visas are good, but there is a problem. Do you have permission from the general in China or Moscow? Because we only accept three nationalities at this border – Russians, Mongolians and Chinese.'

'No, we don't have permission. How do we get it? Do you have their contact addresses? Can you possibly give them a call?' I asked, hopefully.

'Well boys, I have no idea. I don't know the addresses, and in any case we have a pecking order in the army. Phone calls can only come down to us from higher places. We can't call them,' he replied. 'I tell you what you have to do. You have to go to Naushki. It is about forty kilometres from here. There you will have to put your baggage on a train and cross the border as a passenger. If you put your bikes into top gear, you might just make it for the evening train. So, guys, where have you cycled from?'

We set off with a vengeance, pounding the pedals and battering the bitumen as if it was the heart of Russian bureaucracy. Sanity, it seemed, had been left by the wayside in this instance. We didn't know what the time was or when the train was leaving, but our frustration fuelled our speed. My legs became swollen as we powered up that long, steep hill and passed our old camp site.

We managed the forty kilometres in two hours, and arrived screaming through Naushki. Drivers swore at us and I swore back. I pulled into the railway station, bottomed out in a puddle and landed flat on my bum. Chris ran inside to buy tickets.

I lay in a heap with the blood throbbing through my veins. A door slammed and Chris emerged. 'The train is leaving in one minute. They won't sell us tickets and the next train doesn't leave for twenty-four hours. Bugger it!' he growled.

Naushki was a seedy little place overrun by soldiers, drunks and local traders from Suchbaatar, the neighbouring town in Mongolia. With little choice, we spent the night in the station's waiting room. After lying down, we were joined by eight Mongolians, all fighting for a piece of our sleeping mats. In the end I had a thirty centimetre portion and lay squeezed between a man who smelt of vodka, and a couple who wriggled closer and closer, elbowing me in the back.

Along with them came hordes of blowflies that crawled over the floor and onto my face. At 5 a.m. we were kicked out by a furious cleaning woman wielding a broom. At first she told the Mongolians to leave the 'poor foreigners' alone. But when I raised my sleepy head and she got a look at me, she ordered us out as well.

Several hours later the train arrived and we scrambled aboard. After convincing some very unhappy conductors, we squeezed the bikes into the narrow aisle. Once inside, I collapsed onto a bed. 'Finally, it's over,' I whispered.

In transit I felt untouchable – the world lay beyond the thick glass. For a while I could truly relax ... or at least I thought so.

'All right, mate?' said someone with a distinctly English accent. I rose from my dreary half-sleep to see a clean-cut man with a crisp, untainted backpack and a Lonely Planet guidebook.

The comfort and security of the train ride was short-lived. In half an hour or so we arrived at Suchbaatar. The encounter with the Englishman made me feel uncomfortable about myself – I too was 'one of them'. Inevitably, I thought, we were foreigners, and to think we had turned native would just be kidding ourselves. In reality, I hadn't worked for money in more than twelve months. Even living in the forest on four dollars a day had probably left us looking out of place and incomprehensibly rich. Our bikes, for starters, cost more than the average Russian wage for two years. How had the Russians really perceived us?

By the time the train doors opened, I was itching to slip back into our routine. I stepped out of the carriage and made my way across the tracks to the station platform. Before riding on, we would have to reassemble our bags, which had been stripped off at the conductor's demand. The sun had already set and I felt an urgency to get going before total darkness descended. I was nervous. I knew almost nothing about Mongolia. All we had was a very basic tourist map. We didn't know the currency or a single word of Mongolian, and we weren't even sure where Ulaan Baatar was.

There was a rush of activity on the platform as Chris dumped the rest of our bags down. It was already dark and the group of children had multiplied to a seething mass. I caught glimpses of shiny eyes and teeth in the glow of a distant streetlight.

We dragged our gear against a wall so that we wouldn't be totally surrounded. After mistaking a prostitute for a money exchange woman, we eventually changed some Russian roubles for the Mongolian tugrug. Finally, we pushed the bikes into the darkness.

'Which way is Ulaan Baatar?' I asked Chris.

'I don't know ... that way I guess,' he said, pointing into the dark.

In an instant, the kids caught onto the idea. They rushed from behind and clung on, pushing and pulling. Some threw rocks, and I was peppered with gravel. 'Where's the bloody road?' I yelled.

'Shit, I don't have a clue!' Chris called, from somewhere ahead.

I was out of control – the kids were pushing me over bumps, rocks, a gutter, and suddenly towards oncoming headlights. I couldn't stop, yet I couldn't break free. In a last ditch effort I swung my arm violently to the right and hit something. The bike suddenly felt lighter, giving me the chance to break away. I realised that we were riding on a gravel surface. It must have been the main road, but there were no streetlights, and the few motorbikes that chugged by were blinding us with their headlamps.

'Let's find the edge of the road!' I yelled, between breaths. A few more stones hit the road near our bikes, but soon we were in the outskirts.

We cycled until we hit a smooth surface and made for the ink-black sky and earth ahead. When the town lights were finally out of sight we pulled over and made camp.

As we retired for the night, I surrendered to the fact that we were merely tourists in Mongolia. The only thing we could know with certainty was our cycling routine. We were, in effect, just passing through; and I wasn't sure that I liked it.

We woke to a miserable morning. The lack of forest seemed to let the clouds press close to the earth. A light rain fell, and it occurred to me that the narrow corridor between the overcast sky and the ground was liquefying. Something overnight had turned inexplicably stale between Chris and I, and I pedalled behind him without a word. It was close to freezing and I watched my bare kneecaps slowly turn pale blue in the wind. Ten minutes later the cold in my toes returned.

It was probably coincidental that cold weather had arrived on our first day in Mongolia, but the logical reason was that Mongolia is a large plateau sitting at an average altitude of 1,600 metres. From here on we could expect colder temperatures from which there would be no escape until we dropped down to the plains near Beijing, 1,600 kilometres ahead.

By the time I caught up with Chris my big toes were already numb. The frostbite from winter had left the tissue especially susceptible to another dose; I stamped around before putting on my heavy hiking boots. 'I really can't afford to risk frostbite again,' I said. 'My health is more important than getting to Beijing by bike. I'll walk the rest if it means avoiding frozen toes!'

'Yeah, well, there's no way I'm not riding to Beijing!' Chris snarled. He was already counting down the days.

Soon, I noticed a bizarre trend in the road signs. The numbers indicating kilometres travelled from the official starting point of the road were decreasing. After consulting our compass and map, we realised that we were three kilometres from the Russian border at Kyakta. We were heading back to Russia. True professionals, I thought, as we spun around and headed back towards Mongolia.

My spirits soon lifted. We crested a high saddle and before us the land panned out in a sublime, silky blanket of green. The clouds had begun to rise, revealing the treeless landscape and the smooth bitumen road that shrank into the distance. Mountains rose to high, rounded peaks. Time and erosion had mellowed the earth. The beauty wasn't raw and spectacular, but all the same it was awe-inspiring. We rode down and up, saddle after saddle. When sunlight came gushing through a break in the clouds it was warm enough to remove my jacket. Then, as the misty white clouds rushed to fill the gap, I was cold again; such was the fragile balance. With this fragility came a heightened sensitivity to everything. I likened it to the feeling one gets atop a lofty mountain summit.

The only breaks in the view were tiny white flecks – *ger* tents scattered sparsely across the steppe. The *ger* is the traditional home of Mongolians. It is a round, collapsible tent made of felt and canvas. Tendrils of pale smoke rose from the *gers*, horses and sheep milled around. From this distance they looked like armies of grazing ants. There were few major scars to the earth – even the *gers* were impermanent. Several times I heard the muffled pounding of earth and turned to see a horseman galloping alongside. The men sat straight-backed and smiling while their horses chose the path. Their faces bore round prominent cheekbones and wide slanted eyes. Some wore velvet hats with a golden point rising well above the head. Most were wrapped in a long maroon felt cloak called a *dele*. Intricate decorations of silky ribbon lined the cuffs and seams, and they wore knee-high leather boots with similar decoration. All I could do was wave and smile back. Although I couldn't communicate, I didn't mind – it seemed to play into the hands of a country graced with simplicity.

What struck me most was the absence of fences. Come to think of it, the border had been the first real fence we had seen since the beginning of the journey. Without artificial boundaries, the natural lie of the land became clear. I rode a good distance behind Chris and went through much more film than usual. As the bike rolled smoothly along the slick surface, I raised my eyes so that neither the bike, my legs, nor the road was in sight: it felt like flying. Perhaps, I fantasised, we had entered a long forgotten kingdom in the clouds.

It rained almost without break for the next three days. The dampness and a growing exhaustion rubbed out the novelty of the landscape after two days. I sweated profusely beneath my raincoat but my toes still went numb. Although we had ridden approximately 8,000 kilometres, and our legs had become stronger, I was acutely aware of each painful crank forward. Distance, it seemed, was undeniable. The land doesn't lie, and there were definitely no shortcuts by bicycle. Like the hills that were the stumps of an ancient range, I felt worn to the bone. Even with the promise of the Internet in Ulaan Baatar, Chris was looking unusually sapped as well.

We had not had a real break for two months, and even then it had been minimal. We had lost a lot of weight on the Altai trip, and no matter how many bland meals we ate, putting it back on seemed beyond us. The exhaustion made me introspective for most of the time, making me feel guilty that we were not interacting with the people. During the entire ride to Ulaan Baatar we did not stop at a single *ger*.

I felt full of experiences from Russia and unable to face a new language and culture. Russia had been the focus of our journey. Now that the intense battle was over, we were limping towards the finish line. More than anything I just wanted to rest, to lie down on a bed and sleep until tiredness evaporated.

We began ascending higher than we ever had; sometimes it was as much as 1,000 metres before we plummeted into one of the countless valleys. We passed in the shadow of spectacular peaks encrusted with rocky outcrops. Each saddle was marginally higher than the last, and in this way we progressively rose higher. The road seemed long and unending.

On the afternoon of the fourth day, a couple of sumo-wrestling-sized men with frankfurt-thick fingers waved us over to their hut. I was disappointed that they weren't living in a *ger* but a rusty train carriage. With pride they showed us how to slaughter sheep by hand, the Mongolian way. We were obliged to take part in ripping the skin from the carcass and squeezing the faeces from the intestines. Later, in the grimy inside of the carriage, we ate fresh fatty mutton in fist-sized chunks. The infernal buzz of blowflies was relentless as the men slurped and gnawed away at the bones and sinewy pieces of flesh. Their equally big wives shared chunks of meat with their three-year-old daughters. They tore the flesh apart like lions sharing prey with their young. The rain had eased in the morning and been replaced by a blue sky and baking hot sun. I didn't want to ride in the heat, but the thought of spending more time in the carriage made my stomach churn.

In the evening, my bouts of diarrhoea began. Long after dinner, the violent convulsions in my digestive system calmed and I crawled sedately into my sleeping bag. Through the fly-netting of the tent door I gazed at the spectacle of a starry sky. Taking deep breaths, I felt my leg muscles loosen in the warmth of the puffy down, their job over for the day.

As though from a great distance, somebody began to sing. I held my breath and listened. It was a woman's voice. Gradually it became louder, and with it came the rhythmic pounding of earth: she was riding a horse. Her shrill, high tones trailed and echoed clearly across the valley in the still cool air. Although I couldn't see her, I imagined long flailing hair and a loosely fitted *dele* that flapped like a royal robe. The sounds came frighteningly close to our tent before veering away and petering out into the night. For me it was a surreal touch to a world that was already fantastic. Just before zipping up the tent, I was stunned by a momentary flash in the sky: a shooting star. It was moments like this, I thought, that re-kindled the motivation and energy to go on.

The magic was, unfortunately, short-lived. Minutes after closing my eyes, I turned to Chris who was nodding off, too. 'Chris do you hear that?'

'What?' he replied, irritated.

'I think there are horses approaching our tent,' I whispered.

I sat bolt upright and prepared to unzip the tent door. I paused before ripping it open. There were three horses – tall silhouettes towering above me. I didn't dare move, and for a moment neither did they. Then there was a giggle and a teenage boy jumped down from a saddle.

'*Sambaino*. Hello,' I said, nervously.

He said nothing but offered his hand. I was still in my sleeping bag, wearing only stripey thermal underwear. As I reached out my hand, he clenched it hard. Then, with his other hand, he grabbed my wrist and pulled back swiftly. I found myself sprawled out on the grass, centimetres from a pair of hooves and beginning to shiver in the cold. Unseen figures sniggered from above.

Unsure of how to react, I stood and tried to gain focus. Suddenly, the other two riders jumped down and picked up Chris's bike.

'Don't do that!' I shouted in Russian, running to push them away. In the meantime, the third adolescent reached into the open tent door and took my helmet and two spare tyres. The other two jumped back onto the horses and began to run circles around the tent, swinging their fists in my direction. They jeered and screamed insults in an attempt to intimidate; it was the horses that I was really afraid of, though. They snorted wildly and more than once brushed me with brutally strong hind legs. In the dark, and still barefoot, I was paranoid about a wayward hoof.

Seeing that I was distracted, the adolescent on the ground made a break with the tyres and helmet. I was fast to react and cornered him against the tent. He must have been left wondering when Chris lunged out from inside and tackled his legs. He dropped to the ground and I ripped our belongings from his hands. This only enraged the other two who began ordering the third horse to attack.

The commotion went on for half an hour or more. There was nothing we could do but stand and protect the gear. Eventually, fed up and terribly cold, I began shouting abuse in Russian and Finnish. They made a final lunge for our tyres and took off galloping. Chris chased, screaming wildly, until the tyres were dropped and they rode out of earshot.

Afterwards we had little energy left for talking. The matter wasn't helped by further convulsions in my bowels. It was going to be a long night.

The following day we continued upwards, covering the first fifty kilometres in six hours. Several giant eagles followed above, no doubt waiting for me to drop. Beyond them, I could see the fading jet streams of planes. As we neared the flight path, I sought an escape in the distant specks in the sky. Where were they flying to, and from where? Were there passengers flying for the first time? What were they thinking? Probably they were sitting back with an orange juice and settling in for sleep. I tempted myself with thoughts of relaxing in the air-conditioned cabin, completely removed from the bikes. And it wasn't just pure fantasy, was it? In about two months the bikes would be in a box and we would fly more distance in one day than we had cycled in more than a year. The ground would pass below effortlessly as I slept. The specks in the sky represented more than just planes. They were the mechanism with which I would be whisked away from all this and dumped so abruptly in another world. Usually, I found myself dreading the thought of Australia, but in my current state, I found comfort in the idea.

From a high saddle we snaked downhill towards the city that glittered in the evening light. Ulaan Baatar was a collection of apartment blocks, *ger* tents and factories, all squeezed into a steep-sided river valley. It had seemed like such an exotic place for so long. Back in Babushkina people had laughed at the idea of China and Mongolia; now Mongolians laughed in disbelief when we told them of our starting point. The significance of the moment boosted our morale and we took a break at the 'Welcome to Ulaan Baatar' sign.

After days of riding on almost car-free roads we found ourselves swept along in the throng of Ladas and expensive four-wheel drives. A couple of farmers herding their yaks to market were having trouble keeping them off the road. Drivers tooted in frustration and fists came waving out of windows.

Everything – from the apartment blocks, the power station and street layout – were of Soviet design. From a distance it appeared like another Russian city. Yet close up it differed greatly – it was far more congested and chaotic. Elderly men wandered the cluttered streets in the traditional *dele*, shoulder to shoulder with teenage girls dressed in skin-tight pants and platform shoes. There were people wandering around with mobile phones and others carrying bloodied sheepskins on their backs. Some men rode horses on the pavement.

The outer suburbs were a sight neither of us had anticipated: thousands of *ger* tents boxed in by shanty fences of scrap metal and scavenged timber. Each had its own postal address and a minuscule patch of dirt to call home. In a land of wide, open spaces it struck me as bizarre.

As we neared the city centre I had the feeling that life here lacked the vitality of the countryside. Smog collected above the city, turning the sky a pasty grey. The streets, plagued with potholes, were thickly layered in dust. Road workers could be seen sweeping the dust out of gutters and into crude pans, collecting it in rubbish bags; the rubbish disposal system looked horrific. In the courtyards between apartment blocks, adjacent to playgrounds, were enormous metal waste units full of burning debris. Everything from plastics to food scraps was thrown in and set alight, sending putrid black smoke billowing through the cramped living quarters.

In our first hour we saw more bikes than during our entire time in Russia. Children rode cheap but new Chinese-made mountain bikes fitted out with shiny modern parts. Later on we discovered that you could buy 100 puncture repair patches for fifty cents. In Russia we hadn't been able to find one puncture repair kit in 5,000 kilometres.

We agreed that the best plan of attack was to rent an apartment for ten days. The time was needed not just for rest and recuperation, but also for getting Chinese visas, extending our Mongolian ones, and organising plane tickets for the flight to Australia.

I phoned Zula, a woman we had met on the road from Suchbaatar. With the help of her family we soon found a place close to the city centre. Unfortunately, the apartment didn't have beds, and only one light was in working order, but for the time being it was a little patch of paradise.

Our time in Ulaan Baatar began with great promise. I was delighted to find that the streets of the inner city were cluttered with cheap restaurants selling all forms of greasy, fried mutton. A short walk would suddenly turn into an eating marathon as I found it hard to pass by without stopping in each and every shop. My favourite snacks were *khuushurs*, which are a flattened balls of mutton deep-fried in pastry. At five cents a piece there was no stopping me. As they slid down my throat, and the oil spilled over my lips, fast lubricating my beard and sweaty fingers, I fell into moments of pure ecstasy. Even with my stomach at near bursting point, I couldn't help indulging. I was making up for all those desperately hungry times. I spent the first couple of afternoons snoozing in the apartment, my grin oiled with mutton fat. I dreamed of food to come and food past.

While I ate myself towards obesity, Chris was relishing the other luxury of Ulaan Baatar – a million and one Internet cafés. He disappeared early in the morning and returned late at night after epic sessions of indulgence.

On the third day things took a downward turn. After a whirlwind tour to the Buddhist monastery and the *ger* suburbs, we fronted up to the Chinese embassy. Up until this point we had not planned, or even given thought, to the logistics of getting to Beijing. The man at reception was categorical in his response: we could not travel by bicycle through China without the permission of the Chinese Tourist Authority.

The problem with travel in China is that the law restricted foreigners to travel only by government-approved transport. This was probably in place to prevent tourists from straying into 'closed' areas. Getting permission would mean having a Chinese tour guide.

Was this the end then? In a wave of panic we rushed out of the embassy to quell our nerves by writing e-mails of distress. Finishing short of our goal would feel empty. As tired as we were, I was ready for more adventure. Or, rather, I would do anything for more breathing space between now and getting home.

We shot off e-mails to other adventure cyclists, and put up our problem on the message boards of travel websites. After a couple of hours of fierce writing and a few *khuushurs,* I returned to the embassy determined.

Eventually, I came to the front of the queue. 'Hello, I just had some more queries about travelling by bicycle in China.'

'All I can say is that you can't,' the man cut me off angrily.

'Okay. But I was wondering if there are any considerations at all, if the expedition is official, and we have contacts in China?' I asked, pleadingly.

'All I can say is no. Maybe you can, but maybe you can't.'

I stormed from the counter, feeling confused, only to be approached by a lanky European. 'I hear that you are wanting to go by bike in China?' he said. 'Well, don't worry about the embassy too much – don't take them so seriously.' He ushered me outside. 'I have personally ridden a bike in China and, in fact, I know there are people riding there all the time. It's just getting across the border that can be difficult. Just don't tell the embassy you are taking a bike, it's as simple as that.'

A couple of days later we were given visas hassle-free. The only obstacle ahead, we reasoned, would be smuggling our bikes over the border.

Meanwhile, Chris was trying to find the best deal on the Internet for a plane ticket. We had discovered that the cheapest option would be to catch a train from Beijing to Hong Kong, and fly from there. I wanted no part in the ticket discussion. I was reluctant to accept that we were going to be in Australia in the not too distant future. I felt irritated by Chris's persistence, and even more so by his excitement.

When the evening of our tenth and final day arrived, it felt like the end of a prison sentence; contrary to my hopes Ulaan Baatar had not been a good place to recuperate. We were desperate to escape. As we packed I listened to the opening ceremony of the Sydney Olympics on BBC world radio through the one working earphone of my Walkman. It would probably be the first and last we'd hear of the Olympics before they were over. There was, I conceded, a part of me that longed to share the excitement that was going on so far away.

Eventually, late in the evening, we cycled out of Ulaan Baatar. I trained my sights on the black horizon beyond the city's perimeters. Perhaps it was out there that our real refuge lay – in the peace and simplicity of a camp site.

Despite the exhaustion we awoke early, desperate to get beyond view of the city. As dawn broke, the shadows of night peeled away to reveal a puzzling reality. The bitumen had come to an abrupt end. Beyond it, countless dusty wheel tracks trailed off into the distance. There were no signs and no indication that one wheel track was used more often than another. We consulted our map.

'Hey, Chris, which do you reckon is the right route?' I asked.

'Mate, I'm buggered if I know. I guess, in theory, if we just keep heading south-east we'll end up in China,' he replied.

I looked at our tourist map – it was a big yellow blank with a couple of fat red and black lines denoting the train line and the only paved road in Mongolia, from Suchbaatar to Ulaan Baatar. With no contour lines and very few details besides a few happy-looking camels and yaks sketched on for decoration, we were going to have to rely on compass and intuition.

'I guess you're right. We can't really get lost anyway, because we will never know where we are with this blasted map,' I replied.

'I guess if we really get stuck, we just have to remember which side of the train line we're on,' said Chris. He was referring to the fact that our route would vaguely follow the path of the trans-Mongolian railway.

So, choosing the wheel tracks that headed for the easiest gradient in sight, we trundled off. Exactly how long it would take to get to China we didn't know. We approximated that it was 900 kilometres away, but that would depend almost entirely on road conditions. What we did know was that between us and the Chinese border lay a vast stretch of the infamous Gobi Desert.

A couple of hours later we had covered about ten kilometres, and in the last thirty metres of steep uphill climbing I had fallen five or six times. Steeling myself, I sat on the saddle and focused again – I wasn't going to let this stupid track get the better of me. I let go of the brakes and put my legs into action, pedalling as fast as humanly possible. I relied on some speed for balance but I was still going at about half walking-pace. Then, suddenly, the front wheel slid out in some loose rock and I flicked my feet down to earth in an attempt to stay upright. But it was too late. My brakes failed, the bike rolled backwards, my feet skidded hopelessly along the ground and the top-heavy baggage began to lean over. All I could do was try to leap clear of the enormous dead weight as it gained momentum and went plummeting downhill. Wild-eyed I dived towards a patch of pebbly earth that bore the only tuft of grass in sight. I wasn't fast enough.

First came the painful crunch in my hips as I hit the gritty earth. I wanted to punch the earth back. But I was distracted by another blow as the bike thundered down, trapping my right leg beneath the cogs. The sharp metal bit into my calf muscle. I ripped my leg away from the bike's jaw and performed a few commando rolls before rising in a cloud of dust to stare down my foe. It was too painful to stand still so I hopped around and threw handfuls of rocks into the sky. My leg was dripping blood that was already encrusted in sand and dust. It wasn't serious, just infuriating.

The bike lay in a heap, stubbornly refusing to go any further. I thought about giving it an almighty boot up the bum, but was put off when I noticed a horseman trotting by.

'This is bloody ridiculous!' I yelled. Never had the bike been so heavy and cumbersome. The prospect of few watering points meant that we were each carrying seventeen precious litres of water in Chinese jerry cans and soft drink bottles. Along with food for a week, our bikes and baggage weighed about ninety kilograms each.

I cast my gaze into the distance where a few sketchy lines constituted the only break in a land without contrast. A tiny black dot shimmered in the slight mirage, crawling along one of the sketchy lines – Chris.

My energy waned even further as I thought about the stakes. Not only was the bike heavy but I was more worn out than ever, and these were the worst roads we had come across. The prospect of 900 kilometres felt beyond me.

After a drink my nerves settled and I was ready to face the world again. I set off ambling down the track, keeping my eyes on the ground. Gradually, I began to make progress, steering around patches of crumbling rock and following the contours of the tracks. Funnily enough I discovered that it wasn't such a painful ride: without any way of gauging distance, distance itself didn't seem to matter. Hours merged and the rise and fall of hunger became the only indicator of passing time. I was free to move at my own pace, and the open nothingness formed a soothing backdrop. Sometimes it was good just to let the mind wander with thoughts as empty as space. As the sun plodded steadily towards the west my sweat began to cool and the earth came into clear focus.

The second day of riding merged into the first. The large rounded hills began to give way to a series of slightly raised plateaux, like a range of miniature tablelands. From a distance the curvy mounds looked like yellow crests on the sea. The sky melted with the hazy horizon. At times the heat mirage that licked the landscape with clear, molten flames was more real than the earth itself. Now and then we spotted *gers* in the distance but they were far more sparsely scattered than in northern Mongolia. We pedalled on, choosing our tracks on gut feeling and by the odd peek at the compass. Now and then a Russian-made truck or motorbike would hurtle by in a plume of dust and shrink out of sight. They could appear from any direction, rumbling over the steppe, and not necessarily following any tracks at all.

Even though it was only our second day, I was already losing track of time. It was like there was this vague empty land rolling beneath the wheels and I could only keep track of things by the day's events: camp, ride, eat, pee. But with the landscape and weather taking on such uniformity, even those common activities began to merge into one another. Had I peed before or after lunch? Have I had lunch, or was it yesterday's lunch I am thinking of? In the end it was irrelevant. If I am hungry I will eat, and if I am tired I will sleep, I thought. There were just enough signs of life to reassure us that we hadn't stepped off the edge of the world, and enough subtle changes in the landscape to indicate that we weren't living the same day over again. Perhaps the only reality check came from keeping an eye on how much water was left.

One evening we were riding casually along when, out of nowhere, came a young Mongolian man on a mountain bike. 'Hello, how are you?' he said, in English.

'Good ... thank you,' I replied, warily.

'I am a computer engineer. If you want you can come back to my mother's place to stay the night,' he offered.

I had been enjoying the ride but was still craving to spend time in a *ger*, and also to have some well-needed rest. Although Chris was a little bit resistant, this was an opportunity that had come knocking. I watched him bend from his hard-nosed, no stopping attitude to a carefree look.

'Yep, why not? Let's go!' he said.

Half an hour later we were sitting inside a *ger*, feeling as if we had been transplanted into another world. I watched as the elderly woman prepared to stoke the stove, which also doubled as the furnace. She opened it and I caught a glimpse of the red-hot fuel: fifty or so dried horse craps. After shovelling in a fresh load she gracefully drew a ladle of boiling milk half a metre above a pot and poured it back in with a fluid twist of her wrist. Not a drop was lost, as if the milk was somehow bound like elastic. A cloud of steam rose abruptly and escaped through the circular opening in the roof. The woman bent forward into the light that spilled down from above. Silver-grey hair fell from beneath a silky yellow hat. Her face was dark, almost black, and etched with lines that arced from above her eyes to below her cheeks. Prominent cheekbones bulged out, as rough, round and exposed as the steppe itself. Later we learned that she was seventy-five years old.

She stepped out of the light and I looked up to its source. I hadn't been in the *ger* for long, but even so I had taken a liking to the circular ceiling. Close to one hundred intricately decorated wooden rods rose to a small circular opening. Through this the slender chimney exited and the sky was visible. The rods were supported by walls of collapsible trellis. From beneath, the ceiling looked like a giant wagon wheel from which dangled a collection of drying fat pieces and sliced up sheep's organs.

Around the sides on the floor were a couple of mattresses, and close to the centre a few thirty-centimetre-high stools. There was a picture of Genghis Khan on the wall, and a special dresser with Buddhist tumblewheels, icons, candles and incense sticks displayed. The only sign of the modern world was a packet of Kodak Express photos on a tiny table.

In this round little space was housed all of the woman's possessions. With no dark corners, and in such a confined area, everything was on display. The amount of goods paled in comparison to the decadence of an average Australian room.

There was a very good reason, beyond lack of money, to stem the accumulation of material possessions. Most Mongolians in the countryside move at least twice a year, roaming to sites better suited to the changing seasons. They had to be able to bundle everything up, including the *ger*, and fit it onto the back of a wagon. After a year of carrying everything on the bikes, we understood this principle very well: nonessential items usually got the flick. In fact there were many parallels between our travel reality and the Mongolian way of life. For one, the Mongolians were the first people we met who didn't blink an eyelid at the fact that we rarely washed. To them, living in a tent and spending the day outdoors was the norm – it was just that we rode strange bicycles rather than horses. Of course these parallels were pretty shallow, too. While we had to cope with different weather conditions, they had to survive and be self-sustainable. It was pretty obvious that they were born into a life of hardship far more demanding than riding a bike across the country could ever be.

'*Uszhen gotov!*' she announced eventually. (We never did find out what her name was.) This was Russian for dinner is ready! We were astounded to learn that she spoke fluent Russian, and had lived and worked in Moscow in government administration during the Soviet Union.

The woman moved over to me with the large pot and opened it. 'What do you think, boys? Bon appetit!' she boomed with a cackle.

I froze. In the middle of the simmering milk floated the head of a goat: skin, eyes, ears and all. A smell wafted out like a shitted-up milking shed.

'Tim, have you ever tried goat's ear before?' the woman asked.

With a short knife she deftly sliced off a rubbery white bit and held it out. I turned to Chris, who was looking on with just as much anticipation as the mother and son.

I took a hard bite of the warm slimy cartilage and smiled. I chewed for about twenty minutes but just couldn't break it down. Eventually, I swallowed it whole and looked despairingly at the rest of the ear still in my hand. A little embarrassed, I handed it back to the computer engineer. I presumed that it would get passed around and eaten collectively. But, he threw it out the door for the dogs.

'Oh, actually, Tim, we don't usually eat goat's ear,' he said. 'We just thought it was something new for you. The good stuff is the eyes and also the lips. Here, try some.'

Thankfully, the main meal was a delicious bowl of homemade noodles with pieces of mutton. It was followed by goat cheese and yoghurt mixed with sugar and blueberries. The woman, like babushkas in Russia, was adamant that we ate until we couldn't possibly fit more in.

'Boys, boys, boys! Your family must be so worried about you. You are too skinny, eat, eat, eat!' she repeated, shrilly. From there on we decided that she really was the equivalent of a Mongolian Baba Galya: generous, hospitable and jovially eccentric.

With the setting of the sun, there was nothing more to do than settle in for sleep and bask in the feeling of an overly full stomach. We lay our sleeping mats down and slipped under the blankets.

'What a day, hey?' I said to Chris, with a sigh of relief.

'Yeah, I reckon,' came his sleepy response. The babushka blew out the candle and wriggled into her own bed, a foot away from ours. She softly conversed with her son and eventually silence fell.

I listened carefully, feeling cosy and secure in the intimate dwelling. The roaring cold wind that blew outside was barely audible, muffled by the thick felt walls. I could also just make out the sound of a herd of animals approaching with a thousand soft thuds upon the earth. Then, with a cacophony of snorts, they too came to rest. It occurred to me that the animals were like an extended family and they felt safe huddled up next to the *ger*.

I adjusted my eyes to the starry patch of sky visible through the circular hole in the ceiling. Eventually the stars petered out just like the candle.

I awoke once during the night, shivering in the cold with an ice-cream headache. The stove had burnt out and the temperature had plummeted to below zero. I didn't envy the babushka as she woke too, hyperventilating before putting on her warm *dele*. She lit the stove and went back to bed.

Dawn was marked by the rustle of animals rising and a light rain falling. I stumbled into the gloom, bent on capturing the sunrise on film. Before the sun had nudged over the horizon, the babushka and an old man from a neighbouring *ger* washed their faces with a splash of cold water before ambling over to a couple of sedate-looking yaks. I filmed as they sat side by side squeezing rhythmically at teats, often breaking out in laughter.

Around them a herd of about fifty goats, four horses and a few sheep frolicked in anticipation of the first warm rays of the sun. When the sun rose the babushka lugged a bucket of fresh milk over to the *ger*. Next the old man set to catching a couple of goats to clip their hooves; he took chase with a lasso. Through the lens it was obvious that although these people were living a life of survival, there was a real art to it.

No matter how exhausted I was, filming was something that energised me. I loved it, and in recent weeks I had begun to believe that maybe, just maybe, if I kept on trying, we really could make a documentary about our journey.

Chris rose late with good reason: he felt ill. We spent another day and a half with the family, and in that time learnt more about Mongolian life than we had done in the past three weeks. Much of that time we spent drinking the famous *airag* – fermented mare's milk. It came in large bowls, with the added ingredient of a few belly-up blowflies. It was sour and off-putting at first, but I grew to like it. It was slightly alcoholic, and the babushka kept telling us that you could 'live off the stuff'.

Finally, we straddled our bikes and rolled downhill, waving goodbye as the babushka threw ladles of fresh milk into the air for good luck.

Then it was back to the open, almost featureless landscape; crawling into the distance, rolling along on our armchairs on wheels.

A couple more days passed in a blur of parched yellow and the sour taste of *airag*. Our stop with the babushka seemed to have opened the floodgates to Mongolian hospitality. Sometimes trucks would come hurtling out of nowhere and a great big bowl of *airag* and blowflies would be handed down to us. If it wasn't a truck it was a horseman waving us over to another *ger* in the distance.

The hills flattened out altogether until we were on a wide crusty plain. It was so flat that from the low position on the bike only a sliver of earth was visible in every direction. The track became red and sandy, trailing its way through avenues of thorny grass. I felt like we were riding through a moonscape of crushed dry rock beneath a sky that seemed larger than usual. We began to see herds of camels loping across the horizon in search of food.

There was something melancholy and appealing in the openness, and for long periods of time I had no wish to stop pedalling. It left me feeling exposed, as if I couldn't hide anything, even from myself. I remembered the e-mail from my youngest brother Cameron that I had received in Ulaan Baatar, and began to think ahead to Australia rather than reminiscing about Russia.

He had described his excitement about having his braces taken off his teeth. Then, at the very bottom of the letter, he noted that I had never even seen him with braces on. I hadn't been in Australia in twenty-seven months. Especially for teenagers, a lot could change in that time. For heaven's sake, Cameron was thirteen when I had last seen him, and he would be almost sixteen by the time I arrived home!

Jon, two years younger than me, had completed school and was late into his second year living away from home, studying at university. The picture I carried in my head of him was still of a Year Eleven schoolboy. In childhood he had been my best friend, someone I did everything with. I hoped we hadn't grown too far apart. Then there was Natalie, my seventeen-year-old sister. I had been shocked to see how she had grown during her visit to Russia last winter. I wondered how things were panning out in her life as she approached her last year of school.

Somewhere underneath I was beginning to accept the reality of returning to Australia ... and I was looking forward to it. I also had a sneaking suspicion that if we worked damn hard, we could even write a book as well as make a doco! The faster I got back, the faster I could set off on a new journey.

Mongolia, I thought, was the perfect buffer zone. On the home-straight, everything seemed to be crystallising rather than falling to pieces.

Although I had mentally overcome a hurdle, I couldn't afford to assume that we would have a clean run to the finish line. Just outside the small town of Choyr, I was reminded that our journey wasn't all about rosy contemplation.

All night I tossed and turned with growing nausea. It felt as if someone was playing a game of pinball in my stomach and bowels. It verged on agony as I farted heavily, and knew with a sinking feeling that my diarrhoea was far from gone.

Eventually, it came in one great rush. In my desperation, I dived outside and made it just two metres from the tent before an explosion splattered the earth. It was below zero outside, and in my underwear and bare feet I was instantly a shivering mess. The bouts continued for twenty minutes. Progressively I froze in the squat position, unable to grab my down jacket. The wind was the worst of all – it cut like an evil, cold knife. Although it was a relief to return to bed, in half an hour I was out there again. The constant activity made me thirsty, and I discovered to my dismay that our scant water supplies had frozen solid. I scampered out five times before I lost count and began to worry about the deadly landmines that I was leaving around the camp.

I had been asleep for an hour or so when I was woken by horses gently pressing the tent with their snouts and snuffling. I opened the door to see a curious herd silhouetted by the predawn hues. Their manes shivered in the breeze far more fluidly than my body had done all night. This would be a routine that carried on for weeks ahead into China. Herds of horses and camels would surround the tent just on dawn and wake us. It was a special time of morning, when the earth seemed to be exhaling and at its calmest. I thought I might as well get up and do some filming.

By the time Chris rose, I was lying on the dirt outside, cradling the video camera and staring blankly at the tent. I had watched as the frost rose in a vapour with the first rays of the sun. I didn't have the energy to talk and preferred to keep still; it felt like someone had been kicking me in the guts all night. Thank God it's Chris's turn to cook, I thought.

It was mind destroying to wonder how many debilitating nights lay before the refuge of China. The intense cold was another worrying factor – it felt like we were being chased by the onset of winter; frostbite was the last thing I wanted.

'Chris, don't bother with sugar or milk in the porridge. I don't think I can stomach it,' were the only words I could manage.

After breakfast Chris joined me in the dirt and we spread out the gimmicky map between us. For a few days we'd been planning to diverge from the line of the trans-Mongolian and do a 300 kilometre loop into nowhere and rejoin the railway at Sainshand. With several trucks a day passing we had been yearning to go out and see what it was really like away from this major route.

'So what do you reckon?' I asked Chris.

'I don't know. I'd love to get out there. It's just that we aren't in good shape at the moment. It would be harder, but definitely more interesting. What do you think?' he asked.

'Yeah, I agree.'

Somehow, as perverse as it seemed, we decided to take the plunge. With waves of nausea still flowing from my stomach, I was agonisingly aware that we were choosing to make life harder.

In Choyr we filled up with some salty, sulphur-smelling water that was pumped up from a well. It was selling at one cent for every ten litres and was considered very good quality by Gobi standards.

On the way out we asked for directions to the tiny settlement of Ondershil. The men swung their arms out in an arc pointing towards one of any number of tracks that wound aimlessly into the distance. With the compass and some guesswork we set off.

For the next two days we saw little transport, and the only *gers* were tiny flecks in the distance. Time passed and I fell into a lethargic daze. The corrugations and bumps threatened to upset my stomach completely, and the headwind continued unabated. I ate almost nothing except some dry, tasteless biscuits and stopped frequently to relieve my bowels. The nights were plagued with the same draining theatrics, making sleep scarce. This left me constantly thirsty, yet anything I drank and ate went straight through. To make it worse, we had rationed out the drinking water to 1.5 litres per person per day, so there was little water to waste.

The further we headed away from the railway, the wilder the landscape became. The tracks were barely used, and we relied increasingly on guesswork.

On the third morning we came across a shallow lake. The water was brown, salty and only a couple of centimetres deep. But we decided it was the perfect location for an early lunch.

As we were cleaning up, my temper boiled over. For the past few days Chris had taken to licking the knife clean – again.

In the heat of the moment, I cracked. 'Chris, what are you doing licking the knife clean? I thought we decided last year that it was banned!'

'What! Since when? That's the way I do things. It's my knife. I don't think it's unhygienic and anyway, we don't have enough water to waste on cleaning.'

From there side-track arguments grew upon side-track arguments and we continued to scream insults at each other. It went on for an hour until we were both ready to pass out. For a while we slumped to the ground and lay panting for breath. Then we just started again.

By the time we finished I felt more exhausted than after a day's ride, when in fact we had only ridden about ten kilometres. From the lake we struggled five kilometres further and set up camp, agreeing that the day was as good as written off.

That night I had an ominous feeling that I was about to fall seriously ill. In a desperate attempt to revitalise myself I pulled out all the vitamin and mineral tablets I had and popped a couple of each. Then I found a concoction in a small bottle that was some kind of therapeutic oil. The Buryatian family had given it to me to use in case of bad health. I dabbed a bit onto my hands and rubbed it into the beard-free skin on my face and over my chest.

Morning brought with it the unfamiliar feeling of a settled stomach. I sat up and moved ... still no nausea. Chris was already up and for some unknown reason doing push-ups near the tent. With the sudden wave of good health, I decided to join him. Without saying anything, I lay down nearby and started pushing up and down like a maniac. I lasted fifteen before the sudden urge to vomit stopped me dead in my tracks, and I dropped to the dusty earth.

I heard Chris do the same, but he was laughing hard. 'Tim, what the hell have you done to yourself? Your face is bloody bright orange. That oil is for taking as a liquid, not an ointment, you silly bastard!'

I too would have laughed if it wasn't for the fear of throwing up.

The landscape changed yet again and we were met by a howling headwind. Before us rose pointy hills and wide slab-like plateaux. Over every rise, every new rocky saddle, there was another view stretching into the distance ... just hills, wind, vague tracks, hills beyond hills and hills beyond that again. The sea of yellow grass was replaced by the odd thorny tuft of growth and bushes sparsely scattered among the sand and rock. Geckoes often sprinted off in front of the bike wheels.

With the battle against diarrhoea pretty much lost, the only thread of sanity and inspiration came through my increasing obsession with filming. I went to bed dreaming of new angles, new shots, and wrote down lists of scenes that we had to shoot before Beijing. At times it felt as if the journey would never end. And yet time was running out for filming. The shot I wanted most was a silhouette of us riding against a sunset or sunrise. There would be two projects finishing for me in Beijing: the film and the cycling journey. And I couldn't relax until both were over.

We passed through the tiny outpost of Bayanjargalan and continued on to Ondershil. From there we would aim back towards the railway line.

In the late afternoon I was rolling down a sandy, rutted part of the road when I was startled by a shriek from behind. The front wheel dug in and I fell into the sand. I spun in the direction of the voice.

A horseman with a dusty face was staring down at me. In his hand he held a long pole and a lasso. His *dele* was faded and in tatters from years of use. He looked enquiringly, cocking his head, before pointing over a hill, then at Chris and I; an invitation to his *ger*? We had stopped at countless *gers* since the Mongolian babushka experience, but only once since turning off from Choyr. I was keen to spend some time with these 'wilder' Mongolians.

Chris wasn't so enthused, but after some coercion he agreed. We followed the horseman as his *dele* flailed wildly and his horse stirred up a cloud of dust. After some time we came to a pair of *gers*. They were plonked adjacent to a dry sandy riverbed. One was being used for cooking and the other for sleeping.

The horseman's family were as fascinated by us as we were of them. The man's mother and children stared at us, and we stared back. As they didn't speak a word of Russian, conversation was limited, bringing the focus on to food.

Dinner began with a wok of a mash that tasted like sour uncooked cake mixture. The smell alone made me feel nauseous. But I had trouble explaining that I was sick and was fearful of offending. Next came a large bowl of fermented horse milk, complete with flies. I had been feeling marginally better during the day and worried that eating would bring it all on again. But what could I do?

After five or six cups of salty Mongolian milk tea and some homemade noodles with mutton, I lay in the *ger* clutching my stomach. For hours into the night, I tossed and turned, moaning with pain. Eventually, I stumbled out and vomited. Come morning, I had barely slept and felt severely hungover. The thought of more milk and mutton would probably set off another spasm.

I rose from bed warily, careful not to make any sudden movements. No sooner had I rubbed my eyes than I was whisked away by our host. He knew one word of Russian. 'Meat! Meat!' he cried.

He dragged me over to the herd of sheep and without hesitation grabbed one by the neck and flipped it onto its back. While the poor animal shook and shivered uncontrollably, he took a knife and made a neat slit down its chest. He pushed his fist through the slit into the rib cage and pulled out the heart. It sat pulsating for a while above the animal's chest and I thought I saw its eyes look down in terror, then begin to flit like it was in REM, before the shaking reached a peak. Finally, it went still: all over within a few seconds. The man poked at the animal's eyes until there was no response at all. The tongue hung loose from its mouth and the heart was dropped back into the cavity and the limp carcass dragged over to the *ger*. If I'd been feeling pale before, now I was close to fainting.

Our host was eager for me to take part in the butchering. He handed me a knife and I began to cut as he directed. Even though it took intense concentration to control my stomach, I marvelled that I had become devoid of emotion so quickly: it was just a slab of meat now that it was dead.

When we finished, the innards were slopped into a big bowl and sorted out by the mother. She squeezed the faeces out of the intestines and refilled them with blood. Meanwhile, the meat was heaved up on top of the *ger* for drying.

Hoping that our job was done, Chris and I prepared to leave. But we hadn't bargained on breakfast.

As a reward for helping with the slaughter, we were treated to a feast: a steaming pot of boiled intestines, liver, heart and head. The stench inside the stuffy *ger* was overpowering. Chris and I were given a knife each and told in sign language to dig in.

The family laughed, chewed, slurped, sucked and gnawed on the sinewy brown boiled mutton. The sounds of Chris eating paled in comparison to this family – they were real masters at orchestrating a symphony of revolting, irritating noises. Inevitably, we too cut off bits of intestine and sheep's lips, but we were amateurs. It was more like chew, spit, chew, swallow with a look of distaste, and then gingerly pick out another delightful little treat from the communal bowl.

With this last chore over and done with, we rode off. Over the first hill and out of sight of the *gers* we dumped the bikes and collapsed in a heap on the ground.

'Bloody hell, from now on I reckon we should try to stop only for civilized Mongolians. I just don't think I could have taken much more of that,' Chris said, spitting out a leftover bit of intestine from between his teeth.

'As much as I love the notion of this nomadic culture, I have to agree with you. There's not much romance in it when it comes down to it,' I said, rolling over in case I needed to throw up.

'Hey, I've got a thought for you. How does sliced supermarket bread, a meat pie, and homecooked lasagne sound?' Chris said.

We decided to cook up a more palatable breakfast of semolina before continuing. A flush of shame and embarrassment came over us when, mid-way through eating, we turned to see our horseman friend on the hilltop. Presumably he had come out to check on our progress, only to find us scoffing down more food.

After the meal, I put foot to pedal rather gingerly. Chris was already a speck fast approaching the warped heat mirage on the horizon. I didn't get far before dropping the bike and falling to the usual retching position. I watched the intestines lather a patch of rock shards. The foul sight gleamed in the bright white glow of the sun.

I hadn't kept any food down for twenty-four hours. I wondered what the Gobi still had in store for us.

Later that day, between running out of toilet paper and discovering that my bike frame was breaking in half for the third time, a thought struck me: it was Chris's birthday.

For a couple of hours I tried to think of the best way to congratulate him. In the afternoon I finally caught up.

'Hey Chris, you old bastard!'

He grinned wryly and so did I.

Blood, Sweat and Sand

Gobi Desert – Inner Mongolia

Late Autumn 2000

Chris

Cathy Freeman won an Olympic gold medal on the day I turned twenty-two. It was 25 September and the 2000 Olympic games were well under way. Cathy Freeman was winning gold, Ian Thorpe was smashing world records and we were riding peacefully through the desert. Apart from the opening ceremony, I had not the faintest idea of what was going on.

I sat by the tent, stirring the dinner and letting my mind wander over obscure parallels. Sydney was hosting one of the biggest sporting events in history. Thousands of cameras were beaming pictures to billions of people all over the world. The Gobi Desert was hosting my birthday, and it had about as much significance as a camel burping. Admittedly, Tim was catching the action on our little video camera, but even he hadn't remembered until halfway through the afternoon.

But then, why should he? I laughed at myself and swivelled around to take in the surroundings.

We were in the middle of a desert and all morning, we'd seen only endless expanses of salt-bush and a few camels on the horizon. Days ran into one another and dates had no meaning at all. If anyone had asked us the day of the week, we'd have had, at best, a one in seven chance at the right answer. What relevance did my birthday have out here, anyway? It was twenty-two years after the actual event and the passing of the day hadn't marked anything significant.

Tim was up the hill, filming. He steadied the camera on its tripod, hit 'record', then raced back down the slope and skidded to a stop beside me. We were acting out a celebration.

Carefully I opened the present I'd bought for myself back in Choyr. 'Look, it's a block of chocolate!' (Surprise, surprise.) 'Wow. Here, you have half of it, mate.' I offered the block to Tim. 'Good, isn't it?'

Tim raced off to film another angle, and I laughed. At first I'd been annoyed when Tim wanted to film us 'enjoying' my birthday, rather than simply enjoying it with me. But, in the end, what did it really matter?

I crawled out of the tent the next morning to catch the sun sneaking stealthily over the horizon. I yawned and stretched away the stiffness from my joints, then stumbled out into the cold wind to pee, scanning the ground quickly to make sure that I wasn't about to step on any of Tim's overnight 'landmines'. The shorter daylight hours in Mongolia had given us a great routine of eleven hours' sleep per night, but we hadn't covered much ground over the past few days.

We rode strongly all morning to reach the town of Ondershil. It was a rambling town made up of the traditional white *gers* partitioned off into neat square blocks by ramshackle fences.

We did our shopping for the next four or five days in all three of the village shops, then looked around for a place to fill up the fuel bottle for our stove. In the end, we had to visit the town's diesel-fired power station and ask the operator to siphon a litre of fuel from the generator's 10,000 gallon tank!

We finished our chores and packed our bikes, chatting for a short while to a group of people who had gathered around. Just as we were about to pedal off, however, we heard an urgent cry from behind us.

'Waaaiiiittt!' came the shout, in heavily accented Russian. We turned to see a short, stocky man rushing importantly through the crowd, holding a bottle of vodka. He also had a few dirty glasses tucked under one arm.

'Wait, my friends!' He panted as he came to a halt. 'Before you leave, you must drink with us!' He turned to the crowd for confirmation and got a rousing cheer. He glanced back to catch me grimacing. 'No, no, no,' he chided, waving the bottle. 'You *must* drink before you leave. It is an honour!' I looked at Tim and he winced.

'Okay, okay. Thank you for the honour. We will drink, but just one, you understand?' Tim waved a single finger at the man. 'Just one!'

'All right then, we will each drink one.' The man quickly placed the three glasses on the ground then poured steadily, measuring the entire contents of the bottle into equal thirds.

'Just one,' he said solemnly, as he handed me the biggest shot of vodka I'd ever seen.

I gulped and looked helplessly at Tim, who was staring with dismay at his own glass. There was nothing for it. The crowd were chanting encouragement and waiting.

I licked my dry lips nervously, steeled my nerves and braced my body. Then, with a feeling of resignation, I poured the long draught of deathly liquid down my throat.

It hit my stomach like a car wreck and I instantly felt as though my chest had just been carved open with a red-hot butterknife. The backs of my eyelids pinged painfully with a billion multi-coloured stars and there was a sound like an endless, crashing wave in my ears. I staggered around a bit and shook my head to clear my brain. Tim was leaning on his bike, clutching his empty glass and looking ill. Our short friend was standing serenely nearby, an imbecilic smile spreading across his face.

We hopped back on our bikes and pedalled away as fast as possible. We were only wobbling slightly.

We rode out of town that afternoon with a raging tailwind, and blasted a further sixty kilometres on a rough and corrugated dirt track. Along the way, we passed a white felt *ger* with a satellite dish outside the door. Buddhist nomad culture, unchanged in centuries, meets western technology.

We made camp in a wind so strong that we had to lie Tim's bike down and tie ropes to it to anchor the tent. Tim was still suffering badly with a stomach bug and after a little experimenting had found that the only things that he could keep down were plain oats and water, or macaroni. I cooked up my own delicious meal of steaming borsch soup and ate it as he sat gnawing on a crust of bread and shivering in the icy wind. I thought back to the hotel room in Omsk, where I'd been in a similar condition and he'd come back from the market with a bag of hot potato pies.

With a grin, I offered him some of my soup. 'Mmmm. Jeez, this is really delicious. It really warms up the insides. Are you absolutely sure you don't want some? Just before I finish the lot, see.'

Tim scowled at me. 'Piss off, ya mean bastard. I'm feeling terrible.'

Next morning the wind was blowing as strong as ever. The only difference was that it had turned during the night and was now coming from the opposite direction. The anchor line tied to Tim's bike was useless and the tent was flapping crazily about our heads. We crawled out into the freezing gloom of pre-dawn and found that, once again, our water bottles had iced over.

We huddled over the roaring, belching diesel stove as Tim cooked breakfast. Then I packed up and set out – riding in all my clothes – while Tim sheltered out of the wind behind his bike to watch the sunrise and update his diary.

About mid-morning I was startled out of a daydream by the sound of galloping horse hooves. I pulled on the brakes and looked up to see a young Mongolian man in traditional dress grinning curiously down at me.

'Sa sainbaino,' he greeted me politely and I responded in kind. I asked him in careful Mongolian if he spoke Russian or English. This was one of my few and definitely most useful, phrases. The man beamed at me with a gleaming white smile and replied with an eager shake of his head that he didn't. I tried again in a few Mongolian monosyllables and sign language and we got a bit of a conversation going. I understood enough to realise that he was inviting me back to his ger for some tea.

I shared a few mugs of the delicious milky and slightly salty Mongolian brew with the man and his family, and was obliged to have a few nibbles of sour goat's cheese biscuits as well. I walked around the back of the ger to admire his herd of about forty goats, wandering across the nearby hillside. I stayed for about half an hour then set off to catch up with Tim.

We covered a lot of ground on a long and terrible track during the course of the afternoon. The corrugations were shocking, and I alternated between a splitting headache from the constant bouncing and falling over in the sand as I left the track in search of a smoother route. Tim, on the other hand, was feeling great; zooming along somewhere in front he didn't stop for lunch until three. The next day, however, the tables were turned. I was feeling fantastic and raced off, leaving Tim to follow in my dusty tyre-tracks, miles behind.

I stopped to wait for him not far from Sainshand and we rode in together the following morning.

Our first priority was to find food and lots of it. We pedalled up a rare strip of bitumen – the first we'd seen in over a week – then veered off the road and came to a stop outside the door of the first eating house we saw.

It was locked. We prepared to ride on in search of another, but the small crowd that had gathered urged us to stay. They were also waiting for the café to open too, it appeared, and one of the men spoke a little Russian. 'The chief lady will be here soon!' he informed us brightly.

We went through the standard routine of answering questions about our trip. One man asked our Russian-speaking friend to get us to translate some ridiculous techno-babble written in English on the back of a Chinese paint tin. The misspelt, ungrammatical English was challenge enough on its own and what we did manage to translate into Russian, our Russian-speaking friend could not understand well enough to translate into Mongolian. In the end, after ten minutes of heated discussions, we settled on an approximate, one-word summary that survived the trip through all three languages: 'Paint.'

The paint tin owner stared at us in stunned silence, then walked away looking distinctly dissatisfied.

An hour and a half after we'd arrived we finally met the 'chief lady'. She marched up to the door with another woman in tow – the assistant chief lady, I assumed – and cut a path through the crowd and up the steps. The crowd melted away. It seemed that they hadn't been waiting for opening time after all.

Once inside, we sat down ravenous and ready to order but, to our dismay, we had to wait another half hour while they scrubbed the pots from the previous night. By the time our meal finally arrived, my head was resting on the table and Tim had slipped from his chair, a slowly dying pile on the floor.

The food was worth waiting for, though. Hot noodle soup! Afterwards, Tim stripped the baggage from his bike and headed into town to find someone to add yet another layer of welding to his cracked bike frame. Meanwhile, I sortied down to the small but bustling market to restock our food supplies.

On the way back, I was startled almost out of my skin by the unexpected sound of a Scottish voice calling out from behind. 'Oi! Hallo there. You must be a foreigner then. Where are you from?' A lightly built, orange-haired man wearing jeans and sneakers and carrying a briefcase was angling across the road towards me.

'I'm an Australian,' I answered, curious. 'There's two of us, actually. We're just passing through. How about you? Do you live here or something?' Sainshand was a town of no more than a few thousand people. It was hard to imagine what this man could be doing there.

'I've only been here in Sainshand for about a year now, but I've been in Mongolia itself for over five years. Officially, I work for the Mongolian government teaching English to a few paying students. But really, I'm actually working here as a missionary.'

'Oh yeah, what sort of things do you do then?

'Well, the people on the land – the nomads – have generally been all right. But last winter was terrible. It got to minus fifty degrees and a lot of people lost a lot of their livestock and are now struggling to survive. And, of course, their children grow up without any education at all, so that's one of the things that we're trying to address. And in the towns, like this one, things have been going pretty much downhill since the Russians pulled out in ninety one. There's a lot of poverty now, so we're trying to help people as much as we can.'

'I see.' It seemed fair enough. 'How many people can you help, though?'

'We have limited resources, of course, but everyone in the town knows that we're here and we try to help those who come to us. We have a little school and a church where we teach people about Jesus. And we also have funding to help them buy food and clothing, or livestock for the nomads when they need help.'

'Okay, so are there many Christians in the town then?' I had read that nearly 100 per cent of Mongolia's population were devout Buddhists.

'We have a little flock of over two hundred here now, but can you imagine? When we first arrived a year ago, there were no Christians here at all! We're growing faster all the time, too.' He smiled happily. 'About six months ago we were able to send a couple of the younger men over to America to train with our organisation and hopefully, they'll become ordained before returning. They're due back by the end of the year, so we'll be able to leave them to run things by themselves while we move on to another town.' He smiled again and glanced at his watch. 'Oops! Late for choir practise. Sorry, I can't stay to chat, but it's been nice talking to you. Goodbye.'

He hurried off and I was left standing by the roadside with my shopping bags, wondering uncertainly. I admire much about Christianity, and the material help they were giving must have been invaluable to the locals. But I'd always been dubious about zealous missionaries spreading mass conversion through 'undeveloped' countries. Now I'd finally met one first-hand and, try as I might, I couldn't shake the image of this orange-haired Scotsman and his friends spreading their version of God across this land of age-old Buddhist beliefs like an infectious disease. With his words still fresh in my mind, it was hard not to picture churches and gospel-singing choirs popping up all over a country where once ancient Buddhist orders and monasteries had been.

Later, after returning home, I saw a documentary about the missionaries on television. The process was known as 'Cash for Conversion'.

We rode south along the railway with only one more village and 220 kilometres of unknown tracks between us and the Chinese border. At lunchtime, the day after we left Sainshand, we were passed by a motorcyclist on an expensive Japanese machine. The driver said he was heading to the next town of Ulaan Ule and, as that was also on our route, I figured that we could forget about our own navigation and simply follow the distinctive tracks of his slick tyres through the sand for the next 100 kilometres or so.

It was a relief, for once, to forget about picking a route along the myriad intersecting tracks. We hadn't seen a road sign since leaving Russia; and our map usually only showed one road where, in fact, there were many.

For the past month I'd been keeping an excited count of the days left until touchdown at Sydney airport. There were only twenty-nine and a half days to go before I would be reunited with Nat. In a week or so, I would let myself move on to counting down the hours ...

Paradoxically, the closer we got to the end, the slower I felt like going. The plane ticket was booked and the urge to constantly keep on moving had disappeared. Beijing was less than 1,000 kilometres away – we'd get there now, come what may. In the meantime, I was content just to cruise along, meeting people, daydreaming about the year ahead and enjoying the challenge of crossing the Gobi.

Tim, too, had resigned himself to going home. For both of us, the challenge of the past year had been an enormous physical and mental strain and I sensed that Tim was also ready to finish travelling – at least for a little while. He was still returning home to a large debt and uncertainty about his future, but in his own words, he was 'ready to finish up, consolidate, then move on to the next thing, whatever that might be'.

I pedalled lazily under the sun, following the motorcyclist's trail and gazing up at the long, fluffy trails of white jet vapour from an aeroplane that was crawling steadily across the sky. I kept going until I found a nice-looking camping spot out of the wind and close to the top of a low rocky hill, where I waited for Tim.

When he arrived, he was mad. 'What the bloody hell do you think you're doing?'

'Huh?'

'The railway tracks! Look back there at the bloody tracks, mate! The map's got the road following along the tracks on the *other* side of the bloody railway line. And now we're way to buggery off to the west.'

I looked at the map and saw that I had indeed diverged a long way from the line. I'd been in a dream world and had unthinkingly followed the motor-cyclist's trail through a major intersection and under the railway through a stock underpass.

'I'm sorry, I just wasn't thinking, I suppose.'

'Yeah, I know. It's just that you didn't even have the bloody map! Next time, just wait for me can't you, before you go making that sort of decision?'

It was fifteen kilometres back to the intersection where I'd made the wrong turn. The next morning we decided that we'd try our luck with the motorbike tracks, anyway. We pedalled on blind, still heading away from the railway, but we hadn't gone far when we ran across a broken-down four-wheel drive by the roadside.

An elegant-looking Mongolian lady was sitting inside and a pair of male shoes and trousers were sticking out from under the car. The lady greeted us politely in Russian. Tim extended his hand and she winced a little as she shook it. I tried to look at Tim from her perspective and realised with a start that neither of us had washed for over two weeks! The man wriggled out from under the engine and carefully wiped his hands on the back of his well-padded trousers.

'Where are you boys off to then?' he asked jovially in flawless Russian. 'I'm a trader – I import produce to Ulaan Baatar from over the border in China, and I've never seen anyone like you on anything like those out here before!'

We explained our story, then asked him whether the road we were on would take us to Ulaan Ule.

'To Ulaan Ule? *Ho, ho, ho*. No, it won't! *Ho, ho, ho*,' he laughed. 'This road takes you directly to China. *Ho, ho*. If you want to go to Ulaan Ule, you have to go about twenty kilometres back along the way you've come and then follow the railway. *Ho, ho, ho*.'

Tim gave me a meaningful look and I swore at the motorbike rider under my breath. We weren't carrying enough water to go directly to China.

'Do you know if there are any other roads which might take us toward Ulaan Ule from *here*?' I asked hopefully.

He chuckled again and waved an arm expansively in the direction of the featureless plains to the east. 'There are lots of tracks out there, boys. I'm sure that *one* of them might take you to Ulaan Ule, but which it is, I cannot say.'

He said goodbye, his wife gave us a couple of fat, red apples and they drove off, leaving us in a cloud of dust. We discussed the situation briefly, crunched the delicious juicy apples, then pedalled on – still towards China – and ready to take the first turnoff we could find.

Later that afternoon I sat at yet another junction in the wheel-tracks and waited for Tim. We'd turned off the road onto a track that had quickly dwindled and split up into many tracks. From there, we'd made decisions according to the compass and, occasionally, with the toss of a coin. We'd had lunch in a valley a little way back and had been passed by a curious mob of wild camels. Tim had gone off chasing them with the video camera, while I'd carried on, leaving a trail of tyre tracks for him and trying to make sense out of our position on the plain.

I considered the options for a moment, but all of a sudden I was startled from my thoughts by a weatherbeaten old woman who came wandering over the rise, waving a bright blue jacket around her head in giant, helicopter circles, yelling, '*Oiy-oiy-oiy-oiy-oiy!*' She broke off when she saw me and stared. I pedalled over to her to see if she could point me towards the railway.

We communicated, as usual, in sign language and my few Mongolian words. She understood my impression of a Thomas the Tank Engine, and said that yes, the '*chuf-chuf-chuf-chuf*' was certainly over that way, but (I think) that it wasn't due till tomorrow! She invited me back to her home for tea and I willingly accepted. As we walked over the rise and down towards her *ger*, twin boys of no more than five converged on us, each dragging a large hessian sack full of dry horse poo. They were her grandsons, it appeared. She'd been out looking for them.

Tim joined us, and we were treated first to tea, and then to a glorious lunch of noodle soup and chunks of meat. To me, this was a big improvement on the standard autumn fare of freshly boiled gizzards with the blood poured in. These people appeared to be civilized nomads and I was most impressed. Sure, they still had a few cultural peculiarities, like stirring the food with the dung-shovelling utensil, but every Mongolian we'd stayed with seemed to do that. These people washed their hands with soap!

An older boy in the family had a physical and intellectual disability. Instead of a wheelchair, he moved around on a homemade plank on wheels. The constant love and care of his family was deeply moving. Out here, it was all that kept him alive.

After lunch, the man of the family treated us to a magnificent display of horsemanship. He galloped around, wheeling his stocky mount hard and chasing his herd of unwilling horses until he caught an unruly young colt with a long, wooden lasso pole. The horses threw up billowing clouds of dust and their hooves shook the ground like thunder. The whole scene was magical, and I rode away later in the afternoon with the images of stampeding horses and Mongolian warriors etched firmly in my mind.

We stopped that night under a broad, leafy tree. We were in the middle of the desert and it was the first tree we'd seen in 1,000 kilometres! I could think of no explanation for its presence and it was so unusual that we called an early halt to camp under it.

Over dinner, we were treated to a spectacular show of colour as the sun sank below the desert horizon. I sat mesmerised, watching the drifting grey clouds beginning to cycle through an incredible, fiery spectrum of reds and oranges. Tim was frantically hurling clothing from his panniers in an attempt to find a fresh video camera battery.

'Quick, Chris,' he barked, firing off rapid instructions. 'Get your bike and get up to the top of that rise asap I want a silhouette shot in the next minute. *Come on*, mate!' he urged. 'Can't you see it'll be gone soon? We absolutely *have* to catch this scene on film!'

The next evening we camped a little way outside of Ulaan Ule. We'd equalled our longest-period-without-washing record of eighteen days, and were planning a special celebratory dinner with the only delicacy we'd been able to buy – a jar of pickles. When I sat down to fire up the stove, however, I saw that we were in trouble. 'Shit,' I said to Tim. 'I can't get this bloody stove to work.'

'Huh?' He hurried over. 'Here let me have a go.'

Tim carefully disassembled, cleaned, then reassembled the stove before banging it on a rock for good measure. He pumped pressure into the diesel canister, opened the valve and struck a match, but we could only watch blankly as again the yellow flame chuffed a few times and died. It appeared that after months on life-support, our struggling little MSR stove had belched its last.

There was nothing for it. We swallowed our western pride, stalked out to scan the ground and did as the locals do. We collected a big pile of dried horse crap and, after much time and effort, produced an exotic-flavoured, lukewarm meal on a campfire made of poo!

The next morning we entered the town of Ulaan Ule. I let a few kids clamber up onto the back of my bike, and they sat behind me on top of my packs as though they were simply climbing onto the back of a horse. I raced up and down the main street a few times with passengers on board. The little kids were loving it but one little girl took the horse riding analogy a bit too far and started yanking hard on my hair when she wanted me to turn. Enough was enough, I decided, and the game came to an abrupt stop.

We filled up our water bottles and food bags and were given some vague directions to get us to the border. When we set off, the kids set off with us. There was a mad scramble as my gang struggled into position behind the bike to help push me along. The only problem was that they didn't push straight. I had several near misses as a result of over-enthusiastic, sideways shoves from one or other of my helpers. What's more, after the first 100 metres or so, the kids who were still hanging on started to tire. It seemed that they weren't willing to let go! Before long, I felt myself dragging a chain of little Mongolians, despairing at the thought that they'd stay clenched to my panniers, unwilling to give up their new toy until I'd towed them all the way to China!

We pedalled along the dusty road and soon found ourselves in the familiar position of sitting at intersections, deciding which direction to take. We chose to follow a route that would take us along the railway line, even though this meant taking the less established track, and soon found ourselves riding on narrow wheel ruts that were becoming increasingly sandy.

A fat man in a tight T-shirt jumped the fence near his *ger* and scrambled across the train line to greet us. He wanted to invite us back for tea and horse milk but we decided that we really should press on. We'd been in the desert for almost three weeks, and with only 120 kilometres to go until the border, we were itching to move right along.

I smiled politely, Tim declined, then I got in with a quick question: 'Which way to China, please?'

By mid-morning the road was deteriorating and by lunch, after many frustrating falls, we had been reduced to pushing the bikes through deep sand. We must have hit the deck a dozen times each in less than an hour. During this time, I'd noticed an interesting comparison. Tim liked to swear loudly at his bike when it flipped him into the dust, whereas I preferred to kick savagely at mine.

We pushed on for an hour, still following the rails, until it became obvious that the track we had chosen saw very little traffic.

'Doesn't anyone go to bloody China around here?' Tim cursed. 'If this track doesn't improve, then we're going to be walking the next hundred kays to the damn border. And if we have to walk anyway, I reckon I could go four times as bloody fast without having to lug this useless bike along, too.'

We kept on slugging away; the road got worse. Tim stopped at a point where the track petered out in a vast sandy creekbed. He looked hot, sweaty and pissed off. 'It looks like a bloody beach!' he exclaimed. 'How the hell are we meant to get these things through there?'

'It's worse than the beach,' I corrected him. The heat and falls of the past hour had sapped my energy, making me feel demoralised. 'You get hard bits on beaches. This looks more like the place where they make the sandpits for all the kids in the whole bloody world!'

We pushed our cycles tentatively forward and they promptly sank. The bottom bit of my front wheel was completely buried, leaving the spokes extending upwards as though they were growing out of the sand.

'Fuuuck,' Tim breathed, dismayed. 'My bike won't move! What the hell are we going to do?'

I heaved again, exhausted, and my bike moved forwards five centimetres. 'Jeez, mate, I don't know. At this rate it'll take us a bloody week to reach the border!' I said, dejectedly. 'You know, maybe they were right.'

'What?'

'Maybe they were right, you know, all those people who said we'd never make it.'

'What the hell are you talking about?' Tim fixed me with a level stare.

'Well, I dunno. It's just that if it *does* take us a week ... well, there's no way we can carry enough water for a week and maybe we'd just have to bail and ...'

'Chris,' Tim cut me off. 'We're nine hundred kilometres from Beijing. We *have* made it!'

'Huh?'

'Think about it. We're a couple of weeks from Beijing. Not even the pit of hell is going to stop us now.'

His words pierced my gloom and snapped me back to reality. He was right: we virtually had made it. Through all the snow and ice, past the ticks and mozzies. We'd been struggling away for over a year – rarely a moment without its challenges – and now here we were, only a few weeks and one more challenge away from our grand finale. I shook my head as I realised the simple truth. Of course nothing was going to stop me reaching Beijing. After all, a ticket home to Nat was waiting for me there!

'I guess you're right, mate.' I laughed. 'I don't know what I was thinking. All those people and all their warnings – every one of them predicted that we'd be dead by now! Like a pissy little bit of sand's going to stop us! Right!'

Tim grinned and slapped me on the shoulder. 'That's the way; good to see. Now that you've got your head screwed back on ...' He nodded towards the sandy creek bed. 'I'm afraid it's time to start pushing!'

A routine emerged that reminded me of school footy training with the scrum machine. We'd pack down, right arm and shoulder braced around the rear packs on our respective cycles. Then, bent down, left hand extended to clutch at the handlebar, we'd bury our heads into the smelly, dirty covers that had kept the dust and the weather out of our gear for the past year and start pushing.

Laboured steps. Thighs and calves pumping. Driving forward with heaves that buried my tattered sneakers under the surface and filled them with sand. Breathing hard, my legs burning as I inched my bike slowly forward. It was unsustainable. Unendurable! Thirty steps, max. Then a rest. Pausing, slumped over the bike now. Sweat streaming off my face and my heart hammering maniacally. Like it was trying to escape! Wishing it was already in China?

Then again. An endless cycle that seemed to go on and on. A taste of the ultimate punishment. A taste of hell.

I started out following Tim, but later he was behind me. Hours and hours, and I was still able to look back to the hill near Ulaan Ule where we'd begun!

Suddenly, somehow, it was dark. The torment had ceased and we were making camp. We'd come about five kilometres in the past five hours. That, I thought, was *flying*!

'Well, mate, what do you reckon?' Tim asked as he took a slug of water from one of the dirty old soft drink bottles he'd picked up beside the road in Russia. 'At one kay an hour, that's about ...'

'Ninety hours to the border!' I completed his thought. 'And we only have enough water for ...'

'Two more days.'

'Yeah.'

We sat and watched a passenger train go past. It was the Beijing-Ulaan Baatar Express. It had probably crossed the border a couple of hours ago and now we saw a blur of snapshots as lighted windows flashed by: men playing cards and drinking beer. Kids jumping up and down on their sleeper beds. A girl – just a glimpse, but she was probably a foreigner – drinking orange juice and reading a novel. The dining car: a fat man in a suit with a meal and a laptop in front of him.

And then it was gone. The *clickety-clickety-click* of the train was receding into the distance and we were left staring past the tracks at the dark shadows of the dunes and the saltbush extending into the gloom. It was back to us again: just the sand and the isolation.

For us, there was no free ride. Every mile cost effort. Out here, every metre was a struggle. The train had passed through like an alien spaceship in an uninhabited world. Like a time machine from the advanced, civilized future flashing momentarily through our basic, fundamental present.

Tim gingerly prodded another dried biscuit of horse dung onto the stinking little pile of smouldering embers, then balanced a pot of water carefully on top. 'Better pray that this track improves tomorrow.'

We were up before dawn and back to pushing through the sand as the first shafts of sun illuminated the eastern sky. We gradually moved off the plain and into some low dunes which made the going even tougher – sandy and steep. But by late morning, we could see that the dunes were levelling out into a sort of plateau about a kilometre ahead.

We stopped for lunch, having come, we guessed, about ten kilometres. It wasn't nearly far enough in terms of our water supplies; but then, the terrain ahead looked more promising and we could only hope that the going would improve. I smeared jam on my last crust of bread and munched on it thoughtfully. I looked at Tim. He was absolutely feral. Ingrained dirt had turned his skin darker than the locals', and a matted fox-fur collar that he'd added to his windstopper jacket hung limply next to his wild and equally grungy beard. He also looked gaunt and starving. He was staring intently at something near my feet.

'Hey, mate,' he said, salivating. 'If you're not going to eat that, can I have it?' I shifted my gaze down and saw that he was pointing at a small piece of bread that I'd accidentally dropped. The sticky jam topping was covered in sand and dust from the track.

I looked back up, struggling to keep a straight face. 'Why, sure! Help yourself. I've had enough anyway.'

An hour after lunch, for the first time in a day, we were able to ride our bikes again!

'Whooohoooo!' I yelled in jubilation, as I rocketed along at a fast walking pace, then, 'Ughhhh!' I promptly crashed again in a patch of sand.

We snuck under the railway where it crossed over another dry creekbed and made our way along faint tracks – still unused, but slightly firmer – until we saw a man on horseback.

He galloped over, boggle eyed, and politely asked where the hell we'd just come from. We pointed out the route – our tyre and foot tracks were still visible on a dune on the far side of the railway – and he burst out laughing. His look said it all: you are crazy guys! Nobody around here uses *that* road!

By mid-afternoon, we were sitting triumphantly on our cycles and munching greedily on a big bag of biscuits. We'd found the real road, and pedalled no more than a kilometre before a Russian-speaking driver pulled up alongside us. He told us that it was only another sixty kilometres to the border town of Zamyn-Uud and that the road wasn't really that bad at all! This was good news, as the day before we'd lost our one and only map of Mongolia when it dropped out of a hole in Tim's pack. Now that our position was pinpointed, we knew that we'd be at the border by morning.

As we spoke, the driver offered us a sweet cream-wafer biscuit from a huge bag, and we'd absentmindedly munched our way through the lot.

On a huge sugar high, we pushed on for several hours more. The going was hard and we still had to walk through many sandy stretches, but after the ordeal of the morning, and the day before, I felt invincible!

We drank our last drops of water at 3.30 p.m. the next afternoon as the shimmering township of Zamyn-Uud came into sight on the horizon. It was twenty-one days since we'd left Ulaan Baatar and we'd broken a score of records along the way. It had been our longest stretch without washing, as well as our longest stretch without contacting home. Although we'd forewarned that we might be out of touch for a while, our parents had apparently been worried sick. Our bikes had been heavier than ever before – up to ninety kilograms each at times – and at one stage, we'd been carrying enough water to ride completely self-sufficiently for three and a half days at a time. And to top all that? Well, through getting lost from time to time, we'd managed to pioneer a route across the Gobi Desert.

Now, in the distance, we could see a long, glimmering fence stretching across the horizon. It was the border! Beyond that fence lay all the exotic mystery of China. If we could get our bikes through to the other side – illegal – and manage to ride – also illegal – then in a few short weeks, we would be in Beijing. Our very lifestyle would be breaking the law, but other foreigners had managed to cycle in China on conventional bikes. With luck we would manage on our recumbents, too.

I tried to get my head around the idea. A few kilometres away was China! The whole time it had been so far off as to be no more than a dream. Could we really have made it this far?

I looked into the distance and strained to see the Chinese border town of Erienhot on the other side. And when we reached it? Well, the past three weeks through the Gobi had been our biggest challenge yet, and I was ready for a smooth run home. I think that Tim felt the same way.

'What do you reckon?' I asked him. 'What do you think is in store for us over that fence?'

Tim grinned as he replied, his white toothy smile emphasised by the grease streaks in his matted beard and the ingrained dirt covering all his exposed facial skin. 'I've been dreaming about it for the past week,' he said, happily. 'I'd say that once we cross that border we deserve to find a long, flat bitumen highway and a big sign pointing straight to Beijing.'

Four days later, the local train from Ulaan Baatar jerked to a stop at the station in Zamyn-Uud and spilled us onto the platform. We'd returned to the capital for a couple of days to wash, to contact home and to find a way to smuggle our bikes across the border. We'd wanted to book a train straight to

Beijing, then jump off with our bikes at the first station across the border. But the Beijing trains didn't stop at Zamyn-Uud, and that was where we'd left our bikes.

So, clean and well fed, but none the wiser, we returned to the border town to see what we could manage from there. We stretched in the cold air of the platform and sauntered over to the baggage room to retrieve our cycles.

The lady behind the counter peered at me suspiciously with complete lack of recognition. It had taken almost three hours of showering to scrub off all the dirt. Compared to the state we'd been in when we'd first arrived, we now looked as though we belonged to another race.

I slowly packed the bags on my bicycle then wheeled it out of the station, directly onto the town square. We had Chinese visas and a freshly hatched plan. If all went well, this would be our last day in Mongolia.

Zamyn-Uud was a dirty town bustling with busy traders. People rushed about and were sometimes rude. The kids were aggressive. We did a little tour of the shops, buying food and supplies that would see us over the border and at least a few days along the road, then set about searching for a taxi that could take us to Erienhot.

In the end, a Chinese driver with a big van took us across the frontier. We negotiated with him through a Mongolian who could translate our few words of Mongolian into his few words of Chinese, and agreed on a price of US$50. We crammed our bikes into the back of the windowless van, and then, with a wave to the crowd that had gathered, we swung up into the cab and set off along the bouncy strip of bitumen towards the first checkpoint on the Mongolian side of the fence. The Mongolian guards were fascinated with our bikes and we had to spend half an hour dragging them out for a 'customs inspection.' Luckily, at the Chinese checkpoint, the guards waved us through with only a quick word to the driver.

We were in China. It was amazing. They hadn't even seen the bikes. After a month of worry, we had smuggled the bikes over the border.

We were let out near the outskirts of town and the first things that struck me were the bikes. There were thousands of them. Little three-wheeled rickshaws wobbled up and down the streets while shopkeepers and messengers darted nimbly through the crowd on a range of two-wheeled racing machines. Outside of Ulaan Baatar, we'd seen perhaps a few dozen bicycles at most in all of Mongolia, yet here we'd seen a hundred before turning the corner.

My second impression was that the entire town consisted of thousands upon thousands of restaurants! Tightly packed shopfronts lined both sides of the narrow streets, and above each door were the trademark dancing characters I'd seen only on Chinese restaurants back home. It was hard to avoid the impression that the industry of the town was entirely devoted to eating! On looking closer, however, it became clear that these shops sold a huge variety of things.

I left Tim to fix a puncture and went for a walk down one of the streets. I glanced randomly into windows and doors and saw more things for sale than it would have been possible to buy in the whole of Russia. Shelves were overflowing with all sorts of tacky electronics. There were windows full of stationery, cookware and bedding. I came across one little shop that sold bikes and spare parts and ducked inside for a look. Packed onto the shelves between the narrow walls were all the things that we had simply not been able to find in the mega-cities of Siberia. There were thousands of patches and gallons of glue. There were chains and cogs – I even saw a gear-changer! I bought a few patches and some spare tubes, then headed back to Tim. We feasted on a delicious but indescribable snack from a nearby café and then, with the dreamed-of bitumen highway in clear view, we rode triumphantly out of town. Heading south. Heading for home.

Crossing the border into China had worked another silent miracle that revealed itself not far down the road when we made camp. We'd just spent five days being civilized in the city and I wasn't relishing the prospect of reverting back to the old horse-poo emu-parade and meals cooked on a pile of smelly dung. On impulse, I retrieved the stove from the bottom of my pack, banged it on a rock and gave it a thorough clean. I pumped up the pressure bottle then struck a match.

It burst into life with a spectacular two-metre high blast of flame. But amazingly, rather than simply exploding and killing us both, as I was expecting it to, the flame soon settled down to its usual belching. It wasn't functioning as the manufacturer had intended by a long shot, but at least it produced enough heat to cook a good-sized meal.

The next couple of days flashed by in a blur, characterised by perishingly cold mornings, long days of riding along the bitumen and the helpless feeling of being almost completely without language. People in cars would stop to talk to us, and we'd stop in villages and small towns, but we could only sit in silence as friendly crowds full of eager questions gathered around. At first we were unable to communicate at all. It was only after a few days, when we'd worked out the words for Moscow and Beijing, that we were even able to tell people where we'd come from. It was some time before we learned how to pronounce the word for Australia! Before that, I guess, people had assumed we were Americans.

A noticeable feature was the lifelessness of the countryside. Physically, the whole of Chinese Inner Mongolia looked exactly the same as the flat, dry desert of Southern Mongolia. Culturally – although separated by only a 100 kilometres and a fence – the two places were worlds apart. In Mongolia white *gers* dotted the horizon and herds of camels and horses ran free. Here the nomads' homes were replaced by orderly cottages, and the only animals we saw were shaggy goats and sheep, penned behind rows of fences. We had scarcely seen a fence in all of Mongolia, yet here they were everywhere. The wild young men on horseback were now wrinkled farmers, putting along the road on loud, smelly, three-wheeled mini-tractors; the challenge of the endless sandy tracks had disappeared. Many of the people in the two Mongolias were related yet there was no sense of Mongolia's wild, untamed freedom here. Inner Mongolia felt lifeless and constrained.

The towns, on the other hand, were something different again. Their life and vibrancy was a stark contrast to the countryside. I found myself looking forward to reaching each new dot on the map in the same way that I'd longed only for the empty desert a few weeks before. The people seemed diligent and invariably friendly, and the bustling capitalism of the tightly packed shops gave me a reassuring sense of security that had been missing for most of the past year.

We stopped in a large town about 140 kilometres from Erienhot and began eagerly scanning the shops for one that might sell hot food. We parked our bikes against the wall of a promising-looking restaurant and walked tentatively inside. We'd been hoping for a cheap noodle-house, but the moment we went through the door we saw that it was way too plush for such as ourselves. The chairs were upholstered and the tables even had place settings! We began to back out, but a waitress appeared and urged us towards a table. I resisted for a moment, but quickly gave in. We were starving and only two weeks from home. With a quick grin we let the waitress usher us to a table. We'd been living on a shoestring budget of three or four dollars a day for most of the past year, so why shouldn't we spoil ourselves now? Tim grabbed one of the unintelligible menus and quickly perused the

Chinese characters painted across the page. He broke into a beaming smile.

'I'm going to have the second from the top on the right hand side of page three! How about you, mate?'

'Yeah!' I laughed. 'I'll have the one two below that then. What the hell!'

We tried to order by pointing at our choices but the waitress frowned and took the menu. She disappeared then returned a moment later with a pad of paper and a pen. 'Hallo,' she wrote. 'My name is Adeline. Welcome to China.'

Wow, she could write English. I grabbed the pen and we quickly scribbled down an introductory conversation. Then to the serious business: it was time to eat.

Adeline shook her head disapprovingly when we reached again for the menu. Carefully she formed some English words on the pad instead. 'What will you eat?' she wrote, then pushed the pen back towards us.

'Something with beef,' I wrote on the notepaper, hoping for a delicious stir-fry.

'Something with fish,' Tim added, and I grinned wryly. How could I have forgotten? He'd been reminding me about how much he missed his seafood for most of the past year.

'And rice,' I added, as an afterthought. I pushed the pad back to Tim.

'And tea.'

Fifteen minutes later, we could only stare open-mouthed as our meals emerged from the kitchen on two huge carving trays. Adeline had apparently not understood the words 'something' or 'with'. One of the trays contained a huge leg of beef – a couple of kilograms at least – and the other held a gigantic steamed fish!

Was this really their perception of westerners: big, fat, meat-munching machines? I looked at Tim and we burst out laughing. It was going to cost more than we'd planned to spend, but then, what the heck? We thanked Adeline with a quick scribble – 'thank you' – then happily carved in.

An hour later, I staggered outside clutching a painfully bloated belly full of big juicy chunks of meat. The meal was a treat, I told myself helplessly as my insides growled with a long, loud gurgle. I walked over to my bike and confronted the crowd that had gathered. In a country where most of the billion citizens travelled by bicycle, the sudden appearance of our recumbents had been causing even more of a stir than they had in Mongolia and Russia. They were more interested but, at the same time, the Chinese had a different reaction, too. While more people stopped to stare, they stared politely and didn't try to touch. Mongolian kids, in particular, had been the worst. They had invariably dived for the gear levers – *flick-flick-flick-flick-flick* – and we'd suffered more than a few broken gear cables as a result. Here the crowd was standing at a respectable distance, pointing and chattering curiously. Some of them had been waiting for a full hour.

Adeline abandoned the diners in the restaurant and came outside to translate. She carefully wrote down questions on her little pad and we scribbled answers. She even came with me to one or two of the nearby shops to help buy supplies. We couldn't find the macaroni, packets of soup powder and sardine tins that we'd been living on for most of the trip, so we settled on packets of instant noodles, instead.

As we packed our bikes, the crowd grew. A police car came to a halt beside us and a megaphone squealed into life. A crisp voice issued, barking commands. The crowd disappeared in an instant. People fled, vanishing on bikes, motorbikes, in cars and on foot. Suddenly we were alone. The police eyed us suspiciously before driving on. It was my first taste of totalitarianism. We turned to write goodbye to Adeline but she too had disappeared. Associating with foreigners, it seemed, was illegal, and now there was only the swinging door of the restaurant at the top of the stairs to show where she'd been.

We cycled out of town but, somehow, we weren't able to find the bitumen highway we'd been on earlier. We spent the night in a dusty paddock then set off again at sunrise. The wind was howling incessantly, not much warmer than the overnight low of minus ten, and blasting our faces and legs with stinging sand. It wasn't until lunchtime that we found a way over the railway line, and it was late afternoon before we'd found our way back to the highway. We pushed our bikes to the top of the steep, sandy embankment and looked in both directions in dismay.

'It hasn't even been bloody built yet!' Tim exploded. 'This was meant to be our smooth bitumen road to Beijing and they still haven't even finished it!' There were big yellow construction machines shuffling around in the distance. I looked ahead, into the valley, and saw a section of the embankment drop out of sight before reappearing again fifty metres later. It seemed that they hadn't built the bridges yet, either.

We carried on, riding along the sandy tracks on either side of the embankment and sometimes, where piles of gravel and missing bridges allowed, up on the smooth, flat dirt of the embankment. Our slow pace was frustrating Tim. He was pining for his highway, but in a complete reversal of what we'd been feeling three or four months earlier, I was enjoying the challenge of the dirt; the slow pace suited me perfectly. It was 16 October, well into autumn and perilously cold, but I was due home on 1 November.

That gave me another sixteen days and 600 kilometres of riding, and while I was looking forward to seeing Nat again, I was beginning to feel nervous as well. While riding, we were getting twelve hours' sleep per night and the days were flying by. At our slow pace, 600 kilometres could take twelve days (I had this all counted out) and twelve days with twelve hours' sleep per day would simply whiz by. Then – a couple of days in Beijing, a day and a night on the train to Hong Kong, and an overnight flight to Sydney – I'd be back home to Nat. Sixteen days! The numbers meant everything, because they took my mind off their meaning. I was dying to be with Nat again, but scared about what would happen to our relationship as we got to know each other again. I thought down to the heart of the matter and realised my most basic fear. After a year apart, a year when I hadn't been there, would she still love me?

Late the next day the dirt road ended and the countryside underwent a drastic change. For over two months – ever since climbing up and out of Russia – we'd been cycling at over 900 metres above sea level, across the vast Mongolian plateau. Now we'd finally reached its edge and were about to start a long descent to Beijing and the Yellow Sea. Directly below us, although still six to 800 metres above sea level, was Hebei Province and the promise of a different China.

The bitumen reappeared and we raced down a long, winding hill. At the bottom, we emerged into what seemed like a new world. Mud-brick houses clustered together in little villages. Here and there were fields that had been harvested and ploughed in a flurry of activity before winter set in. Winter! There was a startling thing in itself. We'd woken that very morning to find our water bottles frozen solid. The sparse grass on the plain had been dead and brown and the few trees stripped to their bare branches. Now, sixty kilometres further along the road and a few hundred metres down a hill, we seemed to have overtaken the seasons. All around were hills and mountains. There were a few streams and along their banks, more trees than I'd seen in over two months of travelling. They had leaves, too. Brown and red autumn leaves to be sure, but leaves all the same. There were tinges of green in the grass, and the air was noticeably warmer. Somehow, on the way down that hill, we had caught up with the edge of winter and crossed back into autumn. Like migrating birds, we had cycled south and reversed the seasons. Winter was still following along just behind, though, and we'd have to race to stay ahead of it.

We camped the night in a grove of young trees then set off again in the still freezing air of the morning. Our illegal lifestyle had been pretty easy up until now, lots of open flat space and, as in Mongolia, very few people to hide from. Now, however, the countryside was becoming more populated. Already, a day after beginning our descent from the plateau, there were towns and villages everywhere. The traffic had picked up and we spent most of the day riding among a chaotic stream of trucks, bikes and cars. It was going to be a lot harder to find good, tucked-away places to camp, and if the police presence picked up at the same rate as the population, then we might really find ourselves running the gauntlet of the law.

I caught up with Tim a little after midday on the outskirts of a small town; he was surrounded by a group of workers from a nearby factory. The workers had come out, jostling for a look and ignoring their supervisor who was obviously unhappy about the distraction. I held Tim's bike while he went off with a few men to fill the water bottles. When he returned, we both hopped on to do a couple of demonstration laps around the carpark before getting back underway.

Before we could leave, though, we heard a car pull up on the gravel nearby. A door clicked open and a set of heavy footsteps crunched along the ground, heading our way. The men around us ceased their happy chatter and some of them melted silently away. I looked up, confused. The usual, happy grin had disappeared from Tim's face. I turned to see what was going on. There, making his way through the crowd and straight towards us, was a policeman.

End of the Road
Houqi – Beijing
Late Autumn 2000

Tim

'Let's go!' shouted the policeman. He had a slight build but stood square shouldered. His face was striking, with skin tightly moulded over strong cheekbones. Initially, I chose to believe that he was just interested in us. I wasn't convinced that riding a bike was a crime that warranted arrest.

With a joyous smile we waved goodbye to the onlookers, who were now standing at a safe distance, and followed the police car. We didn't know it until later, but we had entered a town that was closed to foreigners. In light of this, I found it ironic that the police made us follow them right into the commercial centre; our cycling route would have bypassed the town altogether.

We rode abreast down the main street, attracting more attention than usual. The pavement was cluttered with stalls selling everything under the sun. Rickshaw riders pedalled alongside us, yelling out a greeting, and bystanders called out for us to stop. I stuck my thumb up and smiled.

'This feels fantastic, hey Chris? Like we are part of a procession or something. Closest we will get to a ticket-tek parade!' I yelled, excited. But I could tell that he was a little more concerned about the whole event.

The parade ended as we turned under a great archway and came to a halt before a fleet of police cars and motorbikes. The rush of interested pedestrians came flocking in behind us like a thundering mob. Thirty or forty pushed into the carpark just to see the foreigners and their bicycles. The arresting officer yelled something that sent them fleeing in panic. He seemed embarrassed that we were such a point of fascination.

Although we were at the centre of the commotion, I felt utterly removed from it. The police, the locals, the hieroglyphics plastered over the shopfronts, and whatever else lay ahead was just so beyond my comprehension that I felt unconcerned.

After retrieving our passports, we followed the officers into a four-storey building. Chris was barely visible beneath a thick film of dust. His usually green jacket was bordering on brown and his face seemed to be blowing away in the breeze. I noticed a couple of dried horse crap 'biscuits' poking out of the pockets – we'd run out of diesel and he'd been collecting them for our cooking fire. Most striking however was his footwear. He wore, like I did, a pair of red Gore-Tex mitts as socks. The sleeve for the thumb flapped loosely over the side. In fact, almost nothing remained of the shoes except the worn soles and the laces that bound his feet to them. As a general rule Chris was the clean one. I could only imagine how I must have looked.

My anticipation of a dirty, dark, windowless interrogation room was crushed as we were ushered into an office on the third floor. We were seated on lavish armchairs facing a large painting on the far wall.

Out the window I noticed a crowd of officials huddled around our bicycles. I wondered how long it would take before our policeman friend would cave in and ask questions about the bike and our journey.

For some time we sat in silence while the officer flicked through our passports. Then another man rushed in. He had marginally better English than the arresting officer. 'Hello. Okay, I will ask you some questions. Where you from?'

'Australia.'

There was extensive discussion before they arrived at a conclusion. 'So, you are foreigners?'

'Um, well, we are not Chinese,' I mumbled.

This seemed to satisfy them. 'When did you arrive in this town?'

'We arrived about five minutes before the policeman met us.'

'When?'

'Just now.'

'And where did you stay last night?'

'Well, we don't know. We stayed in a tent. There were a few trees nearby, probably about sixty kilometres from here,' I said, but the translator was having trouble understanding. Finally, Chris was reduced to miming the idea of sleeping in a tent. When that led nowhere, the translator decided on a new course of action. 'Can you give me your map?'

I reached into my pocket and retrieved a screwed up photocopy of a map that we had made in Ulaan Baatar.

'So where did you go?' he asked, pointing at the map.

'We came from Erienhot, then we came down here,' I said, dragging my finger down the only road south from there. 'But where are we now? What is this place called?' We hadn't been able to read any signs, and our map only had place names in English.

'Houqi,' he replied. 'So when were you in Erienhot hotel?'

'No, we were not in a hotel. We were in a tent,' I replied.

The translator skipped to the last question on his list. 'Do you have permit to travel?'

'Permit? We have visas.'

'This town is closed to foreigners, and this road to Beijing from Erienhot is also closed to foreigners. You can only go on train.'

'Oh, really?'

'Yes. So do you know you have broken Chinese law?' He smiled smugly, closed his folder and stood to leave. 'Have a good journey,' he said, with a smile as he walked out.

'Good luck!' I called after him.

The policeman was replaced by a woman who came rushing in with wet, freshly washed hair and a contagious smile. She couldn't mask her excitement. I immediately felt comfortable with her in the room, like it was the beginning of a party; she had such a bouncy energy about her.

'Hello, my name is Xiao Wei. I am the English teacher from the local school. They have asked me to come and help with some questions that they couldn't ask before.'

In between questions, we began a casual conversation about our journey and Australia. We also asked her some questions about China and found out how to pronounce 'Australia' in Chinese.

At some point we were asked to show the film footage we had shot in China. The arresting officer squinted at the tiny LCD screen, looking for who knew what in scenes of a donkey and cart, a few trees, our bikes and a sunset.

Xiao Wei was eventually asked to translate the basic problem. 'So, you understand that our town here is closed to foreigners. And you rode right through our town,' she said, trying hard not to laugh. 'You broke Chinese law and for this you must be punished.'

'But we didn't know.'

'I know, you are very brave, you boys. It's quite cold to be cycling at this time of year.'

'Do you meet many foreigners here?' I asked.

She blushed and laughed a little. 'It is a closed town, but yes there was another Australian on bicycle one time, and she was here too in this office. By the way, if you want I can take you on an escorted tour of our town,' she replied, eagerly.

'Oh, that would be great!'

We moved to another office, and while the officer flicked through some fat law books, Xiao Wei handed us a booklet. 'Look, you can read what others wrote so you can write also,' she said.

It was a booklet with statements from all the other poor foreign cyclists who had wandered into the forbidden zone and been arrested. There were two parties in all – an Australian woman and a group consisting of an Australian, a Japanese and a Canadian. I read the statements with interest and flicked over to see their fingerprints and copies of their passports.

Then I looked at Xiao Wei and smiled. 'So you do meet a lot of foreigners here!'

After writing our own statements, we had to dip our fingers in red ink for fingerprinting. 'It's just like finger painting!' I said to Xiao Wei, who blushed and put her hand over her mouth to hide her smile. Then it was Chris's turn.

My spirits were high. I was wondering when the formalities would be over so we could give the officer and Xiao Wei a ride on the bikes. But I overdid my confidence. 'Can I film Chris signing the statement?' I asked. Xiao Wei blushed again, as if it were an inappropriate question, but translated my request to the arresting officer.

The atmosphere changed immediately. He slammed his fist on the table. I was acutely aware of his glare and a supremely stubble-free face. Xiao Wei tried to fall in line with the seriousness of the situation but failed. She just couldn't suppress her giggle and curiosity. I realised my mistake and tried to look appropriately intimidated.

The officer said something to Xiao Wei.

'Did you see the Olympics?' she translated.

'No, we were in the Gobi and missed the whole thing, actually.'

She translated my response for the benefit of the policeman and then handballed his response back to us. 'He said maybe then you do not love your country.'

When we were done with paperwork, it was dark outside and I was getting hungry. All that was left, it seemed, was saying sorry and goodbye. Xiao Wei read out the final details of our crime: 'This says that you have broken the Chinese law Section forty-six for riding through a closed town and for riding in China. For this you must pay ... five hundred Yuan. If you agree with this then please sign here. If you disagree you can take the matter to court.'

'Shiiit! Five hundred Yuan!' Chris shouted. That was about US$62! On a budget of about four Australian dollars a day, this was mind boggling. In fact, we only had US$150 cash left in total for Beijing and the train to Hong Kong.

'Five hundred Yuan!' I repeated.

'Yes, and this is only for one person, so together that will be one thousand Yuan.'

I turned to Chris who had already become a quivering mess. 'But we just don't have that kind of money!' he pleaded.

'So you want that I ask to lower the price? I think also that it is too much,' Xiao Wei said. She put her arm around the straight-backed officer and whispered into his ear in soft, seductive tones.

After a lot of haggling, and a point at which I thought she was about to sit on the man's lap and start kissing him, we agreed on an awful 600 Yuan. It still amounted to US$75, but at least it was less.

As we stormed out of the building, my joviality felt well and truly squashed. In the carpark the police wanted a ride on the bikes. Of course, now that we had paid the fine, the officer in charge seemed more amenable, although he hinted that his motorbike was by far the superior machine.

We were taken to a dumpy hotel room opposite the police station and placed under house arrest. Tomorrow, we were to be sent to Beijing on the train, and no more riding would be permitted. The next train out of Houqi didn't leave until the following evening. Only then would we be given back our passports.

All was not lost, though. As our friend waved goodbye for the night, she promised to take us on a tour and, if possible, would organise for us to talk to her students.

When we were finally alone, we flopped exhausted onto hard narrow beds and flicked on the crappy television. The opening ceremony of the Paralympics in Sydney was on. Despite our money woes I found some pleasure in having a shower and lying down on a real bed to vegetate, something I hadn't done for a long time.

'At least it's a nice prison cell,' Chris mumbled, dejectedly.

'Yeah, and let's just make sure we make the most of our 'tour' tomorrow. It was a bloody expensive ticket!' I said.

It seemed incredible that we were only 400 kilometres from Beijing, yet getting there by bike still seemed uncertain! I reflected that there had been many times when we could have or should have given up: the desert, the snow, the BAM railway; just getting the trip off the ground had seemed improbable. Then again maybe that was just the nature of adventure: uncertainty is relentless and it's never easy. It kept us on our toes. There was never a moment to take for granted; the whole journey could be thwarted at any given time. Perhaps that was why the sunset at the end of a day's ride always felt like the equivalent of gulping down ice-cream after a meal of vegetables. The constant challenge made moments of reward exquisite.

I awoke early in the morning feeling hungry. The police didn't turn up until midday, by which time Chris and I had resorted to soaking semolina with hot water from the tap; it was like eating spoonfuls of warm, lumpy sand.

After a real meal in a nearby restaurant, closely guarded by our police escort, Xiao Wei took us on a tour of the town. I jumped at the offer, but Chris was keen to have some time alone. For me, the real purpose of the tour wasn't sightseeing but buying food supplies. Although we were supposed to take the train to Beijing, Chris and I had no intention of doing so. Somehow I had to convince our escort that we needed five loaves of bread, four tins of fish, two and a half kilograms of biscuits, eight packets of noodles and some breakfast cereal just for the train ride. Both women were dubious, but asked no questions. What's more, with a guide and interpreter I was certain not to get ripped off.

When the time to leave Houqi came, I felt disappointed and a little sad. There hadn't been time to talk to the English students, but every moment spent with Xiao Wei had been a joy. Despite Chinese regulations, she had offered us the warmth that had characterised our Russian experience. In her presence, I swelled with optimism.

Consequently, I wasn't terribly upset when the police realised that they had forgotten to bring our passports. Much to their embarrassment we missed the train. The next service wasn't scheduled for another twenty-four hours.

As we trundled back to our cell, I talked with Xiao Wei, who seemed just as relieved. I was more than happy to spend more time with her, especially if it meant visiting the school.

'So maybe you can come to school tomorrow,' she said, with a contagious smile.

The next morning our escort failed to show again. As time passed I began to worry. I didn't want to miss the opportunity to talk to the students.

By midday, starving and fuming mad, I decided to break out. I crossed the courtyard and strode into the police station. On the stairs I ran into the policewoman who had been assigned the task of escort. When she saw me, she looked as if to say, 'Not you again!' Five minutes later Xiao Wei came running into the building. Then we all walked back to the hotel.

After packing our bikes, we set off through the congested traffic. Behind us the policewoman struggled to keep up on her own bike. I turned to see her chubby face reddening as she panted heavily. In front of us two officers on motorbikes led the way with Xiao Wei. It was a windy day and dust clouds rushed through the town, scattering litter. I had attached the video camera to my bike with hose clamps and discreetly pressed the record button. Part way down the main street I stopped to adjust the angle of the camera. When I looked up again Chris and the motorbikes were nowhere to be seen, and the policewoman had fallen hopelessly behind. Before a crowd could gather, I took off.

'Bloody hell, I've lost the escort,' I muttered, chuckling.

Everyone was looking concerned when I eventually arrived at the school gates. From there, under close guard, we cycled across a large square and came to a halt next to some classrooms that looked like rows of army barracks.

Before going any further, Xiao Wei translated the orders from the police. 'You are to tell the children how to study English and something about your homeland. Okay, then, you are welcome. Go in.'

Putting my foot into the classroom was like stepping onto a trigger. There was a hysterical shouting and wild cheering. It was overwhelming, deafening, consuming. I turned to face the students with a triumphant smile; I just couldn't help it.

A sea of faces. Boys, girls, just faces from wall to wall. There were probably over 100 students squeezed into a tiny room, all staring wide-eyed. More children were climbing through an open window and somersaulting onto what seemed a mass of humanity. Suddenly, the expensive fine we had copped seemed irrelevant.

Everything took on a slow, dreamlike quality. Chris followed and the jubilation continued. A surging mass of students from outside almost knocked the police off their feet and through the door.

'Hello, I am ...' I started, but more cheering washed over me.

Eventually, the crowd grew silent and Xiao Wei stepped forward to address them. 'These are our guests from Australia. They will introduce themselves, and please use the opportunity to ask them questions in English.'

Then it was over to us. We spoke about our journey, Australia, and what had happened to us along the way. Chris even recited 'The Man From Ironbark'. Everyone just gazed, spellbound. Quite possibly no one understood a word of what we said, but it didn't really matter.

After about twenty minutes Xiao Wei broke in with an emotional address to the children. 'Students, do you understand that our Australian friends had much trouble coming to our town. They were taken by the police. Students do you know that our town is closed? That foreigners are not to come here?'

'Yes!' cried the children.

'They have had much trouble with our police, but they have asked and got permission to talk to you. This is a great opportunity so ask questions,' she continued.

I was so caught up in the euphoria that I jumped onto a table from where I pointed out our route on a map.

I was angered when the police finally called an end to the presentation. Following them back through the town, I cursed and swore under my breath. It was then that I realised we weren't heading for the police station.

We pulled up outside a shop and the policemen loosened their collars. It was a restaurant. A table had been booked and orders placed. Several familiar officers were already sitting around the table, waiting.

It was as if the policemen were temporarily leaving behind their jobs. Even the man who arrested us smiled as he flicked through photos and calendars of Australia. Questions were asked and laughter flowed as Xiao Wei translated our answers. The meal was on the police, and I could only feel a little guilty for disliking the officer for doing his job. He was human. And he was interested. Perhaps he was as much a victim of the system as anyone else.

As I slurped down noodles and drank a shot of wine, I couldn't help feeling that we had once again been graced with unbounded hospitality. It wasn't deserved, asked for, or even expected; and it wasn't something that we could ever repay. We were living our dream, perhaps a selfish one at that, yet people were willing to support us! I felt like the luckiest person alive.

After the meal we headed for the train station, where a group photo was taken before we boarded the train. Xiao Wei's last words summed up the whole occasion perfectly: 'Goodbye and good luck. We have to go back to work now!'

Just before dark the train pulled into Jining station, sixty kilometres or so from Houqi.

Chris and I alighted and dashed for the exit, wheeling our bikes and dragging all the gear. Our aim was to get out of Jining before being spotted.

I packed and was ready before Chris. A curious crowd was already forming, 'umming' and 'ahhing'.

Chris was having problems with his rack so I went off to hunt for potatoes and noodles. By the time I came back the crowd had grown and, much to my horror, a group of uniformed men were standing over Chris. He was still working away, oblivious.

Finally, he was ready. An unseen face in the crowd handed out some potatoes. I took them, yelled out a thank you and cut a path through the crowd. Someone volunteered to lead us out of the city on a motorbike. I turned onto the street and powered after him. The motorcyclist picked up speed. Ignoring leg pains, I accelerated too. I was flying, blinded by a blur of lights, weaving between a throng of rickshaws, motorbikes and cars that tooted in a shadowy chaos.

Chest heaving, legs ballooning, heart trying to beat its way out of my rib cage. But I couldn't feel it. I was an engine and all I had to do was click into a higher gear before overtaking cars and shooting off into the night at a blistering pace.

After some time I turned to look for Chris but was blinded by headlights. He must be there. Just keep going, Tim, you can't afford to stop!

Then came a distant call from inside this swirling mass of speed, lights and rampant urgency. 'Tim, waiiiiiiiiiiit! Tiiiiiim! Waiiiiiit! Fuuuckiiing biike brokeen!'

As I stopped, everything snapped back into focus. The blur of lights was suddenly a stationary glare. The world was catching up! 'C'mon Chris, c'mon, c'mon!' I yelled.

There was a problem with his back wheel, which prevented him from going further. 'Piss off, Tim. I am trying!' he called.

With the bike lying down on the busy street, people flooded in, keen and curious. The crowd swelled at an alarming rate and spilled onto the road. Within minutes three lanes of traffic were blocked. Tooting, yelling, cars banking up by the second, lights, a mass of commotion ... and we were in the middle of it. So much for being subtle.

Finally, Chris was ready. I jumped aboard for our last chance to escape.

My bike stopped one metre later. 'Chris, hang on! My brakes are stuck!'

I thrust my hands under the mudguard and yanked and fiddled but they refused to loosen. A thousand faces breathing down my back and 2,000 eyes, the end, just half a kilometre from the station.

Then finally the brakes loosened. 'Let's go!' I stood up to see a policeman's face centimetres from mine. But I didn't stop. 'Excuse me, get out of the way!' I urged.

Twenty minutes later the rush of traffic had diminished to a few trucks and cars trickling out of the city. We turned off onto an exit ramp into the safety of darkness.

We continued for hours as the temperature dropped to below zero and my ears burned in the intense cold. At a roadside café we stopped for a meal, and later avoided a police checkpoint. To get around it we had to lift our bikes over a fence, push through a dark field and rejoin the road 300 metres or so further on. Finally, we rolled into the quiet of the countryside. At some point my back wheel went flat and we decided to give up for the night and make camp in a ploughed field.

Next morning I rolled out of bed feeling groggy. Chris was still snoozing, so I took the opportunity to write in my diary. In recent days I had fallen behind and feared that if I didn't get the events in Houqi down on paper, I never would.

Eventually, Chris rose and went about cooking breakfast. For him, waiting was the activity he hated most. Even if it was for half a minute, his anger and frustration seemed to simmer. On most occasions it didn't matter because we could leave at different times and catch up later in the day. But with the risk of getting arrested, we decided that it would be prudent to ride together.

I was acutely aware of this as I rushed to finish scribbling my notes. I was also aware that we were most prone to arguments in the morning, especially when we were extra tired.

Chris finished his porridge and packed up the tent as I continued on in my own world. 'Tim, how much longer will you be?'

'Oh, probably about ten or fifteen minutes.'

I didn't have a watch, but I was longer than that – a lot longer. Chris asked again and I underestimated yet again. In hindsight it was understandable that when I looked up for the third time he was preparing to leave.

'Hey, Chris, you can't leave, mate, it's too risky!' How dare the bastard jeopardise the whole trip just because his 'happiness' was temporarily compromised.

'What! I've asked you several times, and I've done everything I can. I can't stay here any longer or I'll go crazy!' he yelled.

'What do you mean? We can't afford to split up. It could stuff up the whole trip. What if one of us gets arrested?' I said.

'Oh, piss off, Tim! I've given you your chance. Fact is you just say one thing and do another. You're a bloody hypocrite. At least if I say something I stick by it.'

'Bullshit, mate! All right, I was wrong. But c'mon, sometimes I have had to wait for you and I never complained. It's bloody life! Usually you can just leave when you want, but this is an exception. My diary is important at the moment. Anyway, you also don't do everything you say.'

The argument spiralled out of control. Without the energy to return to a more civilized debate, it seemed inevitable that it would only become worse. Although we had argued on a number of occasions during the journey, there was something about the malice in our voices on this occasion that told me we had stooped to a new level. We attacked each other for shortcomings that we had never brought into the open before. Even as I yelled obscenities at him, it scared me on the inside.

How could we ever reconcile after treating each other so badly? He was one of my best mates and there I was, calling him the lowlife of this world. His insults struck home, too, and welled up as feelings of anger and sadness. Was that what he really thought of me? God, was I really such a bad person? Could I be so wrong? But I couldn't stop. I had lost my head and so had he.

Eventually, he rode off in a stink and we flung final insults across the fields until the words would no longer carry the distance. Then he was gone, out of sight, over a hill on the road towards Beijing.

I was left shaking, suddenly unsure of what had happened. After thirteen months or so, and with less than 400 kilometres to Beijing, had I blown it? Would Chris ride into Beijing on his own?

Looking back now, I guess it was a time during which we were both at the point of mental and physical exhaustion. The end was tantalisingly close, and yet we still had to get there. Maybe we were just letting our guard and our diplomacy down too early. Or maybe it was just natural that after such a long time of trying to tolerate each other's differences, we spoke out.

Whatever the case I couldn't help feelings of hatred as I took off fifteen minutes or so later, a terrible energy throbbing through my veins.

Cycling, as always, was a good remedy for working out the important things – you can't waste energy on being angry on a bike because you need all you can get just to keep riding! You can yell, curse, feel bitter, whatever, but you live in the knowledge that it's not getting you anywhere. If you want to restore some inner peace, you just have to come to terms with it.

After an hour or so I calmed down and the paranoia of being caught returned. Just about every second car on the road seemed to be a police vehicle.

Since leaving Houqi we had entered an entirely different part of China. Gone were the sandy tracks and isolated mudbrick villages – in fact, in this new environment they were almost unimaginable. We were still high up on an arid plateau, but even so we had obviously hit the rim of fast-developing China.

The road was a wide, smooth bitumen highway complete with large signs, heavy traffic and impressive bridges. Fleets of Chinese trucks rattled along with all kinds of goods, and expensive Japanese cars often zipped by in near silence. Everything was shiny, new and prosperous. This was an alien world, unlike anything we had seen in Russia and Mongolia.

By early afternoon there was still no sign of Chris. I tried to not let it bother me and pedalled on, content to eat my biscuits and marvel at the changing environment. The road wound through steep hills which, in turn, rose into rugged desert mountains. Most of the yellow-red slopes were cut neatly into a series of terraces. On rare occasions, I spotted old men walking behind cattle, directing drays. In general, though, it was a barren, sparsely populated place. Between the slopes, where you would usually expect to see streams and moist gullies, there were deep, eroded gorges with sandy bottoms that looked like the savage, random cuts of a giant machete.

When my biscuits ran out, I began to worry about Chris. With each kilometre that passed, terrifying thoughts began to manifest. Had he really decided to go it solo to Beijing? Had he, in fact, been arrested? If so, how on earth could I find out? I spoke no Chinese, was travelling illegally, and was utterly alone.

I continued until the sun was nudging the rugged mountain skyline. The air was cooling fast, and with it waned my energy.

I was bordering on tears, partly out of anger and partly out of fear, but mostly from exhaustion and the thought of having ruined the end of the journey.

Chris, where are you? Where the hell are you? But the empty landscape had no answers.

Eventually, I stopped, lay down on a terrace and chewed on a raw packet of noodles. It settled my nerves and restored some rationale to my thinking. Well, if he hasn't gone ahead, then he's either been arrested or somehow I've passed him. In any case, I am not moving.

After finishing the noodles, I put on some warm clothes, rested my head on the bike, and let my eyes drift with the dimming sky. I wondered what Chris was thinking at that moment.

Although we had been travelling together for over a year, the fact remained that we were very different people. As individuals riding bikes we had lived parallel lives, but for much of the time it had been a solitary journey. It wasn't like a rowboat, where the hardship is split among several rowers; we had to ride every inch alone, and come up with the motivation and energy by ourselves; we battled through mental turmoil of different kinds.

Now that it was all winding down, were our parallel lines diverging and leaving nothing but memories?

As staunchly independent people, our relationship had never been one of dependence. Nor had it been reliant on us agreeing with everything the other thought. Beneath our conflicts and differences was surely something stronger than just a wish to 'see it through'. For even below the differences, at a grass-roots level, we shared a lust for life and a will to be the best we could. We had convinced each other that living out a childhood dream was possible, and that in the end, we only needed permission from ourselves to do what we wanted. It hadn't been easy, but life wasn't supposed to be.

Our differences had also been our strengths. It had given us the opportunity to feed off each other and grow as individuals. Alone on that terrace, I suddenly missed him.

I had fallen into such a reverie that it took several seconds for me to react to the black couch on wheels that went whizzing by. 'Chrriiiiiiiiiis!' I screamed.

He returned, panting heavily. Even in the dark I sensed that his smile reflected my own.

'You silly bastard!' I giggled.

Early next morning the road was littered with patches of ice. The air was biting cold under a clear sky and even with Gore-Tex mittens for socks, my toes began to freeze. I found it fitting that we had almost come full circle since being dragged off the street with frostbite in Babushkina. Once again, birch trees in Russia would be blazing with colour, leaves ready to drop.

Upon arriving at the peak of our first high mountain pass for the day, I set up the video camera on the bike to film us going down the other side. Then, releasing the brakes, we began to roll effortlessly downwards. Soon we were rocketing along with the rush of air in our ears. After ten minutes the bottom was still beyond view, so I stopped to put on an extra layer of clothes over my stiffened limbs. Never had we encountered such a long downhill slope. An unspoken thought lingered between us: This is it! This is the final plunge down from the plateau, safely into the haven of warm weather. Surely nothing can stop us now! I turned off the video camera. These were moments to savour.

Eventually, we hit flat ground and rolled into the fierce sunlight of the valley floor. It was another world.

Aspen trees lined the road, their canopies thick with green leaves. Rice paddies and crops of corn formed neat squares and cut a patchwork quilt into the land. The road widened to allow for four lanes of traffic: two for conventional cars and the others for hordes of cyclists, donkeys and carts, rickshaws, tractors and an array of small engine-powered contraptions. On every spare space of concrete or tarmac, people were spreading out wheat grain for drying and sorting. We were startled by a fleet of motorbikes that zoomed past, each with about five live sheep strapped onto the front and sides. Their legs and heads were dangling perilously close to the ground and had been grazed on the bitumen, leaving a trail of blood.

It wasn't a town or a city, just a dense band of population. The land above had been a comparable wasteland.

With spirits high, it felt like we could join the throng and be swept away to the end; as far as we knew, it was only another 200 kilometres or so.

After a brief stop for lunch we hurried towards a halo of smog in the distance. We weren't too concerned about the police anymore. If the law was widely enforced, then we wouldn't have made it out of Jining. Since then we had probably passed 300 or so policemen, and most had given us a friendly wave. Presumably, it was only a law exercised in closed areas.

By early evening we were beneath the smog and closer to the city of Zhangjiakou. As we were discussing where to camp, a motorbike with two young men pulled up. I recognised them as the pair that had been following us for about three and a half hours.

'Hey, come, my home, you sleep there,' one of them said, pointing in the direction of Zhangjiakou. I thought it strange because it is illegal for foreigners to stay with Chinese locals unless permission has been granted. But the idea of sleeping in a bed and seeing the inside of a Chinese house was an inviting idea. 'What do you reckon, Chris?' I asked.

'Why not?' he replied, shrugging. Everything else had gone our way for the day, and this just felt like a well-deserved ending.

A few hours later our patience was at breaking point. It had already been a long day, but the extra thirty to forty kilometres through heavy traffic had taken its toll. What was more, we still didn't have a place to stay! First the men had taken us to a house where an old man yelled angrily at them. Then they drove to an expensive hotel. After several hours of this, we began to question their intelligence. When we finally decided to cycle out of the city into agricultural land to set up camp, they were still following.

Just outside the city centre we stopped to say goodbye one last time. One of the men motioned that we should make camp on the concrete embankment of a nearby river. It was surrounded by busy streets and tall buildings. When I declined, he grabbed me by the arm. 'No, you stay here camp! Money and no policeman. You go and very bad, very bad!' he said, visibly angry and pointing at a police station across the road.

'Sorry, I don't understand. Goodbye, we are going!' I replied.

They began to yell in Chinese. One man grabbed my shoulder to prevent me from cycling off, while the other sprinted towards the police station.

'Bugger off!' I yelled. I turned and thumped him in the stomach with my elbow. His grip relaxed and I pedalled away. I dropped over a kerb, swerved into the busy traffic and was gone, pushing at the cranks like my life depended on it.

'Chris, let's get off the road and hide. Let's get off the road!' I yelled. He was somewhere behind me, but in the pitch black I couldn't see a thing.

Is that their motorbike coming? When will a police car give chase?

I called out to Chris again. 'Well, let's get off the bloody road then!' came his reply.

I turned into the darkness and ploughed straight through a garden bed. When the wheels ceased to turn, I dropped the bike and ran blindly until my legs gave way. I fell clumsily into a ditch; Chris promptly followed.

We sat panting heavily and peeping above the line of the ditch towards the traffic. There was silence for a long time, until our heart rates fell back to a more leisurely pace. At some stage, a police car drove by with its lights flashing, and our 'friends' in tow.

At first we agreed to stay another half hour, but in the end even the ditch seemed inviting. It was just deep enough to lie in and be hidden from view. So, squeezed between a busy major road and a field of lettuce, we settled in for the night.

Morning came quicker than expected.

'Hey Tim, wake up.' Chris was shaking me by the shoulder. I opened my eyes to see his face and the pale sky beyond. 'Tim, it's time to move. We're already pretty obvious.'

My vision slowly cleared and focused on the heavy stream of traffic. There were donkeys and carts, cyclists, cars and even pedestrians. In the sitting position, I would have been visible from the waist up. People paused to gape before the banked-up traffic willed them on. It was no wonder; I was wearing only my rainbow coloured thermal underwear. More intriguing was my headwear. I had lost my beanie near Houqi and in recent days had taken to wrapping an old pair of thermal long johns around my head. It must have looked like some kind of bizarre turban.

'Chris, mate, how do I look?'

'Like you spent the night in a bloody ditch!'

We couldn't help laughing. There was nothing to hide anymore.

Chris wet his fingers with some spit and attempted to give his face a wash, but just succeeded in smearing some dirt over his brow. 'Time for breaky, hey?' he said, with a grin.

'Yep, let's go.'

Zhangjiakou was a shock by day. The alleyways were congested with a moving sea of people. In one side street alone there was probably more commercial activity than in an entire Russian city. The pavements and squares were cluttered with crowds dancing to music and stretching in perfect synchronicity. And what's more, there were bike highways, and we were two among thousands.

As a heavy rain set in we took refuge in a cheap noodle restaurant. After four hearty serves it was still pouring. Begrudgingly we returned to the bikes and within minutes were soaked to the bone; my waterproof clothing had worn out long ago. Miserable, but with a belly full of noodles to keep me warm, I put feet to pedals and followed Chris. We turned off in the direction of Beijing and didn't stop for lunch.

The downpour did not ease and eventually the liquid bullets beat me into submission: there was no point in resisting. They penetrated everything. My skin felt as soft and fragile as soggy cardboard. Water streamed down my back, my chest and the underside of my legs. It collected in pools in the sleeves of my jacket and the cuffs of my pants.

We passed through busy little towns where the buildings were blackened with coal soot, and smoke stacks billowed thick grey smoke, which merged with the low clouds. As the unseen sun dimmed, the clouds drooped and cloaked the earth in fog.

Just before the evening faded into black we turned into a small cornfield to make camp. I leaned my bike against a lone tree, and didn't bother to look for cover. I just stood, unmoving. There was no escaping the discomfort. The tent was soaking, my sleeping bag was drenched and all my clothes were soggy. I pried a pocket open to find the swollen remains of a Chinese biscuit and lifted it slowly to my mouth. Chris stood nearby, up to his ankles in a puddle. He was trying to shrink into his Gore-Tex coat and hide, but it clearly wasn't working.

I took a quick look around and just hung my head. I started shivering. Our little cornfield was besieged by a railway line, busy roads, factories, cluttered brick homes and giant power lines. A heavy clanging noise came through the fog from a nearby factory, and every few minutes a loud explosion boomed. A thousand cars, motorbikes, trains and trucks filled the air with a dull vibration that I knew would never quieten. The solitude of the taiga forest and the empty Mongolian steppe seemed worlds away. Long ago, I thought, there would have been a spirit to the land, but it had been wrung dry by the grip of civilization and a heavy-handed regime. The sky wasn't dreamy and the true landscape was masked by what man had carved out of it. There was little vitality, just a race to produce, develop and survive.

Clenching my fists, I tried to imagine life beyond this moment. What would it be like to throw away these shoes held together by the laces alone? To wear fresh, clean clothes, and not sleep in that dank tent? To wake in the morning and have a shower and rub myself dry with a towel? To store food in something other than rank old pannier bags? What was life like without the constant worry of getting a puncture or fixing the brakes? And what about life without meeting daily distances and the agony of tortured thigh muscles?

I tilted my face into the rain and let the drops hit my tongue. In all the discomfort, it suddenly occurred to me that I wouldn't have it any other way. We had lived the dream and spent our energy. All that remained was the exhausted shell of our journey and the task of nudging it over the finish line. I had left my heart behind the moment we dropped off the plateau into this so called 'land of the living'. Now that we had been through the hardship of living a simple life, my passion was spent.

Down here in the bustling plains, everyone rushed about, oblivious to the serenity of a campfire in the taiga, the humour of Baba Galya and the hospitality of our friends on Lake Baikal. They didn't understand the luxury of stepping off the bike after a day's ride and spooning in a mash of sardines, potatoes and Russian soup mix. In the past year, they hadn't wondered what it was like over the horizon, nor had they ridden off to find out. Here, we just looked like a couple of ragged tramps.

It made me acutely aware of just how lucky we had been. The million and one unique experiences had been more than just sights, people and places; they were pots of happiness and growth to hold close to the heart.

Eventually, we were brought to life by the intense cold.

'C'mon, you lazy bloody New South Welshman, let's get this tent up!' I murmured in an attempt to rattle some life into Chris.

'Yeah, all right. Gee, glad I'm not on cooking tonight!' he replied, with a cheeky smile.

We went to bed in the wet and woke with the ugly task of sliding sopping wet socks back onto our feet. I climbed onto a bike that was in tatters. Many parts were held together by grey tape like a crude life-support system – the bikes and our gear should have died long ago.

Two days later we crossed a mountain range, saw the Great Wall of China at a distance and pulled into an apple orchard on the outskirts of Beijing.

All day my mind had flicked over fond memories: the shimmering lakes of Finland where I took a rowboat out in the morning fog and watched the waterbirds flutter off, leaving ripples in the glassy water. My first time in an abandoned village in Russia, where I had been transfixed by a white line of hooting swans flying over the taiga forest. I remembered the bitter cold and haunting beauty of my first winter in the Arctic, when it had dropped to minus 37 degrees Celsius. Then there was the meeting with Chris in Moscow, Baba Galya, Baikal, the BAM railway, and everything else that had filled my life in the past fourteen months. Alone with my thoughts, I didn't feel as if it was just the end of a journey. It was the end of a way of life, and of two and a half years away from Australia. Now that we were so perilously close to finishing, I realised that relief wasn't the overriding emotion. There were two others: a sense of achievement and a sense of great loss.

We worked quietly in the dull evening sun to set up camp and cook dinner. We were both deep in thought, quietly contemplating the gravity of the moment.

Although there was something comforting about having a gander down memory lane, I also found it unnerving – each and every experience was unique. Although I could think about the past, I could never truly experience it again. Rosy predictions of the future also seemed to fall short. As I peered into my last ever stodgy bowl of macaroni and canned sardines, it was obvious that although the mind could conjure up and recreate beautiful things, it was never as real as the moment. It is the ground upon which we stand, not that of two paces behind or in front. So quickly the taste of macaroni would fade; life wasn't just about reflection and anticipation, but about continuing to push into new things.

And damn it! Maybe I really had changed, and I wasn't just returning to the past. Australia, too, would be a chance to live and learn. And Russia would wait for me.

I set up the tent for the last time and rolled out my filthy sleeping bag. Then I lay down and closed my eyes next to Chris.

'Only one more day of freedom, hey, Chris,' I murmured.

'Nup. Ten days until freedom.'

An Incredible Journey

Beijing

24 October 2000

Chris

I packed slowly in the grey light of dawn then sat on a half-rotten log next to a stunted apple tree. Tim was cooking breakfast – our last breakfast – and I was filling in the final few pages of what would be my last letter to Nat for a good long while. Tim served up and we ate, mostly in silence.

'Guess this is the last time I'll ever have to wash this pot,' Tim remarked as he scraped the last granules of semolina from the corners.

I smiled. In my opinion, what he did to that pot every couple of days could hardly be called *washing*. 'Yeah, I guess so. Are you taking it home with you then?' I asked.

'Bloody oath!' he replied, emphatically. 'This pot has some great memories. Some of the best times of the entire trip – *my* best memories, anyway – are of eating.'

'Yeah.' I laughed.

'How about you? Are you taking yours home? It'd be a shame not to. Yours is a good pot.' Tim's question held a hint of sadness. I smiled for a moment as I looked at the dented blackened thing in my hands. The inside was tarnished and the outside was coated in layer upon layer of hardened black tar, a residue that had built up over the course of around 500 campfires. I found myself remembering some of the more memorable moments of our incredible journey. There was the one time, recently, when the stove had died for the first time and we'd been forced to burn horse shit. And another, back in summer, when we'd nearly started a bushfire. Then there was that time on the BAM – in the rain at two in the morning – the day I'd tried to alter our bikes. And not to forget that campsite a few weeks earlier when we'd burnt half a ton of wood while we sat up into the early hours of the morning arguing and yelling our heads off. And then – I laughed as I remembered it – the camp, early on in the snow, when I'd cut down an entire dead aspen tree because I needed a log to sit on. That pot sure did bring back -memories, but they were memories that I'd have to store elsewhere.

I shook my head slowly and looked at Tim. 'Nah, mate.' I waved the pot in the air. 'There's a baggage limit on aeroplanes, you know. And besides,' I measured him up with a steady grin, 'I don't think Nat would appreciate it too much if I took this home and tried to cook up a romantic dinner for two. I've already told her about us using it to cook our meals on horse poo.' Tim laughed and I continued. 'I reckon I'll just have to go and get a new one. They're about three bucks, as far as I remember, from Woolworths.'

Tim's face darkened. He was a Victorian and this was an issue of contention. 'You mean Safeway.'

I finished my long-rehearsed, almost automatic, morning routine with a new awareness. I shoved my sleeping bag into the rear pannier for the last time and let my thoughts wander.

We'd come through a lot this year, Tim and I. More than a lot actually. More than I ever could have imagined, but the journey had run its course and now we were returning home to different lives. I wondered if we'd ever travel together again. Tim seemed to sense this too, and he broke the silence, adding his voice to the few birds and the distant rumble of early morning traffic.

'You know, I've just realised ...' I waited as he let his words hang in the air. His voice was neutral. I didn't know what it was he'd just realised, but I could guess. He let the pause extend a dozen heartbeats and seemed to be considering the mood that hung around us like a fog. Then the moment passed and he broke into a smile. 'You know that private concert of yours that you and your pot make every day when you're eating?'

I scowled half-heartedly back at him. 'You mean your hyper-sensitive hearing? Sure, what about it?'

He grinned with huge satisfaction. 'I've just realised that I won't have to listen to it ever again.'

We wheeled our bikes slowly out of the orchard and back onto the road. Beijing was big and there – a thick pall of pollution and the beginnings of a vast build-up of population. Our map was dodgy – just the photocopied corner of some large-scale atlas – but as far as we could figure, we had camped about fifty kilometres from the centre. We'd rung the day before and spoken to Helen, a British girl we'd met on our second visit to Ulaan Baatar, and she had agreed to meet us there – right there, in the very centre, Tiananmen Square.

For the very last time, I climbed onto my bike and flexed my fingers around the brake levers. Then, with a deep breath and a glance at Tim, I clicked my ragged shoes into the squeaking pedals and pushed off into the crisp morning air.

The morning was a tumultuous blur of traffic, shops and people. Beijing was the biggest city I'd been in by far, yet all of the millions of people seemed to be crammed into a tiny space, one on top of the other. It was like a huge, bulging city squeezed into the shell of what was really only meant to hold, at best, a large township.

We became caught up in a surging crowd of cyclists. There were thousands packed across the road and taking up more lanes than the honking traffic. We darted forward, from one traffic light to the next, while the buildings on the roadside became taller and more sophisticated. We passed a McDonalds – the first we had seen in (I counted back) about 10,000 kilometres and over a year – but it flashed by in an instant and we were back to surging ahead with the crowd.

We didn't have a map of the city and we had no idea which road we were on, but the direction still seemed good, and the buildings were getting more impressive and city-like all the time. We pulled over and sheltered from the muggy heat under a loudly vibrating overpass bridge. Neither of us had a watch – we'd been riding without knowing the time for most of the year – but experience and the first hints of fatigue in my legs told me that we'd been going for several hours already. It had all passed in a flash of sights and sensations though, and I'd been running on adrenaline the whole time. It was only now, as we stopped for a breather and to take a drink of water from our dirt-encrusted bottles, that my thoughts slowed enough to return to the mood of the morning.

Was it possible that only a few weeks ago we'd pushed for days through the heart of the desert without seeing another soul? Beijing was overwhelming and confusing, and as much as I'd so often longed for the end of the journey, nothing during the past year had prepared me for this mass of people. While I might have found the experience of Beijing exciting another time, right now it represented a huge transition, a new beginning and a final end.

I closed my eyes and wished I didn't have to be there. Just a week from now, I'd be home with Nat, and only a week before we'd still been cycling. I longed for both, equally. I was yearning for the past. And the future! I just didn't want the now.

For so long I'd been looking forward to everything that was waiting for me in Australia. But now, for almost the first time, I turned my thoughts to reflect on what I was leaving behind. I looked across at Tim and realised that this was very nearly the end. Soon we'd both be packing up our bikes and heading for our respective homes. Tim would be in Gippsland, down south in Victoria, and I'd be starting out on my new life with Nat in Canberra. We'd made a lot of tentative plans for big talks and presentations in the new year, but in reality, we were both returning to a good deal of uncertainty. I acknowledged, with a weird kind of pang, that it could be a long time before we saw each other again.

I reflected on the year we'd spent together. 'Friends' was the best word I could think of to describe our relationship. But at that moment, it wasn't exactly what sprang to mind. Our relationship had been unique and indescribable. Sometimes it had seemed more like a business partnership than anything. We'd come together – for better or for worse – for a single purpose and we'd stayed together to see it through. It had been 24/7 for most of the year and often we'd had no one to talk to but each other. Almost everything that either of us had done had had an effect on the other, and in that sense – in its intensity – it had been more like a marriage than anything. Yet there had been very little love lost on either side, and at times our relationship had been a hell of a stormy one.

So many times during the past year I'd decided that Tim and I simply rubbed each other fundamentally the wrong way. So many things about him pissed me off and yet there were so many things about him that I couldn't help but admire: his unflagging drive and his unshakeable optimism, to name but a few. We'd had so many explosive arguments and early on, especially, I'd sometimes hated him. A sad reflection of my intolerance, I guess, but then, I don't doubt that his feelings for me had often been the same. Over the long, rough course of time, we'd both learned to live with a thousand little compromises, and the learning had changed us both. That change in each of us had been for the better, of course. But it had also changed the nature of the friendship that we'd started off with, too. I remembered back to the beginning of the trip and a poignant prediction I'd made in a letter to Nat: *This journey will either make or break our friendship for good and all.*

I looked wanly at Tim. I decided that it had come pretty close to being both in the end. We'd had definite boundaries during the year, privacies that our conversations did not touch, but despite that, I probably knew Tim and all his weaknesses, ambitions and dreams better than anybody else alive. Tim probably knew me better than anyone else as well. My weaknesses at any rate. He definitely knew my weaknesses better than Nat did.

And for all that, what did it all mean? I glanced at him again, then shook my head with a private grin. A year or so with a thousand kilometres between us would probably do the world of good. After that? Well, I was 100 per cent sure that we'd end up lifelong friends.

We pedalled off into the crowd again and soon found ourselves heading down a long, straight promenade lined with tall, important-looking buildings and buzzing with eight lanes of traffic. We stopped at a traffic light to give way to pedestrians and saw, amid a sea of Chinese faces, a tall, elderly European-looking man.

'Hi!' Tim yelled. 'Over here!'

The stares of the crowd doubled but the man in the green golfing cap almost stumbled over us before he noticed our bikes. 'Oh! Hello there,' he said in a pleasant English accent. 'I'm sorry, I didn't see you.' His face showed a gentle kindness and not a bit of surprise. He seemed ludicrously out of place in this bustling city – even more so than we did!

'Um, hi,' Tim continued. 'Could you please tell us how to get to Tiananmen Square?'

'Oh! What? Oh, yes. Tiananmen Square. Just let me think. Why yes. It's about a mile ahead, but a few blocks off to the left. Take the next left, then turn right again after several hundred yards. That should take you straight there, I'd say. Jolly good!' The lights changed and we were on our way again.

Tim's brake cable snapped – our last one. 'Great timing,' he groaned, but it didn't matter. Ten minutes later, we crossed an intersection and rode past a gigantic portrait of Mao Zedong. There it was, right before us, Tiananmen Square. The heart of Beijing and the final destination of our dream.

We fell into a silent reverie, overcome by emotion. There was a deep sadness that the long adventure had finally come to an end and, of course, an overwhelming euphoria. But mostly there was just a bewildering sense of uncertainty – or maybe it was a sense of freedom? The journey that had occupied us both for so long was finally over and now only the daunting prospect of the future remained.

We met up with Helen by the fence at the top end of the square. She gave us bunches of flowers, and she'd brought her Chinese teacher and the whole class along too. A camera flashed somewhere, a newspaper photographer maybe, but I couldn't see. A gate opened and we were allowed to wheel our bikes onto Tiananmen Square.

'You're not allowed to ride them though,' Helen translated for the stern-looking guard.

I wheeled through the crowd of tourists, feeling numb. We stopped and I turned to Tim. 'That's it, mate. That's fourteen months, finished.'

He shook his head. He breathed out slowly. 'Unbelievable.'

Afterword

A week after finishing the journey Tim and Chris flew home to Melbourne and Sydney respectively. They secured the interest of an Australian film company and a documentary was subsequently made about their journey. Australian Geographic recognised their adventure with the 2000 'Spirit of Adventure Award'.

In June of the following year, Tim returned to Siberia with three others to row a wooden boat 4,500 kilometres down the length of the Yenisey river to the Arctic Ocean.

Chris was reunited with Natalie. In 2002 he returned to the Australian National University to study psychology. He and Nat were married in Canberra on 7 December 2002 – the anniversary of their relationship and Tim's twenty-fourth birthday.

Tim is still passionate about Russia and among other journeys he plans to return and circumnavigate the world via the Arctic Circle between 2003 and 2005. He will travel using reindeer sleds, kayaks, skis, ships, bikes, skidoos, tanks and on foot. Chris and Nat are planning a year of adventure in 2004 and are toying with several ideas, such as walking the length of the Andes or travelling extensively throughout Central Asia. Chris also dreams of trying to cross Antarctica on a specially designed, pedal–powered skidoo.

For more than twelve months after the journey Tim and Chris lived 1,000 kilometres apart and barely spoke. In the process of writing this book, however, their friendship has been rekindled and strengthened. In a strange way, they find themselves back at square one, inspiring each other with e-mails and phone calls and dreaming of adventures to come.

Contact the authors and see more photos and stories about this and other adventures at: www.timcopejourneys.com

Acknowledgements

It was a huge effort to turn our dream into a reality. Many people thought we were mad, and organising the journey seemed at times to be a constant uphill battle. Throughout this struggle, however, there were occasional rays of sunshine. These were our friends and family, the babushkas who chided us for being out in the cold, then dropped everything to look after us anyway, and the teachers in Russia, Finland and Australia, who saw value in our journey and gave students the opportunity to keep in contact with us. Moments of optimism also came from our generous sponsors.

Finally, there were the people, including the staff at Penguin, who believed in our dream of writing a book and making a film, and who encouraged us to share our experience with others.

To everyone else who supported us we extend our sincere thanks. We hope we have warranted your belief and your faith, not only in us, but in other young people as well.

With kind regards
Tim Cope and Chris Hatherly

Thanks to our sponsors:

Australian Geographic
Outdoor Survival Australia
Mountain Designs
Energizer
Kodak
Gear, Australia
Roman Sleeping Bags
Adventure Designs
Maxwell Optical Industries (Nikon Australia)
Nomad Travel Equipment and Ortlieb
Everwarm Thermalwear
White Mountain
Velocity Australia
Rosebank
Snowgum
Lonely Planet
Wayne Kotzur

In Finland, Tim would like to thank:

Halti Outdoor Equipment
Ruovesi Medical Centre
Kuru College of Forestry
Hiking Travel Oy
Ruovesi High School
R-Cycles, Tampere
Ruovesi Library
Anna Korpoo
Liisa and Pekka Tyllilä

In Bathurst, Chris would like to thank:

Peter Rogers Real Estate
ChemMart Plaza Pharmacy
Coleman Office Products
Surf, Gym & Street
Winning Edge Cycles
St. John's Ambulance
Fletchers Fotographics

Special Thanks to:

Our families: Jon, Natalie, Cameron, Anne and Andrew Cope
Meredith, David, Alex and Mike Hatherly
John and Alison Kearney
Baba Galya, Mama Tatyana, Baba Sveta and all in Babushkina
The Kleshnok family in Petrozavodsk
The Chuginov family in Kvitok
Dmetri Kakmi, for showing so much heart and perseverance
with our manuscript.
Eric Philips for his unflagging encouragement and advice.
Rob Devling, friend, mentor and teacher

And to all those individuals we have not named, but who
helped, encouraged and supported us along the way.

Don't Mention The War!

A shameful European rail adventure

Paul Bassett, Stewart Ferris

£7.99 Paperback

Follow the authors on their latest morally reprehensible trip around Europe. Experience the fatigue, the smells and the total lack of appreciation of the cultural pearl that is continental Europe. Discover how they played their part in making a gendarme crash his police car; marvel at the undeserved adulation heaped upon them by the inhabitants of a small town in Provence; wince in embarrassment as they demonstrate how not to represent their nation when abroad.

Don't Mention The War! follows the exploits of three young men as they gallivant across Europe gorging themselves on junk food, funded by their questionable ability as buskers.

Provided you're not an anxious parent or a member of the clergy, or French, German, Italian, Swiss, Belgian, Dutch, Eastern European or American, this book is guaranteed to make you laugh at least once.

Good Vibrations

Coast to coast by Harley

Tom Cunliffe

£7.99 Paperback

Tom Cunliffe and his wife Roz take life in the saddle and onto the American highways and byways astride the quintessential 'dream machine' – the Harley-Davidson.

Bikes Betty Boop and Black Madonna are chrome steeds for an extensive road-trip: from Maryland on the east coast to San Francisco on the west (and then back again), they thunder their way over the sun-beaten plains, through scorching Death Valley, neon Las Vegas, the deep South and everywhere in between.

With flashbacks to the Sixties, the eclectic assortment of moonshiners, bikers hard and not-so-hard, cowhands, Sioux Indians, strippers, bible-bashers, war veterans, southern gents and the occasional alligator, this book delivers a unique insight into the diversity of the USA.

An easy-riding peepshow into today's America through British eyes and between the handlebars of the great Harley-Davidson.

The Trail To Titicaca

A journey through South America

Rupert Attlee

£7.99 Paperback

It seemed like a mad enterprise: three inexperienced cyclists setting out to pedal 6,500 miles up the Andes, from Tierra del Fuego to Lake Titicaca. After nearly a year and against the odds – contending with grasshopper storms, deserts of volcanic ash and trigger-happy police – the trio succeeded in their objective, also raising tens of thousands of pounds for Leukaemia Research Fund.

Battling with the language barrier, an addiction to chocolate and fuelled by copious amounts of vino, this is the story of the physical and emotional ups and downs experienced by three friends: the romantic, the stoic and the writer. Their journey tells of the awe-inspiring wilds, history and peoples of Chile, Argentina and Bolivia. What started as the adventure of a lifetime evolved into a voyage of discovery, comradeship and humour.

Trans-Siberia

Inside the grey area

Paddy Linehan

£7.99 Paperback

It all started in the mind of a child with the desire to travel. Siberia was full of darkness, struggle, cold and desperation.

Years later, haunted by a shadowy image that he just can't shake off, Paddy Linehan decides to pursue his Siberian dream. He learns to think on his feet and travels 'like a Russian' in a culture struggling with post-Soviet, post-communist flux.

Traditional after-bath beatings, bonding with a love-sick Siberian boy, bizarre occurrences on the 44A Trans-Siberian train: this is an extraordinary and very human journey.

'...very cold and very far...' You almost want to go there yourself. Almost.

www.summersdale.com